Child Development

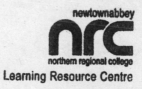

HARPERCOLLINS COLLEGE OUTLINE

Child Development

Bill Cunningham, M.S.
Thomas Nelson Community College

■ HarperPerennial
A Division of HarperCollins*Publishers*

An American BookWorks Corporation Production
Project Manager: Judith A. V. Harlan
Editor: Thomas Quinn

Library of Congress Cataloging-in-Publication Data

Cunningham, Bill, 1950–
    Child development / Bill Cunningham.
        p.   cm. — (HarperCollins college outline series)
    Includes bibliographical references and index.
    ISBN 0-06-467149-6
    1. Child development.   I. Title.   II. Series.
HQ767.9.C85   1993
305.23'1—dc20   92-53288

93   94   95   96   97   98   ABW/RRD   10   9   8   7   6   5   4   3   2   1

Contents

Preface

This book, *Child Development*, is one of the titles in the HarperCollins College Outline series, and is written with a dual purpose. First, the book can be used to supplement most of the major textbooks in the field of child development. Whenever there is a topic that is confusing to you, or that needs additional clarification, consult this outline book. Additionally, if you find a classroom lecture puzzling, this book can be helpful in demystifying the material.

Although it has been written to serve as a supplement, it can also be used as a stand-alone textbook. Despite the fact that this book is briefer than a standard textbook, it is *complete*, and can satisfy the need for an easy to use, inexpensive textbook. It presents all of the major issues in the field, and carefully examines all of the topics that are normally covered in a Child Development course in college.

The book features an extensive index to help make your work easier in finding topics. Additionally, there are charts and tables to help illustrate material that may be somewhat complex.

In short, it is a multifaceted book, and should help you in your studies.

Bill Cunningham

1

Child Psychology

Child psychology is a portion of the larger science of developmental psychology, which looks at the development of people throughout the whole of their life-span. The area of child psychology assumes that childhood and adolescence have a formative influence on the entire life-span, as most changes in life are assumed to occur within this time frame. Childhood has been viewed as something different from adulthood only in the last 300 years and was not studied extensively until the last 75 years. Currently, the psychological development of children is studied within the context of the physical, intellectual, and social/emotional changes that occur over time as well as how those changes may be influenced by the whole environment surrounding the children.

Different controversies have fueled the questions that child psychology attempts to answer, including what controls development and how development proceeds over time.

WHAT IS CHILD PSYCHOLOGY, AND WHY SHOULD WE STUDY IT?

The study of child psychology is actually the first portion of the larger field of developmental psychology. Developmental psychology essentially looks at how and why people change throughout the whole life-span as well as how and why people stay the same throughout the life-span. Specifically, then, child psychology looks at those same "how" and "why" questions from the moment of conception (when human life is believed to begin) on through the end of adolescence. This emphasis on childhood and adolescence is due primarily to the assumption that these two periods encompass the periods of the most dramatic changes and provide formative influences for development over the lifespan.

There are three reasons for studying child development/psychology separately and with more intensity than one might study other portions of development. First, on a personal level, we get a chance to see how the events of our own childhood may have influenced us to become the people that we are today. Second, on a practical level, if we know how different events can influence development, then we have the opportunity to help all children reach their full potential both as children now and adults later. Third, on a theoretical level, as we learn more about how children change over time, we should be better able to explain why they change the way they do and why they differ in their responses to similar events.

History of the Science of Child Psychology

For much of recorded history, children were seen as miniature adults, only not as smart. Not until the writings of the seventeenth- and eighteenth-century philosophers John Locke (1632–1704) and Jean Jacques Rousseau (1712–1778) did childhood appear as a stage distinct from adulthood. Essentially, Locke assumed that children entered the world absolutely blank, like a clean chalkboard, and that whatever they became was purely the result of their interactions with the environment, that is, whatever was "written" on that chalkboard. Rousseau, on the other hand, assumed that children entered the world with a naturalness that was sufficient to guide them through their early development.

This division in thinking over what controls development, the environment or an inborn naturalness, was a driving force for the establishment of a more objective effort to understand child development. Observations of the behavior of developing organisms, including humans, by naturalists such as Charles Darwin (1809–1882) demonstrated that significant changes in the development of any given species occur over time. This use of observation to examine the developmental changes of organisms allowed a method of testing the relative importance of each side in the Locke-Rousseau debate. Thus the science of developmental psychology was born.

G. Stanley Hall (1844–1924), the first developmental psychologist, was influential in the growth of this new science in two ways. First, he asked children for information about childhood. He did this by observing children in a laboratory and by surveying schoolchildren. Second, he introduced two new theoretical concepts: the concept of adolescence as a transitional stage between childhood and adulthood; and, by bringing Sigmund Freud (1856–1939) to the United States and attracting attention to his theories, the concept that events in the early years shape later life and personality.

Developmental psychology expanded when Alfred Binet (1857–1911) devised a test for assessing the amount of intelligence that individual children might possess. Hence a tool was made available for measuring intellectual changes over time within a single child and for measuring differences between children as well as changes over time for them. This step was quickly followed by the work of Arnold Gesell (1880–1961), who developed the methodologies for conducting systematic short-term comparisons between groups of children and long-term studies of changes within a group of children. See chapter 2 for a further discussion of developmental methodologies and chapter 3 for a more in-depth discussion of developmental theories.

Current Approach to Presenting Child Psychology

In looking at the development of children, the different influences present at every age have been divided into three general categories or domains: physical (encompassing all of the changes that occur in growth—musculature, the nervous system, motor skills, nutrition, health, etc.), cognitive (encompassing the mental processes of perception, learning, memory, language, thinking, and so on), and psychosocial (encompassing personality, social, emotional factors).

It is important to remember that these divisions are not separate from one another. That is, each domain influences the other two. For example, a child who believes (cognitive domain) that he is clumsy may avoid interaction with other children, for fear of being ridiculed (psychosocial domain), and also avoid the physical activity (physical domain) that could help him overcome that self-concept of clumsiness. Dividing all of these influences on a child into categories at any given age is purely arbitrary.

In addition, child psychologists recognize two other areas of developmental influence that can interact with the domain approach. First are life events. These are occurrences within a person's life that are generally out of the person's control but for which some personal adjustments must be made. Examples are the death of a family member, birth of a sibling, puberty, and moving to a new neighborhood. Second are critical periods. This refers to the timing of the events in one's life, that is, the time when an event will have its greatest effect. Many birth defects, for example, are the result of the child being exposed to something harmful during a critical period of physical development before birth.

In general, child psychologists view all of these influences beyond solely their effects within each developing person. They assume that individual children and adolescents are integral members of a social environment (i.e., ecology) that not only supports or interacts with their development but that in turn is influenced by that development. For example, all family members are now seen as contributing in some way to the psychology and development of a new child; likewise, the child will contribute in some way to the stability of the family and interactions of its other members. Also such nonfamily events as the economy, politics, and parental job satisfaction will have some effect on the development of a child.

Currently, then, the science of child psychology seeks to understand each child's perspective as well as the events and influences that help form that perspective.

Major Controversies in Child Psychology

Anyone who studies children and their development, whether this "anyone" is a parent or a child psychologist, will confront many of the fundamental issues that have been around since Locke and Rousseau. These issues are usually presented in the form of two extremes—for example, is A more influential than B?—even though it is rare for there not to be some form of interaction between the two competing alternatives. In any event, the issues that child psychology and development have addressed from the beginning are presented below.

WHAT IS THE STRONGEST INFLUENCE ON HUMAN DEVELOPMENT?

This controversy concerns the major controlling influence on development and dates back to the Locke and Rousseau debate mentioned above. That is, are the hereditary characteristics that we acquired from our parents a stronger influence on what we will become or is the environment that we grow up in stronger? It is an issue that examines the relative roles of internal versus external forces in determining who or what we become.

The internal force is usually referred to as maturation, which is how the hereditary (genetic) message shows itself to the outside world. Some of this message is visibly present in a wide range of traits, such as eye or hair color. Many more hereditary characteristics are less immediately present. That is, maturation describes at what time many events are likely to occur (e.g., when a child can sit up by him/herself) as well as the order of events necessary to produce a particular behavior (e.g., in order for a child to run, he or she will usually proceed through the steps of crawling, standing, and walking). Even though the maturation process is fairly universal, differences in development between children can be explained as the result of slightly different genetic patterns.

The external force is usually referred to as the environment (sometimes also called experience or learning), which encompasses all of the influences on development that are not genetic. These may include everything from a mother's health during pregnancy to the number of siblings in a family, even the presence or absence of a family pet or the type of church one attends. Basically, any event in the physical or social world can have some effect on development. The type or nature of the event in conjunction with a child's response to it is what will determine the effect of that event on development.

Hence, the differences between each person's environment or history of experience are what make each person different.

In reality, the influences of each of these forces on a child do not create an either/or situation but rather an interaction. Simply put, maturation has a greater influence on some characteristics than the environment, and vice versa. But rarely is either force the sole determinant of development. For example, being able to throw a ball requires that sufficient muscle and bone development has occurred to hold the ball and coordinate the actions of throwing and releasing. Being able to consistently hit what you throw the ball at requires practice.

HOW DO PEOPLE CHANGE AS THEY DEVELOP?

This question relates to the observations of the naturalists like Darwin: are the changes that occur in development over time the result of a continuous progression of small changes or do they occur as the result of some radical change in the developmental process?

The continuous point of view assumes that changes in development are constantly ongoing and are quantitative in nature. That is, development is nothing more than a sequence, or orderly progression, of changes in whatever it is that you are examining. A child, for example, becomes a little taller or friendlier with each passing day. One can imagine the continuous view as being similar to walking up a grassy hill: Each step upward is a minimal rise in elevation so that you may not really notice the differences between steps. Basically, every change that is observed results from the cumulative effect of all the changes that have gone before. That is, you get to the top of the hill through slow, gradual climbing.

The discontinuous (radical change) viewpoint assumes that development occurs in stages. Each new stage is qualitatively different from the previous one; that is, some underlying developmental process is totally different in type or in style from what previously existed. For example, walking is a qualitatively different stage for a child than is crawling: it requires a new set of skills, like balance and coordination, and necessitates a change in thinking about dependence on parents. In this regard, the discontinuous view is not unlike climbing a flight of stairs: each new step is distinctly different from the previous one, and the change between steps is both large and apparent.

A major difference between these two viewpoints has to do with the passage of time. The continuous view sees little time passing between changes since by definition change is a continuous process. The discontinuous view, on the other hand, sees a period of time as needing to pass before each new stage.

Two things happen while a child is in the period between abrupt changes. First, the new abilities (characteristics, traits, experiences) are explored and practiced so that a child can understand what is required in order to meet the demands of the new stage. For example, when a child first begins to walk, steps are short, hesitant, and interspersed with periods of falling down while the child tries to maintain the requirements of balance and movement on two feet. Second, once the basic skills of the new stage are mastered, then slow, gradual change predominates until the time for the next new stage has arrived. In the above example, over time and with more practice the child will be able to control walking faster when he or she wants to get somewhere and slower when a parent wants him or her to get somewhere.

As you can see, then, both views use the concept of slow, gradual changes over time. The discontinuous view adds the component of periodic abrupt changes that significantly alter the abilities of the child as well as the interactions that the child will have with the environment.

One other point may also be apparent: Neither one of these viewpoints takes a strong position on the previous controversy. Both continuity and discontinuity can assume that heredity and the environment interact equally or that one is stronger than the other. The outcome of this controversy does not hinge on the outcome of the previous one.

HOW PREDICTABLE IS A CHILD'S FUTURE FROM WHAT IS KNOWN AT PRESENT?

This question has its roots within the theoretical musings of Freud (mentioned earlier and in greater detail in chapter 3) and is part of the general scientific desire for prediction: is there a stable relationship between behaviors (characteristics) that are observed now and those we may see in the future, or is every person's development dynamic and changeable?

To put this another way: how strong is the environment in influencing a person's development? In this light the question directly relates to the first controversy. That is, if heredity and maturation are the strongest influences in development, then prediction of the future is easily definable. All child psychologists need to do is understand the biology of genetics and how that biology will manifest itself through maturation; then they will able to see the future of an individual child simply from knowing the early infant behaviors and traits.

But if the environment can mold or change a child, then biology and heredity might take a back seat to the effects of the environment on child development. All child psychologists would need to know in this case is the influence that different environmental situations have. Changing the situation, then, would change the future of the child.

How to access the NRC Student Intranet from outside the College

1. Go to www.nrc.ac.uk
   Click on the **NORTHERNi** icon at the bottom of the web page, left hand side [see circled area below]

   NORTHERNi f 🐦 You Tube

   Alternatively, type this into your internet address bar http://www.nrc.ac.uk/nrc/nrci/

2. Click on 'Login' in the 'Student Intranet' option [as the arrow indicates below]

   STUDENT
   Student Intranet
   Username: nrcusername@nrc.ac.uk
   Password: nrcpassword
   Login

   NB Username should read: nrcusername@nrc.ac.uk
   e.g. DYN1236578@nrc.ac.uk

3. Enter your student email address [as your username] (e.g. DYN1236578@nrc.ac.uk), followed by your password. Click OK.

   Connect to student.nrc.ac.uk
   Connecting to student.nrc.ac.uk.
   User name: DYN1236578@nrc.ac.uk
   Password: ●●●●●●●●●
   ☐ Remember my password
   OK   Cancel

4. If your details have been entered successfully, you will be directed to the NRC Student Intranet.

   STUDENT INTRANET
   Library

For example, children raised in intellectually unstimulating environments will often show low intelligence scores. If they are left in these environments, one can predict that their scores would not change much over time. However, taking the same children and placing them in remedial education programs (like Head Start) will usually improve their current and future intelligence scores. Hence, knowing that certain past and future behaviors are linked gives child psychologists the ability to alter patterns of development.

Yet, sometimes behaviors that are viewed early in life seem to have no apparent relationship to ones viewed later. For example, children who are rated early (ages seven and eight) as behaviorally troubled, or even deviant, may easily be those children who are rated as normal by the time they are aged 16 or 17, sometimes without any special intervention.

The issue of predictability of development shows that both stability and change occur and that, as the science becomes better, our knowledge of the links between early and later behaviors, characteristics, and traits should also improve.

SPECIAL ISSUES

What Constitutes "Normal" Development?

Early researchers in child psychology/development assumed that a universal pattern of development existed that constituted "normal" development. Indeed, many of the early research projects centered around taking a large group of children, observing them over time, and then averaging the results that were obtained on many different measures. From this research a set of norms was developed for the average age for different behaviors or traits, for example, standing unaided, walking, riding a bicycle, speaking in complete sentences, and the like. Essentially, the research gave us the concept of the "statistical," or average, child. It did not matter what influenced the occurrence of these behaviors (heredity or environment), only that they were routinely observed to occur at these average times with most children.

The logic that subsequently followed this research was that if a child did not follow the normal pattern, then something was abnormal in either the child or the child's environment. In any event, that child's development was considered abnormal and probably inferior.

In recent years a growing movement in child psychology has been to view differences from the statistical child as representative of alternative paths of development rather than deviant paths. The reason for this change in interpretation is based in part on the fact that much of the early research that developed the "normal" child concept was based almost entirely on white, middle-class, American, male children. Any other racial, socioeconomic, ethnic or sexual group would most likely then be viewed as deviant, which in effect would include most of the world.

In addition, child psychologists have also realized that every environment that a child grows up in is different from every other one. One cannot neglect the unique factors in those environments that may have influenced individual development within some universal pattern.

The result is that we now have "bench marks" or times and patterns that might be expected in lieu of hard and fast normal deadlines. For example, we would expect a child to be saying understandable single words around the age of 18 months; however, this may be seen as early as 15 months or as late as 22 months. Either way, early or late from the bench mark, would be viewed within the context of the child's environment and evaluated appropriately, rather than categorically assigning terms like *genius* or *retarded*, respectively, to describe the child, based on a "normal" child pattern.

Child development looks at the hows and whys of human development from the moment of conception on through the end of adolescence. The emphasis on this part of the life-span is because it encompasses a time period during which most of the dramatic changes of the lifespan occur. The study of child development began with the philosophers John Locke and Jean Rousseau (seventeenth and eighteenth centuries, respectively) but achieved scientific status with the work of G. Stanley Hall in the early 1900s. Today, for ease of understanding, most child psychologists look at development from three perspectives: physical (body growth and maturation), cognitive (thinking and intellect), and psychosocial (personality/social/emotional).

Currently, work in the field of child development is fueled by three controversies: Is our hereditary past or the environment we grow up in a stronger influence on development? Is development a process of slow continuous change or is it characterized by almost sudden abrupt changes? Can you reliably predict a child's future from what you know about the child in the present?

Child development takes the approach of a broad perspective, assuming that children are not only influenced by the world around them but that they influence it as well. The field has broadened its view of development to assume that each child is an individual with his or her own developmental path.

Selected Readings

Applebaum, M. I., and R. B. McCall. (1983). Design and analysis in developmental growth. In *Handbook of child psychology*. 4th ed., ed. P. H. Mussen. NY: Wiley.

Aries, P. (1962). *Centuries of childhood*. New York: Vantage Books.

Borstelmann, L. J. (1983). History, theory and methods. In *Handbook of child psychology.* 4th ed., ed. P. H. Mussen. NY: Wiley.

Bronfenbrenner, U. (1979). *The ecology of human development.* Cambridge, MA: Harvard University Press.

Flavell, J. H. (1982). The concept of development. *The Minnesota symposia on child psychology.* Hillsdale, NJ: Erlbaum.

Hottinger, W. (1980). Early motor development.: Discussions and summary. In *A textbook of motor development.* 2d ed., ed. B. Corbin. Dubuque, IA: Wm. C. Brown.

Lerner, R. M. (1986). *Concepts and theories of human development.* 2d ed. New York: Random House.

Sommerville, C. J. (1982). *The rise and fall of childhood.* Beverly Hills, CA: Sage Publications.

Weisfeld, G. E. (1982). The nature-nurture issue and the integrating concept of function. In *Handbook of developmental psychology.* ed. B. B. Wolman. Englewood Cliffs, NJ: Prentice-Hall.

2

Methodology of Child Psychology

The theories that help explain development are only as good as the data (observations) on which they are based. Those data are only as good as the methodologies used to collect them. Each method available to the child psychologist answers particular types of scientific questions and has its own set of advantages and disadvantages. These methods run the gamut from observing children in their natural environments (home, school, and playground; alone or with other children and adults) to finding not only relationships between events but also determining if one event truly causes another. An examination of the methodologies that explore developmental changes over time will also be presented. Most important, a review of the research ethics for experimenting with children as well as their rights will end the discussion.

THE SCIENCE OF CHILD DEVELOPMENT

The specific goals of child development as a science are similar to the goals of psychology in general—description, explanation, prediction, and control of behavior. First, child psychologists attempt to provide a detailed analysis of each of the behaviors of children and adolescents (description). Second, child psychologists attempt to understand why each of these behaviors occurs (explanation). Third, child psychologists attempt to further their understanding of these behaviors by predicting when and under what conditions they are likely to recur (prediction). Finally, when the goals of description, explanation, and prediction of the behaviors of children and adolescents have been achieved, then child psychologists can move to the goal of the control of behavior. This means that children, parents, schools, and society in general can then work to provide the appropriate environments so that children and adolescents can, individually and as a group, reach their full potentials.

It is through the methods child psychologists use that the information (data) is obtained that helps in the achievement of these goals. Data are information gained through research. However, data also serve as the starting point for all research. That is, data generate hypotheses (educated guesses about, or potential explanations for, a particular problem), which in turn promote research that generates data either in support of or in conflict with the hypothesis.

At first glance, this would appear to be like a dog chasing its tail, continually running in circles and never getting anywhere. This is where the role of a theory enters. Theories are general statements that attempt to integrate all of the data that have been obtained into some unifying package, that is, to make sense of everything that we have described. Theories also attempt to explain current behaviors in light of past behaviors, that is, to help us understand the behaviors of children and adolescents in general. Finally, theories attempt to predict future behaviors. The better a theory is, the better we have met our goals of description, explanation, and prediction. In chapter 3 we will have a more in-depth discussion of the major theories of child psychology/development and of how well they attempt to meet these goals.

Keep in mind two final points about data. First, a theory is only as good as the data on which it is based. If for some reason the data are not reliable, the theory will not be reliable as well. This situation might occur if: (1) the data cannot be replicated; that is, other researchers using similar methods cannot come up with the same or similar results; (2) the data are not collected in a controlled and systematic manner; that is, the psychologist does not use the same procedures with all the children in the study; and, (3) the data are influenced by the researcher's subjective bias, that is, data-recording techniques are not objectively and understandably defined. This brings up the second point. Data are only as good as the methods used to collect them. The procedures discussed below each have advantages and disadvantages making them appropriate or inappropriate for testing different kinds of hypotheses.

METHODS THAT DESCRIBE THE BEHAVIORS OF CHILDREN AND ADOLESCENTS

Naturalistic Studies

Naturalistic studies are techniques that depend on simple observation of the behavior of children and adolescents. The main characteristic of these methodologies is that the researcher makes little or no effort to interact with or alter the naturally occurring behavior of the subjects. In so doing, these methods provide much of what is known concerning the description of the behaviors of children and adolescents.

NATURALISTIC OBSERVATION

These types of studies simply observe children in some natural environment, such as a child's home or school. For example, one could determine if there were differences in politeness (as defined by a child opening a door for an opposite-sex child) between boys and girls entering and leaving a school. This method could not tell you why the politeness occurred. It may, however, give you information about which gender is more polite at a certain time of day, given those specific conditions.

These methods suffer from a lack of control of the environmental conditions; that is, you have no idea what caused what you saw. In addition, they suffer from observer bias (the researchers may specifically look for what they expect to occur). For example, if you expected boys to be more polite, a boy's reaching for but not necessarily opening a door might be seen as an instance of politeness. They also suffer from the observer effect. That is, when people know that they are being watched they will act differently from when they do not know. Boys may indeed be more polite when they see an adult watching the front door to a school.

Baby Biographies. This is an example of a naturalistic observation that provides normative types of data concerning development. It is nothing more than a journal of "what happens when" in the development of an individual child, not unlike the sort of thing most parents keep on each of their children. These provide data concerning, for example, when a child first stands or what his first words are. Besides helping parents, doctors, and psychologists chart the development of individual children, baby biographies can help in the formulation of new theories. Darwin, for example, used the observations of his own son to theorize the concept of child observation as a way to better understand the development of humans as a species.

INTERVIEWS AND QUESTIONNAIRES

These methods acquire data from a large number of people about one or more specific questions. G. Stanley Hall, the first developmental psychologist, was the first to use questionnaires to discover how much children know. He developed the questions and then had schoolteachers ask them of their students. With this approach one can make easy comparisons among the extents of knowledge of different-aged children. Generally, the questionnaire approach works well with parents and teachers (such as in studying parent-child relationships), whereas an individual interview works better with older children. Despite Hall's success, these approaches do not seem to work well with young children (age five or less).

The main disadvantage of this question-and-answer approach, whether in person or on paper, revolves around courtesy bias, meaning that people sometimes answer questions depending on what they think the researcher wants to hear. This may be particularly troublesome if the events in question occurred some time in the past. For example, parents being asked about the past childhood behaviors of their now-teenage children may remember those behaviors in a much better light than when they actually occurred. In addition, people may reluctantly answer questions if they feel that the answers may make them look bad to the researcher. This might occur if children are asked about their own aggressive behaviors.

CASE STUDY

This approach utilizes both naturalistic observation and interview methods: a single child or a limited number of children are followed and intensely observed and studied for a period of time. To corroborate the observations made, interviews are also given periodically to get feedback from the subjects. One can thus obtain a large amount of information on the development of an individual with regard to changes in the surrounding environment. This technique provided the basic information that allowed Jean Piaget to advance his cognitive theory of development (see chapter 3 for further information).

The disadvantages of this approach are the same as with the observation and interview approaches. In addition, the amount of time needed to acquire data is enormous and their applicability may be limited to just the children from whom they were obtained.

METHODS THAT DESCRIBE CHANGES IN BEHAVIOR AS CHILDREN AGE

Methods under this heading have the characteristic of incorporating age into the overall design of the study so that the data reflect the changes that occur in development over time.

Cross-sectional

Studies of this type are the simplest for exploring the age-related differences in development: children of different ages are measured at the same time on the behavior or characteristic in question, and then the results are compared. For example, one can measure the differences in friendliness to a new teacher in a classroom with 6-year-olds and again with 12-year-olds. These studies are quick to do and show age differences very easily. However, the researcher has no information about the sequence of development between the behaviors of the younger groups and that of the older ones. That is, one only knows that different behaviors exist, not how they got that way. Cross-sectional studies also tell nothing about the consistency of behavior within individual children over time; for example, does a friendly 6-year-old remain friendly at age 12?

Finally, each age group may have more than age as a difference between it and the other groups. That is, life experiences for one age group may be very different from those for another age group (commonly called the cohort problem). In our example, the 12-year-olds may have had much more experience with having new teachers in their classroom settings over the years than the 6-year-olds, who are likely only just starting school.

Longitudinal

This methodology deals with some of the problems of the cross-sectional procedure by following the same group of subjects for a long period of time, usually a number of years. Therefore, researchers can observe the sequence of development as well as the consistency of behaviors or characteristics within individuals, allowing an overall view of the process of development rather than a view only at an isolated point in time. Because of the expense in time, money, and planning involved in following a large number of people from childhood through adulthood, longitudinal studies longer than just a few years are uncommon. Also, they follow only one particular group born at a particular time in history; no guarantee exists that the results from one study are germane to any other group at any other time. This is another example of the cohort problem.

Methods Dealing with the Cohort Problem

TIME-LAG

This procedure supplies a way of measuring the effects of cultural, historical or life-experience variation over time that might influence either development or the task being measured, that is, the essence of the cohort dilemma. Simply put, a researcher measures different groups of subjects in different years while the test age is held constant. For example, a group of two-year-olds is tested at the beginning of a study, another group of two-year-olds is tested one year later, and a third group of two-year-olds is tested one year after that.

CROSS-SEQUENTIAL

This procedure is essentially a combination of the three methods listed above. First, set up a cross-sectional study. Second, using the same subjects, repeat the same study in a longitudinal fashion at regular intervals, for example, every year. Third, conduct repeated time-lag studies to examine cohort effects with data from same-age subjects across the years of the study. Although extremely complicated and time-consuming, this procedure allows for examination of three areas: the differences between age groups; the continuity and sequence of development within a particular age group; and whether cultural, historical or life-experience factors were a part of the collected data.

METHODS THAT DESCRIBE RELATIONSHIPS AMONG VARIABLES (THAT INFLUENCE DEVELOPMENT)

Correlation

With this methodology a researcher examines how likely, or unlikely, it is that one event will occur if another event has taken place. This procedure asks the question: how are two environmental events related? These are the types of data that one might collect from a naturalistic study. In a positive correlation, the occurrence of one event predicts the occurrence of another event; and in a negative correlation the occurrence of one event predicts the nonoccurrence of another event. The reliability of the prediction is represented by a number between 0.00 and 1.00, 0.00 representing no predictable relationship between the two events, and 1.00 representing perfect predictability. The nature of the relationship, positive (+) or negative (–), is given by the sign in front of the number. Therefore, a correlation between two events of "–.70" is stronger than one of "+.60." Although a correlation gives researchers some predictability about events, they cannot tell if one of the events caused the other to occur. For example, there is probably a positive correlation among elementary schoolchildren between their shoe size and their spelling ability. This means that if you lined up all the children in an elementary school according to their shoe size from smallest to largest, you would also generally see that those children with the smallest sizes spelled worse than those children with the largest sizes. It would be incorrect to assume that those facts are related because one of them caused the other (e.g., as you learn to spell new words, your feet grow). Rather, it is more likely that they are related because of some other factor. In this case, normal biological maturation would explain and cause foot growth over the years, and older children (those most likely to have larger feet) will have been in school longer, with more experience in language and spelling than younger students with smaller feet. Therefore, correlation does not mean causation.

METHODS THAT EXPLAIN DEVELOPMENT

Experiments

Experimentation is the only method that can demonstrate cause-effect relationships in development. It is essentially a comparison of two groups of subjects. The subjects got into their respective groups through the process of random assignment; that is, before the experiment started, every subject had an equal chance of being in either group, such as through the flip of a coin. Therefore, both groups are equivalent when the experiment starts.

This equivalence is maintained by having both groups experience all aspects of the experiment except for the event in question, the "independent variable." Specifically, the experimental group receives the independent variable (that thing that is being examined and whose occurrence is tightly controlled by the researcher) while the control group does not. The control group serves as a point of comparison for determining if the application of the independent variable caused some change in the "dependent variable" (the thing that changes or depends on the application of the independent variable). In their simplest form, experiments use only two groups, but it is possible to have many levels of the independent variable used in an experiment, with each level represented by a different group.

For example, the popular assumption that refined sugar causes hyperactivity in young children can be tested with this methodology. First, choose a hundred four-to-five-year-old children who are equally healthy and come from similar backgrounds, and then randomly assign them into two groups of 50 children each. Second, tell all of the children that they will be receiving a treat, for example, a Popsicle. Third, include a specific measured amount of refined sugar in the Popsicles made for the experimental group but not in those made for the control group. Last, one-half hour after consumption of the Popsicles, all children have a rest period during which the researchers measure the following: the time it takes each child to quiet down; how many times each child gets up and walks around; how many times each child talks to another child; and the number of times a "teacher" has to talk to each child. Presumably, if sugar had the hypothesized effect, then the experimental group would show higher numbers overall in those dependent measures than the control group; that is, sugar would cause those measures to increase.

Experiments can be done in a laboratory where subjects are brought to a location that will allow the highest degree of control over environmental factors that may inadvertently affect the dependent variables. They can also be done in the field, as in the above example, which can occur in a school setting.

In any event, a major concern of the researcher is the exclusion, or control, of all events that could influence the dependent variables other than the independent variable. To be sure of the cause-effect relationship, the researcher must be sure that the only difference between the experimental and control groups is the independent variable.

SPECIAL ISSUES IN DEVELOPMENTAL METHODOLOGY

Children and the Ethics of Research

Researchers need to constantly be aware of the potential negative effects their experiment or study might have on the children being examined. Such is the case with the issue of deception. Deceiving children or keeping them in the dark about the real purpose of an experiment is often crucial to obtaining objective results. If children know that they are being observed for instances of aggressive behavior, they might not act aggressively. However, when the researcher notifies the children about the results of the experiment, will they be mistrustful of adults because they were lied to or have a reduced sense of self-esteem because they feel used and mistreated? The answers are not easy to come by, and the majority of research on children must be reviewed by ethics committees to be sure that the design reduces any potential negative impact. Usually, this procedure will necessitate the use of "informed consent." Basically, this means that the subjects (or their parents/guardians) will be informed of the purpose, procedures, risks, and benefits of the study. In addition, all subjects (and their parents/guardians) are debriefed when the study is over to answer any questions they might have. Even though there is no guarantee, such procedures usually make the risks to the children negligible.

Children's Rights and the Self-fulfilling Prophecy

Inherent in this discussion of the ethics of research is one on the rights of children in research. Even though the risks of some research project may be negligible and may be outweighed by the benefits to be obtained, that cannot be an excuse for disregarding the rights of the subjects involved. These include not only a right to not be deceived, and to be fully informed, both of which are mentioned above, but also a right to privacy. This means that any private information that could be used to the disadvantage of a child should remain privileged communication in much the same way as it might for doctors, lawyers or clergy.

The reason for this relates to something called a self-fulfilling prophecy. This can be a label, prediction or even just a description of behavior that can bias people to act as though it is, and will be, true in all situations. For example, if a child is described as hyperactive in school records, it may be that the child is indeed hyperactive; however, teachers, principals, and assistants will expect to see that type of behavior, and thereby treat the child as though it is expected. Then when the child fulfills those expectations in their eyes, we have in effect "created" a hyperactive child.

The science of child development has the same goals as psychology in general: detailing an accurate description of development; being able to understand or explain why a particular change in development occurs or does not occur; predicting when and under what conditions developmental events are likely to happen; and, with all of the aforementioned information, providing the appropriate conditions to allow children and adolescents to reach their full potentials. These goals are attained through the collection of data (observations), generation and testing of hypotheses, and formulation of theories.

The methods used to achieve the above goals range from simple observation of a single child to experiments or studies utilizing hundreds of children. Each method gathers different types of information ranging from descriptions of the general behaviors of children (naturalistic observation, baby biographies, interviews, questionnaires, case studies, correlations) to studies of developmental changes in behavior over time (cross-sectional, longitudinal, time-lag, cross-sequential) to a determination of the causes of some types of behavior (experiment).

Each methodology has its own particular set of advantages and disadvantages so that no one technique is best suited for all types of research questions. For example, studies that attempt to gather general descriptions of behavior in varied situations may be significantly influenced if the children know they are being observed. Likewise, studies examining how people change over time may find very different results depending on the generation those people were born into. Finally, studies that attempt to discover the single cause of a particular behavior by necessity must exclude all other possible variables that in reality may influence the occurrence of the behavior in question.

Regardless of the methodology, all child psychology research must be done ethically to balance the need for good objective information with the need to respect the rights of the children involved.

Selected Readings

Applebaum, M. I., and R. B. McCall. (1983). *Handbook of child psychology. Vol. 1, History, theory and methods.* NY: Wiley.

Cooke, R. A. (1982). The ethics and regulation of research involving children. In *Handbook of developmental psychology.* ed. B. B. Wolman. Englewood Cliffs, NJ: Prentice-Hall.

Forman, G. E., and I. E. Siegel. (1979). *Cognitive development: A life-span view.* Belmont, CA: Wadsworth.

Harrison, N. S. (1979). *Understanding behavioral research.* Belmont, CA: Wadsworth.

Mitchell, A. M. (1975). Experimentation on minors: Whatever happened to Prince *v.* Massachusetts? *Duquesne Law Review* 13.

Repp, A. C., G. S. Nieminen, E. Olinger, and R. Brusca. (1988). Direct observation: Factors affecting the accuracy of observers. *Exceptional Children* 55.

Scarr, S. 1985. Constructing psychology: Making facts and fables for our times. *American Psychologist* 40.

Schaie, K. W., and C. Hertzog. (1982). Longitudinal methods. In *Handbook of developmental psychology.* ed. B. B. Wolman. Englewood Cliffs, NJ: Prentice-Hall.

Society for Research in Child Development. (1977). *Ethical standards for research with children.* Chicago: Society for Research in Child Development.

3

Theoretical Approaches to Development

*I*n this chapter, the theories that underlie the study of development are presented. Beginning with the psychoanalytic theories, the two most comprehensive examples (Freud and Erikson) are outlined along with their major stages of development. This discussion is followed by a presentation of the most extensively studied cognitive theory (Piaget), including its associated stages.

Nonstage theories of development are presented with discussions of learning, biology, and humanistic approaches. Finally, a comparison of all of the approaches together is presented along with an argument for taking an eclectic viewpoint.

What is presented in the following chapter is an introduction to the individual theories about development. They will be further expanded in the chapters on psychosocial development within each age group, namely, chapters 9, 13, 17, and 21.

THEORIES IN GENERAL

Theories serve two general purposes. The first is to explain all of the data, or behavioral observations, that are available for scrutiny. That is, they are general statements that attempt to integrate all of the collected data on a given topic into some unifying package to give meaning to those data. In so doing, they attempt to explain current behaviors in light of past behaviors, to give continuity to one's development. The second is to provide hypotheses about what will happen in the future either very generally or with an eye to specific environmental conditions. The data from tests of these hypotheses serve to measure the accuracy and usefulness of the theory that generated the hypothesis.

The size of the theory does not necessarily matter. Some theories are very narrow in scope. They are made to explain a certain amount of data and not to cover the whole lifespan. Other theories are much more global in nature and attempt to put together all the major events coming from the environment that would influence development at all. This means that one of the things a good theory can do is to differentiate central issues (those paramount to development) from minor issues (those on the periphery, providing little if any influence on the overall course of development).

No one theory is accepted by all developmentalists because no one theory can explain all the particular influences on development. This is an important consideration because each theory supports its own set of hypotheses since each theory has its own perspective, its own way of looking at how development occurs. Developmental psychologists may get a biased viewpoint by utilizing only one theory. Hence, much of the study of development considers an eclectic approach. Quite often to understand a given problem, observation or pattern of development, more than one theory may explain it well. In addition, they may provide additional hypotheses of what the outcome will be of this particular pattern or behavior, given a specific set of environmental conditions. It is easy to see the usefulness of theories: they take us beyond specific individual events and give us a much broader understanding of the entirety of human development.

PSYCHOANALYTIC THEORIES

Psychoanalytic theories are stage theories, meaning they take a discontinuous approach to development (see chapter 1). Basically, development occurs within a specific stage until either biology or experience (life events) takes the person into another stage. During this next stage, the person will learn, change, and develop until biology (maturation) or experience is such that a new stage begins. Within a given stage, certain conflicts occur or are presented, based on the environment and the biology that the person has to deal with at that particular time. In this way, what the psychoanalytic theorist is looking at is the influence of unconscious drives and motives that may be beneath the behavior currently seen, and how those unconscious drives not only influence but are changed over time and experience. Within any given stage, a child is both passive (i.e., responsive to the environment that changes the child) and active (i.e., the child is born with certain characteristics that aid in making changes on the environment). So, the psychoanalytic approach is both a passive and an active approach to development.

Freud

Theories of development were initially the musings of what are called armchair philosophers, meaning they were simply thoughts with little effort to evaluate those thoughts against observations of actual human behavior. However, in the late 1800s, Sigmund Freud, a medical doctor living in Vienna, Austria, took his observations of the neurological and behavioral problems of adults and tied them in with the neurological models being presented by medical institutions. He then postulated the first overall theory of human development that attempted to combine observations of people with a medical model of activity.

Freud's psychoanalytic theory is based on an assumption that there is a drive present at birth that is seated within the unconscious of an individual. This unconscious is called the id. At different points in a person's lifespan, this drive, which he called the libido, or sexual energy, will be expressed through different body parts. Freud divided a person's overall personality into three main sections: id (the unconscious), ego (the outward signs of the individual person), and superego (the internalized parent of an individual, an internalized conscience). These three sections serve different functions and interact differently in order to help create the individual as seen on the outside.

Id. The id seeks gratification for all of its wants and needs. It is basically hedonistic. It wants what it wants when it wants it. So it desires pleasure and attempts to avoid pain. It is also a repository of all of the hurts and pleasures that a person experiences throughout his or her life. The id works on the pleasure principle. Since it seeks nothing but gratification of its own individual needs, the id has a very difficult time waiting; the id has no patience. For example, from birth to the age of two years, children have a very difficult time accepting the concept of waiting for something. They want to be fed *now.* They want their diaper changed *now.* They want pain removed *now.* They want discomfort removed *now.* Therefore, the id is a "I want it *now*" sort of mechanism.

Ego. Over time, the infant learns that things do not always occur when they are desired; the infant learns to wait. This is the function of the ego. It ameliorates the id by helping it accept the concept of patience. Whereas the id responds to the pleasure principle, the ego works on the reality principle, that is, the reality of the situation or environment. For example, a child may want to eat dessert now instead of eating his or her vegetables. The parent responds by saying, "No, you must eat your vegetables first." The id would be upset, but the ego would calm it, thereby allowing the child to wait until the vegetables are eaten and then have dessert. Over years, what develops into adulthood, quite frankly, is the ego. This is what we normally see on the outside of the individual. It is what is presented to others as the adult personality.

Superego. The superego is the internalized parent; that is, it works on the parent principle. It gives us a conscience of what is good or bad about our particular behaviors. When a child does something that a parent does not like and the parent disciplines the child in some way, the child begins to learn the difference between right and wrong, to differentiate between appropriate and inappropriate behaviors. The superego part of our personality gives us the concept of guilt. It tells us whether our behaviors, regardless if they are seen or not, are wrong or not. It is the part of our personality that guides us just as a parent would guide us.

DEFENSE MECHANISMS

Accordingly, when the id attempts to gratify itself for a particular need, it may come into conflict with the ego, which says, "You can't do that now," or with the superego which says, "It's wrong to want that," or it may come into conflict with both. When this conflict occurs, the result is often anxiety: a generalized uneasiness about life or the events surrounding the situation that is being viewed or is currently happening. In order for the id to deal with this anxiety, defense mechanisms are developed. These are gimmicks that the ego and id use together to help deflect anxiety until a later point in time when it will be easier to deal with.

Repression. This is a defense mechanism whereby something that is excruciatingly painful, or for which there is a great deal of anxiety, is literally forgotten. It is an unconscious, motivated forgetting. If a father or mother dies, the child, or later the adult, may not remember all of the particulars revolving around the death, burial, wake or any of the funeral ceremony. This happens not because the person was absent or did not participate, but because the person's anxiety over the death of this parent was so traumatic that it was much easier to repress or forget that information. In another example, a teenage boy may repress, or "forget," his ex-girlfriend's phone number after their traumatic breakup. His anxiety over his loss is so great that, in Freudian terms, his id does not want him to remember.

Regression. This occurs when a situation is anxiety-producing and the person reverts to behaviors of an earlier time that were less anxiety-provoking. For example, a four-year-old may "rule the roost" with no brothers or sisters. If a new baby comes into the household, this four-year-old may start wetting the bed, wearing diapers, throwing tantrums, and in effect act more like an 18-month-old. The child is reverting to behaviors that are either indicative of a time when there was much less anxiety in life or when those behaviors were ways to deal with anxiety. Regression can also occur in order to gain attention. For example, a four-year-old has very good table manners and is sitting at a table with a two-year-old brother or sister. If the two-year-old starts throwing food and the parents start giving a lot of attention to get the two-year-old to stop, the four-year-old may also start throwing food in order to gain the same kind of attention. The cause may be envy or jealousy of the attention given to the younger sibling.

Displacement. With this defense mechanism, a child or an adult has a difficult time expressing anger or displeasure to a person who causes them some amount of emotional hurt. This anger, or upsetness, is subsequently taken out either on someone or something that cannot hurt the person. For example, if a child is angry at a parent because the parent requires the child to sit still or act in a mannerly fashion, the child may either push a younger sibling or a dog or break something in the house. This happens because the child is having a difficult time expressing anger to the parent. The anger is displaced to the younger sibling or the dog or the broken object, thereby helping the child alleviate his or her anger.

The voicing of defense mechanisms and timing of their use depend greatly on the ego strength of the individual, the actual events occurring, what is provoking the anxiety, past history that exists within the id of hurt or pain around similar situations, and so on. It is important to realize that defense mechanisms, while they serve to keep us from anxiety, are not necessarily bad things to have. According to Freud, a defense mechanism can be useful to keep us from painful anxiety until our ego strength is sufficient to handle the anxiety directly. If defense mechanisms are continually used, however, they keep us from dealing with anxiety and from attaining our full growth as an individual within any one of Freud's developmental stages.

Freud's Five Developmental Stages

Freud saw development as occurring over five distinct psychosexual stages, meaning the id, ego, and superego worked to channel libidinal energy through five different *erogenous* zones (areas corresponding to physical/sexual pleasure) on the human anatomy over the course of the lifespan. Table 3.1 presents the five Freudian psychosexual stages in order with the ages they represent. Freud saw an individual's personality and development arising from a number of biological instincts. Each of these instincts would have to be gratified throughout life, and the sexual instinct, according to Freud, was the most important of them. Depending on the age and sex of the individual, gratification would be achieved through a major body part. The biological function of maturation determined which body parts would be the locus of gratification.

Accordingly, as the libido is channeled through different body parts at each psychosexual stage, important developmental tasks are learned. During the oral stage, the child becomes attached to whoever meets the oral needs of getting the child fed, usually the parents. During the anal stage, issues of

Psychosexual Stage (Freud)	Psychosocial Stage (Erikson)	Cognitive Stage (Piaget)
Oral (birth to 18 months). Zone of gratification is the mouth. Baby gets pleasure from eating and sucking.	*Basic trust versus mistrust (birth to 18 months).* Baby gains sense of what to trust and appropriate degrees of mistrust.	*Sensorimotor (birth to 2 years).* Infant develops from a being who responds instinctually to one who relates actively to the environment.
Anal (18 months to 3 years). Sensual interest is focused on the anal region. Child learns to control withholding and expelling feces, thereby experiencing gratification.	*Autonomy versus shame and doubt (18 months to 3 years).* Child gains a sense of balance between independence and feelings of shame and doubt.	*Preoperational (2 to 7 years).* Child uses a system of symbols such as words to relate to the world and the "objects" therein.
Phallic (3 to 6 years). Child begins to learn male and female role models. Parents are models for gender identification. Genital region is zone of gratification.	*Initiative versus guilt (3 to 6 years).* Child gains confidence to try out new skills and is not inhibited by lack of success.	
Latency (6 years to puberty). Period of relative quiet. Child puts gender-appropriate behavior into practice.	*Industry versus inferiority (6 years to puberty).* Child practices skills of the society while overcoming feelings of inferiority.	*Concrete operations (7 to 12 years).* Child handles concrete situations, using logic for problem solving.
Genital (puberty through adulthood). Sexual interest matures, shifts from parents to peers.	*Identity versus identity confusion (puberty to young adulthood).* Adolescent experiments to forge an understanding of self.	*Formal operations (12 years to adulthood).* Individual can resolve hypothetical and existing problems through abstract reasoning.

Table 3.1   Developmental Stages According to Various Theories

control and self-control are important so the child develops independence. Through attaining control over his or her own body, the child figuratively begins to develop control over his or her own destiny. During the phallic stage, the individual begins to learn gender identification with the same-sex parent, because of the interest in the parent of the opposite sex. Hence, a child begins to learn male and female roles. During the latency stage, a time of quiet between the phallic and genital stages, the child's physical body matures for subsequent puberty and adulthood, and the child puts the gender-appropriate behaviors acquired during the phallic stage into practice. During the genital stage, the child learns to channel the desire for opposite-sex contact from parent to peer and to develop mature sexual interest from this point onward.

Erikson

Whereas Freud's theory centered on biological and maturational forces that drive the development of the individual, Erik Erikson, a student of Freud, centered his psychoanalytic theory more on social and cultural influences, that is, how these forces shape the development of the individual. In addition, Erikson gave more credit to the conscious part of the individual rather than the unconscious part as Freud did overwhelmingly.

Rather than seeing an individual's development as centered on a particular body part, Erikson saw development as an interaction between the person's individual characteristics and his or her interactions with the social environment and any support therefrom. According to Erikson, the individual is going to be confronted with different environmental, social, and cultural dilemmas throughout life. Some balance must be achieved between a strictly positive result and a strictly negative one in these dilemmas. Table 3.1 presents Erikson's psychosocial stages in comparison with the same age ranges of Freud's psychosexual stages. For example, in Stage 1, trust versus mistrust, the infant enters the world with certain biological as well as social and cognitive needs. These needs can be met by the child's caregivers, that is, mother and father, thereby giving the child a sense of trust that his or her needs will be met. Within that first year the infant must also learn a sense of mistrust. This means that the infant must also learn to discriminate when those needs might not be met. Therefore, a child must come out of each stage with a sense of balance between his or her needs and the ability of the culture, society, and family to meet those needs.

Erikson's counterpart to Freud's libido is something he called the *epigenetic principle*. Essentially, the eight dilemmas that Erikson believed people face in life are actually parts of each person that achieve maturity at different points in the lifespan. In each of his stages, the specific part, or developmental task, matures with a crisis that must be faced. Rather than being seen as a catastrophe, each crisis is viewed as a time of potential for achieving healthy development.

In comparison, Eriksonian theory appears as a more positive theory in terms of conflicts and outcomes that individuals will face as they go through life. In addition to a sexual instinct, Erikson takes into account other instincts of achievement, success orientation, and self-fulfillment within each and every child. Both theories are seen as global theories to aid in understanding where a child is in the current state of development and how that level of development has been influenced by past events and past stages.

In summary, psychoanalytic stage theories provide a framework, under which an unconscious, driving force exists, as well as a way of assessing the interaction between innate biological maturation principles and the overall environment (including the caregivers the child comes in contact with). Psychoanalytic theories, by their nature, are good at explaining the influences that have occurred in the past and good at explaining how those influences interact with present-day development. However, they are not good at being tested, because they tend not to generate hypotheses that can be explored in a laboratory or natural environment. Likewise, psycho-analytic theories give us an overall perspective of the lifespan. This means the people we are as adults, or teenagers, can be viewed in the context of having developed from children. The problem with this approach, however, is that it is never clear just how influential childhood events are on adolescent and adult behaviors when those ages are reached.

COGNITIVE THEORIES

There are number of cognitive theories of development, the most prominent of which is one that was promoted by Jean Piaget, a Swiss psychologist. According to cognitive theorists in general, and Piaget in particular, the emphasis on development is in the way a child thinks and on the child's interactions with the surrounding inanimate and animate world. Because Piaget sees children as active in their environment, the concept of knowledge acquisition is not a static event. It is a lifetime developmental process, and the ways of acquiring knowledge change as children react and interact differently with the environment and with the world. It is as though Piaget equates knowledge acquisition and development as the same sort of process. Piaget's theory is a stage theory as were the two psychoanalytic theories; one stage builds upon the information attained by the previous stage. Hence, each stage builds on what came before and provides a basis for what will follow. Table 3.1 presents the stages of Piaget's cognitive theory in comparison with the psychoanalytic stages of Freud and Erikson.

Certain basic assumptions underlie Piaget's cognitive theory. First, in order for a child to attain all of the stages listed in Table 3.1, the child must experience normal, healthy, biological cognitive growth. Any child who is in one way or another impaired intellectually may develop slower, or not reach one of the higher stages or not attain many of the concepts within a given stage. Therefore, the individual stages coincide with development of the brain and myelinization, which will be presented in chapters 5 and 6. The second assumption is that, all things being equal, an individual will indeed go through all of these stages following biological growth of the brain, provided the environment allows sufficient experiences to help in practice with the newly developed abilities of each new stage.

The third assumption is that there is a homeostatic mechanism that promotes cognitive changes. This is the mechanism of "equilibrium": essentially every individual wants to maintain a sense of cognitive balance or organization. When new information is presented or biological growth causes a new thinking process to be available, a period of disequilibrium is presented. This happens because the new information or process confronts our organization. In order to regain equilibrium, our thinking must be changed to either include the information or adopt new thinking principles. This involves refining old "schemas" or constructing new ones. Schemas are mental concepts which guide or influence interaction with the environment. For example, an infant's first schema with regard to its parent might be that crying causes an adult to come. However, as the child develops language capabilities, that schema may be broadened to include not only crying but also yelling for "Mommy" or "Daddy" and having an adult come. With advanced development and advanced language capabilities, the child's schema about how to get an adult to meet its needs expands to include language as well as possible other behaviors.

When new situations or information cause disequilibrium, a process of adaptation helps return the individual to a state of equilibrium. Adaptation involves bringing the new information from the world or about the world into the schema and either incorporating that into the existing schema or changing the schema. The process of bringing information in and letting the current schema handle it is a process known as *assimilation*. With the above example, a child learns that crying will bring an adult, screaming will bring an adult, and whimpering will also bring an adult, that is, any variant on the form of crying. However, with new biological processes ongoing in the brain and the ability of the infant now to use language, the infant learns that something entirely different or qualitatively different from a scream can also bring about the presence of an adult. This changing of a schema is a process known as *accommodation*. In essence, then, people achieve balance through adaptation of schemas that are used to deal with the world: either the schema can handle new information and processes with slight expansion (assimilation), or the schema must change (accommodation). Generally speaking, if the process changes, it results in new schemas.

Lastly, all organisms actively seek knowledge and stimulation. Therefore, cognitive development will occur as individuals handle all new forms of information. This can be seen simply with habituation, a process whereby something is continually presented to an infant until it is no longer of interest to the infant. According to Piaget it is no longer of any interest because there is no new knowledge in the presentations, and therefore no further cognitive development can occur.

Comparison with Psychoanalytic Theories

Whereas psychoanalytic theories explain emotional and personality development, cognitive theories explain intellectual development. They help us understand the individual structures and thinking processes of thought as well as the internal needs for new thoughts when old ones are outdated or outmoded. This understanding of the thought process that has come from cognitive theories has been applied almost exclusively to theories of education. Where education used to involve teaching students such concepts as math through lectures or demonstrations, it now appears that teaching new concepts is much easier to do if children can have hands-on experience with objects that they can manipulate. In this way, they can develop abstract possibilities and solutions using specific concrete activities.

On the other hand, this discussion would lead one to believe that cognitive growth will occur regardless of the individual's place in the culture or society, and there is some evidence to suggest that may not be the case. In other words, where the cognitive theories of development do not take into account the role of the culture, the society or the home environment in providing a mix of equilibrium and disequilibrium, the psychoanalytic theories do as well as some of the other theories soon to be mentioned. In addition, these stages that Piaget presents are not universal. The ages may be different depending on the culture or the environmental experience the child has, and some stages are never reached. For example, the stage of formal operations is possible for all adults, but depending on one's practice with it in school or in young adulthood, it may very well not be attained at all. Hence, these individual stages may not happen at an even sort of schedule but rather at some sort of uneven and nonuniversal rate.

LEARNING

Where the psychoanalytic and cognitive theories take a stage approach to the development of individuals, learning theories do not. The learning theory approach assumes all events are a continuing process of development. Accordingly, the learning theorists see the ability to learn as an evolutionary survival mechanism. It must be present at birth or near birth for an infant to survive. Therefore, stages of learning do not actually exist. What happens is that an infant begins learning from birth about how to interact with the environment and how the environment will interact with the infant. Change in that infant's development, whether in terms of personality, coping skills or simple associations, is a process that continues throughout life. The same skills that are used by an elderly person are used by an infant and vice versa. Therefore, according to the learning theory approach, there are three basic learning skills, or learning processes, that humans utilize.

Classical Conditioning

Table 3.2 describes the classical conditioning process. It is based on a very simple reflex. This means that some stimulus produces some response on a reliable level. Every time the stimulus occurs the response occurs. This is called an unconditioned or unlearned stimulus that produces an unconditioned or unlearned response. If some other event occurs close in time to the unconditioned stimulus, it can be paired with that. In other words, it can signal that the unconditioned stimulus is about to occur. As in the table, the sight of a baby bottle would come to mean that the nipple in the mouth that would produce the sucking is about to occur. With repeated pairings of the sighting of the bottle with the nipple in the mouth, the sucking would occur with the bottle sighting alone. When that happens, classical conditioning has taken place.

Classical conditioning is often considered an association type of learning. It gives a signal that something else is going to happen. It is not unlike hearing plates rattling in a kitchen before dinner. You do not know whether dinner is on the table or not, but you do know that dinner will arrive soon. This occurs even though you do not see the food or taste it, because the two things have occurred close enough together in time that hearing the plates means that food is about to be presented. This type of learning is essential for many developmental processes. For example, it appears to be important in learning language. The way an infant will learn the names for objects and actions is by having the word associated with a picture of the object or action or with the actual object or action. It is also a method that explains how children develop their initial emotional responses to either things or objects or people. This process explains why a mother or father may be a safer object for a child to be around than a stranger: the child has come to learn that the presence of the mother or father is a signal for the child to feel good. The parents represent love, nice things happening, being cared for, caressed, and comforted. Likewise, if one of those parents consistently presents punishment, for example, spanking, then that parent will become associated with painful sorts of stimuli and might even be avoided. This process is important not only for learning about individual objects and their attributes, but also for giving emotional cues related to people, things, and actions within the environment.

Two other processes are important in the development of the individual. The first is stimulus generalization. This process can describe what happens the first few times any bottle is seen by an infant. Not only would the sight of the original bottle promote sucking, but so would any other similar looking bottle. However, after repeated pairing of one specific bottle with

Step 1		Step 2		Step 3	
Stimulus	Response	Stimulus	Response	Stimulus	Response
Nipple in the mouth (Unconditioned stimulus: UCS)	Sucking (Unconditioned response: UCR)	Nipple in the mouth (Unconditioned stimulus: UCS) + Sighting of bottle (Conditioned Stimulus: CS)	Sucking (Unconditioned response: UCR)	Sighting of bottle (Conditioned Stimulus: CS)	Sucking (Conditioned response: CR)

Table 3.2   The three steps in the development of a classically conditioned response. In step 1, the unconditioned stimulus automatically triggers the unconditioned response. In step 2, an additional stimulus occurs at the same time as the unconditioned stimulus. In step 3, the additional stimulus—called the conditioned stimulus—triggers the original response.

the nipple in the mouth and the sucking response, the infant would come to tell the difference between the different bottles (i.e., the second process of stimulus discrimination) and begin to suckle at the sight of only one bottle. What we see is a process by which children learn cues and then learn to discriminate what the cues mean even if they are very close in sound, sight, or proximity with each other.

Operant Conditioning (Instrumental Conditioning)

This process describes how the consequences of some behavior influence the behavior itself. Basically, any behavior that is reinforced in some way is more likely to occur again. This can be a positive reinforcement in which something desired is obtained; therefore, the behavior that acquired the desired object is more likely to be repeated. The second type, termed negative reinforcement, occurs when a behavior removes something unpleasant, making that behavior rewarded and more likely to be repeated again. Both positive and negative reinforcement strengthen the behaviors that caused them. For example, examine the situation where a young child comes into a kitchen while dinner is cooking. The child starts whining or crying for a cookie. The parent involved decides not to give in to the whining. But as the child continues to whine, the parent becomes more upset and irritated because the whining is getting on his or her nerves. At this point the parent decides, "Well, what can it hurt?" and gives the child the cookie.

The child's behavior has been positively reinforced; that is, the child has learned that whining will get the cchild what he or she wants. The adult's behavior has been negatively reinforced; that is, the adult learned that if he or she gives in to what the child wants, the irritating behavior will cease. Therefore, both the whining and the giving in are likely to recur despite the parent's insistence in thinking, "Oh, I will never do this again."

Punishment, on the other hand, is designed to weaken or remove some undesired or undesirable behavior. This might be done by eliminating something positive or evoking something negative following the behavior. Therefore, a child's misbehavior might result in the loss of TV privileges, or it might involve a spanking.

COMBINING REINFORCEMENT AND PUNISHMENT

Important in understanding the processes of reinforcement and punishment is something that is essential to both of them: what is reinforcing or punishing may be different for individual children or situations. For example, one would assume that a spanking would be a punishing thing and would probably reduce the behavior that caused it. However, for a child who may feel that he or she does not get enough attention from a particular parent, it may very well be that when a child does some misbehavior and gets a spanking from a particular parent the child may do the behavior again just to get a spanking. What the parent perceives as punishment, the child might perceive as reinforcement. A prime example of this is with the problem of hyperactivity in classrooms. Quite often, hyperactivity is viewed as a symptom of attention deficit disorder (ADD will be covered in later chapters). ADD has often been viewed as a biological problem, whereby a child has not developed the appropriate brain mechanisms, or a biochemical dysfunction. The child has a difficult time controlling his or her attention and maintaining quiet when asked to follow directions. In most cases where this is truly the problem, some form of drug therapy brings the child's behavior under control so that the child is manageable. However, recent studies indicate that as much as 50 percent of what appears to be hyperactivity in children is not ADD-related but is rather a learning disorder; that is, the children have learned that if they act up in class, they get the attention they want. Getting attention from parents, teachers or other classmates is reinforcing, and the child will be more hyperactive. A child who feels in need of a lot of attention yet is not getting it in a classroom of thirty students with a single teacher, may feel he's getting even less attention than he desires. All the child needs to do is stand up once in the middle of a classroom when it is supposed to be quiet and the child finds that the teacher and other students direct all their attention to him. It becomes reinforcing for him to stand up, run around, make noise, or generally act hyperactive.

A way to change this behavior is to change the punishment and reinforcement characteristics. When the child is quiet or doing some appropriate, socially accepted behavior, the teacher should reinforce the child by praising him or her. When the child does act hyperactive, the teacher should simply remove him or her from the classroom. This is a form of "punishment" called non-reinforcement, whereby the child is removed from a situation where reinforcement is potentially possible. Therefore, the child is not reinforced for the disruptive behavior and it should quickly decrease. Both reinforcement and punishment can be active forces in development.

As with classical conditioning, the processes of stimulus discrimination and stimulus generalization are also at work in operant conditioning. For example, a child may realize that he or she can get away with all sorts of behaviors and not be punished for them with one parent but also realize that another parent is very strict and therefore the child needs to toe the line. This constitutes stimulus discrimination. What the child will do is to push the limits of what can and can't be done in an attempt to see if stimulus generalization, that is, with same-sex adults, occurs. These processes are very important in the early years of development because they tend to establish patterns of understanding, learning, and behaviors that the child will then continue to follow over time.

Social Learning Theory and Modeling

A variant of the learning theory approach to development has been presented by Albert Bandura. This variant is based on the concept that all learning happens with regard to other people. In other words, an interaction involving other people occurs during the learning process, one that goes beyond simple reinforcement and association. Bandura calls this social learning. It involves the imitation or copying of the behaviors of a model and is easily seen in other species because it has significant survival value. Some behaviors, if they were required to be learned by trial and error, would result in the death or significant harm of some species or members of a species. For example, an animal learning to avoid particular situations would only have to observe its parent avoiding similar situations.

Social learning theory says that if you look beyond normal trial-and-error learning (operant conditioning) or association-and-meaning learning (classical conditioning) you can gather a great deal of information simply by imitating behaviors of other individuals. This modeling process requires the observer to do five things. First, the observer must pay attention to the model and be able to physically repeat the model's behavior. This means, for example, that if a model is showing a child how to tie a shoe and that child is handicapped or too young to have the necessary coordination, the child will not be able to imitate that behavior. Second, there must be some retention of that behavior. For example, the observer must be able to see it, pay attention to it, and then remember it over a period of time. It is absolutely useless in the imitation process if the observer cannot remember two hours later the behavior that was modeled. Third, the model should be someone who has some status with the individual observer. Hence, parents will be the most significant models for a child. As adults, we imitate the behaviors of athletes, movie stars, and people with notoriety because we see these people as those we admire. Fourth, we have to see that when the behavior is done, the model gets rewarded for doing that behavior. If a child is watching a parent tie a shoe and the parent does a bunch of stuff that doesn't work, then the child is not going to imitate the behavior. Imitation happens when the child can see the behavior working and reinforcement occurs for the model. The last step is that when the observer does the behavior, the observer must also then be reinforced for that behavior (by imitating the model's behavior, the child successfully ties his or her shoe). From that point on normal operant and classical conditioning reinforcement techniques will rule whether that behavior occurs or not. And at that point, then, the behavior (shoe tying) becomes a part of the child's repertoire.

Traditional operant and classical conditioning theories do not deal with thought or motivational principles on the part of the child, whereas social learning theory does. It assumes that the child wants to imitate the given behavior, rather than just do it as a trial-and-error process. This means that when the child does imitate a behavior and gets some positive feedback for doing that behavior, the child may be motivated to continue the behavior again. Therefore, the concepts of cognition and motivation are intimately involved in social learning theory, meaning that other kinds of behaviors can be imitated besides simple survival and maintenance behaviors.

Children can test out alternative patterns with their own thoughts and choose the ones they prefer because of the desirable outcomes that may come with them. Children can practice forethought as they get older. This means that the thought process for learning theory, with social learning theory attached, becomes an integral part of the developmental scheme. One would assume, then, or predict from this, that the younger the child, say an infant or a preschooler, the more mistakes made, resulting in more regrets over mistakes. However, by the time the child has acquired a sufficient memory of failures and successes (cognition), he or she could bring past experience to bear. In addition, children's observations of other people would help in making choices to achieve what they want to achieve, getting the reinforcements they want, and avoiding the punishments they don't want.

In looking at learning theory, we have a continuous theory of development. Individuals can acquire specific behaviors as well as life styles and thought processes, based on the principles of reinforcement and modeling. This theory is easy to test as well as to explain past behaviors, and lends itself easily to setting up new hypotheses for subsequent behaviors and testing them.

Much of what we know about learning theory, however, was acquired from the use of animals, and therefore it has to be consistently tested to see if human learning follows the same principles as animal learning. What worked for animals may not necessarily always work for humans. Concepts of interpretation, very complex reasoning skills, and understanding the meaning of items that are not included in the framework of animal learning may have been seen to be intimately involved in human learning, had the study of learning begun with humans. The reason this is important is that learning theory paradigms make it difficult to test those sorts of mental processes and assumptions about cognition and thinking. They are difficult to define and therefore difficult to test with controlled experiments. This also means that learning theory tends to not accept the concept of an unconscious which arose from the psychoanalytic framework and that seems to apply very well when looking at therapy. The concept of an unconscious, since it is not involved in the learning theory concept at all, may make the learning theory approach less relevant and less applicable to the totality of human experience.

LESS COMPREHENSIVE THEORIES

Biological

Biological theories attempt to explain development throughout the lifespan with a heavy emphasis on heredity and the genetic bases for behavior. They have come in different forms over time. The sociobiology theory tends to see many of our sociological interactions as biologically determined. Attachment behaviors an infant shows to a parent would be biologically determined and transmitted through genetic material just as hair color or eye color might be. The ethology approach views humans as having species-specific hereditary traits, just as every other animal species has its own specific traits that are instinctual and passed from generation to generation through the genes. The third more general biological approach was formed by Albert Giselle in the 1920s and incorporates both sociobiological and ethological approaches. Basically, it says that genes and their hereditary influences are the major determinants of development in the human. Biology also determines the sociological implications, the personal interactions, and the behaviors that are seen in humans.

Outside of basic genetic patterns (as discussed in chapter 4), the process that guides development is that of maturation. It is the genetic pattern that unveils itself over the course of time in a prescribed series of events. As presented in chapter 7, the development of motor behaviors in infants follows a prescribed series of events in order: raising the head, holding the chest up off the floor, sitting up on its own, crawling on all fours on the floor, standing with support, walking with aid from an adult, and finally walking under its own power. This process happens in a prescribed order, in a prescribed way, and at the prescribed time.

Maturation not only guides the body's individual development; it makes interaction with the environment possible at different levels. Biological theories do not exclude the environment as being important, but rather the environment takes a second-hand role. The environment really only becomes possible for interaction once the biology has determined the course of development. This will show up in later chapters under different sorts of principles. For example, in the development of the human, we see the concept of the principle of motor primacy: it does not appear to be possible for an infant to acquire some particular behavior until its body (the physical structure) is capable of doing that behavior. Therefore, you can't train an infant of two months to have control of its body for excretory purposes (toilet training). This can only happen once the child has developed sufficiently, matured, to have control over its bowel and bladder and is able to understand those sensations as they are approaching and communicate that understanding to an adult or travel under its own power to a bathroom.

In addition, two strong influences for the biological approach come from the way maturation generally occurs, that is, from head to tail, and from the inside outward. These are called the cephalocaudal and proximodistal principles, respectively.

Biological theories work well for explaining both infant and adolescent development. For example, the emotional and sociological changes that occur in adolescence, which are different from those that occur in middle childhood, are only possible because of the hormonal, bodily changes due to maturation at around puberty. When those changes occur and hormonal changes are present, they prompt the child, now adolescent, to begin to see the world differently. Hence, biology is the important determinant of environmental interaction.

According to these theories, all of development is guided by the maturation process. Maturation here is not the same thing as growth. Growth is a change in quantity or in size, not necessarily a change in quality that might develop because of new abilities made present by the maturation process. Growth occurs because of maturation and not vice versa.

Humanistic

A relatively new theory in the study of development is "new" only in terms of its being applied to children. Abraham Maslow devised a theory of human motivations that outline a progression of development across the adult portion of the lifespan. According to Maslow, every adult has an inherent drive to achieve full potential in life. This potential is termed self-actualization. The attainment of one's full potential in life can only be achieved, however, after one has met some more fundamental motivations.

These include (in order): physiological needs (those for food, shelter, and basic needs for surviving as an individual); safety and security (to be sure that one is taken care of, or for familyor for insurance); love and belongingness (to feel a part of a group, to feel cared for, to feel whole emotionally); and esteem and self-esteem (to feel a sense of self-respect and respect from the community at large). Accordingly, when one has achieved each of these lower levels, when the individual feels that it is under control, he or she is able to move on to the next higher level.

This theory, although interesting to adults in its own right, does have problems in application to children because of the child's inability to have control over many of these kinds of needs, such as esteem and self-esteem and safety and security—ones that the child must depend on others to provide. In addition, whereas Maslow saw self-actualization as occurring most likely in late adulthood or middle adulthood, it is difficult to see this sort of process as it may apply to children. However, the theory is only currently being applied to explain development, and it may be worthwhile to look at it in terms of the development of motivation processes.

COMPARISON OF ALL THEORIES

In evaluating or comparing all of the theories presented above, it would be easy to take the viewpoint that some are stage theories, some are not, some take a continuous view of development, some do not, and then try to show the pros and cons of each theory. In doing so, one could come to the conclusion that these theories compete to try to explain all of human development. And in that competition, each theory would be found to have some strong points and to be lacking in other areas.

However, it may be more appropriate to look at all of these theories together and, in effect, take an eclectic view of development. What this means is that each of the theories presented looks at one aspect of development and tries to use that one aspect as an explanation for all other facets of development. Some of the theories stress nature more, some stress nurture more, and some stress an interaction between the two. If you compare them, what you see is that each one has a central focus that is very different from all the other theories. Psychoanalytic theories stress the emotional development of the individual. Cognitive theories stress the thinking or intellectual development of the individual. Humanistic theories stress the motivational development of the individual. Biological theories stress the genetic or maturational component of development for the individual. Learning theories stress the development of an individual's interaction on a day-to-day basis with the environment: how he or she acquires information and uses that information.

All of the theories put together may actually describe the totality of human development; that is, each one looks at human development from a different perspective. One theory's emphasis on development from a specific perspective does not mean that all perspectives follow the same developmental pattern. This is not unlike the story of the blind men who tried to describe an elephant by describing the individual part that each blind man was touching. The man who had the trunk described the elephant in vastly different terminology from the blind man who had hold of the elephant's tail. If we view human development as the elephant and view each of these theories as different blind men, we can conclude that different theoretical perspectives examine and try to describe different parts of development. Human development may actually be best understood by a combination of all of these theories.

*P*sychoanalytic theories attempt to analyze the mind of the individual as essential to development. Freud views that development as a process of guiding certain basic instinctual urges, the most powerful of which is sex. These urges provide the drive behind all of our interactions with other people and the environment. If these urges are met, then development proceeds normally; if not, then the process becomes bogged down. For Erikson, however, instinctual drives are secondary to our social interactions. Basically, our experiences with our parents and others, as we grow, provide an environment in which our needs can be met in a balanced fashion.

Cognitive theories look at development from the viewpoint of how an individual processes information from the environment. According to Piaget, we begin life as basically a set of reflexes but quickly advance through a series of changes in our ability to think. As these abilities change, our perception of the world changes and subsequently we change.

Learning theory takes a viewpoint that stresses the responses of individuals to daily events and how the consequences of those responses may change our expectations of future events. Whereas the previous stage theories look at development from a very broad view, learning theory allows us to see the developmental process and its resultant changes from the viewpoint of the effects of individual events.

The last two theories presented, biology and humanism, tend to be more limited and less supported than any of the other theoretical approaches. Biological theories of development stress the influences of heredity and maturation and see the environment in a more supporting role. Humanistic theories see the developmental process from a motivational point of view; that is, you can understand development if you can understand what motivates individuals.

Most developmental psychologists tend to endorse an eclectic theoretical stance. Basically, they use the parts of each theory that may explain a current situation best. Thus, the process of development can be seen as being explained by the combination of a number of different theories.

Selected Readings

Arndt, W. B. (1974). *Theories of personality.* NY: Macmillan.

Baer, D. M. (1970). An age-irrelevant concept of development. *Merrill-Palmer Quarterly (16).*

Bandura, A. (1977). *Social learning theory.* Englewood Cliffs, NJ: Prentice-Hall.

——— (1986). *Social foundations of thought and action: A social cognitive theory.* Englewood Cliffs, NJ: Prentice-Hall.

Erikson, E. H. (1963). *Childhood and society.* NY: Norton.

Freud, S. (1938). *The basic writings of Sigmund Freud.* NY: Modern Library.

Gesell, A. (1926). *The mental growth of the preschool child: A psychological outline of normal development from birth to the sixth year including a system of developmental diagnosis.* NY: Macmillan.

Immelmann, K. (1980). *Introduction to ethology.* NY: Plenum.

Miller, P. H. (1983). *Theories of developmental psychology.* San Francisco: Freeman.

Piaget, J. (1954). *The construction of reality in the child.* NY: Basic Books.

——— (1983). Piaget's theory. In *Handbook of Child Psychology.* Ed. P. H. Mussen. NY: Wiley.

Skinner, B. F. (1953). *Science and human behavior.* New York: Macmillan.

Strachey, J. (1957). *The standard edition of the complete psychological works of Sigmund Freud.* London: Hogarth Press.

Thomas, R. M. (1979). *Comparing theories of child development.* Belmont, CA: Wadsworth.

4

Conception and Heredity

The natural basis for development begins at fertilization, when an ovum and sperm unite to form one cell with a complete set of chromosomal material. This material contains millions of genes, the "signals" for the hereditary traits that are inherited from the mother and father. The individual genes from each parent combine their signals to produce a genetic blueprint for the individual. Because of the ways that these combined signals may exist, it is possible to have a genetic pattern for an individual (genotype) that is not completely expressed to the outside world (phenotype). Primary influence for determination of the sex of a child comes from the genetic material provided by the father.

Genetic errors, the result of either genes for specific diseases or improper cell division, occur with a variety of patterns and are passed on to succeeding generations through a variety of different routes. Eugenics, selective breeding of specific traits, has been hypothesized as a way to deal with genetic errors. In any event, most development is normal, meaning that the vast majority of people are born with no obvious genetic (hereditary) abnormality. Also, the occurrence of some personality trait, behavior or even physical characteristic may depend largely on the interaction between heredity and the environment.

CONCEPTION (FERTILIZATION)

Development of every human being begins with conception, the moment when a single sperm cell from a male unites with a single egg cell from a female. Although this union can occur anywhere within the female reproductive system, fertilization usually occurs within the fallopian tubes. (See Fig. 4.1 for a diagram of these events and concepts.) The single sperm that fertilizes the egg (ovum) is one of as many as 350 million that may have been deposited by the male during intercourse. Those sperm, which individually are much smaller than an ovum, are capable of "swimming" through the uterus and up the fallopian tubes. When the ovum is encountered and a single sperm is able to penetrate the outer covering of the ovum, the ovum becomes immediately impervious to other sperm. The resultant newly fertilized ovum is called a zygote, and it contains all of the hereditary information that will "naturally" guide this human throughout life. (See chapter 1 for a discussion of the relative importance of the influences of nature vs. nurture on human development and chapter 5 for an outline of prenatal development from fertilization onward.)

You who are reading this material are actually in the minority considering all the possible fertilizations that apparently take place. That is, it is believed that at least 50 percent of all fertilized ova either do not implant themselves in the wall of the uterus, where prenatal development will take place, or are spontaneously aborted during the first weeks of the pregnancy. In addition, another 10 to 25 percent of fertilized ova are spontaneously aborted sometime later during the pregnancy (this is usually termed a miscarriage). Only about 25 percent to 40 percent of all fertilized ova ever become living persons.

BIOLOGY OF CONCEPTION

Genes and Chromosomes

The fundamental unit of hereditary transmission from one generation to another is the gene. It is composed of molecules of deoxyribonucleic acid (DNA) that are arranged in a specific order for that gene. In other words, the organization of DNA molecules, which is different for every gene, gives each gene its individual and exclusive function. That function is to control, or influence, the development of some specific characteristic or developmental process for the developing human being. Current estimates place the number of genes within every human cell at about a hundred thousand.

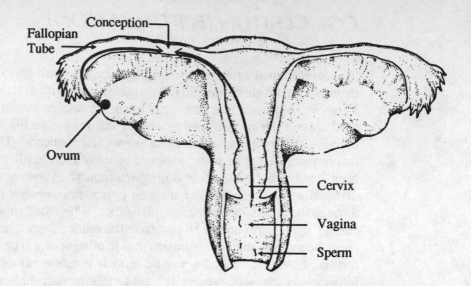

Fig. 4.1   As the ovum travels down the fallopian tube, it is met by sperms that have been deposited by the male during intercourse. When a single sperm is able to penetrate the ovum's outer covering, no other sperms will be accepted by the ovum. At this point, the zygote contains all the hereditary information needed for guiding development of this particular individual.

Just as each gene carries its own specific developmental "message," its location on its respective chromosome is also important. There are 46 chromosomes, arranged in 23 pairs, in every normal human cell. One of each of these pairs is supplied by the sperm, and the other member of the pair is supplied by the ovum at conception. Each chromosome is nothing more than a string of genes with each gene having its own specific location (locus), or spot. For example, the locus of the gene concerned with determining blood type (A, B or O) is found on chromosome 9 and nowhere else. At conception, the blood type gene on chromosome 9 from the father interacts with the blood type gene on chromosome 9 from the mother to determine the blood type of the child.

Types of Cells and Cell Division

Although there are many different types of cells and cell functions within the human body, they can all be subdivided into one of two classes: those that are required for some body process (including growth and tissue replacement), commonly called body cells; and those that are required for reproduction (sperm and ova), commonly called germ cells. Body cells are formed through a process of cell division called mitosis. Basically, all 46 chromosomes within one cell are duplicated and then evenly divided so that when cell division is complete the old and new cells are exact copies of each other. It is with this process that all body cells throughout a person's life have a copy of exactly the same genetic material that was in the zygote at conception.

Germ cells (sometimes called gametes) undergo a different cell division process from body cells. Although the early stages of a germ cell are ruled by the process of mitosis, the last stage before becoming a sperm or an ovum is governed by meiosis (from a Greek word meaning "to make smaller"). During meiosis the pairs of chromosomes are simply split apart rather than duplicated. One-half of each pair of chromosomes then ends up in the resultant germ cell; that is, each sperm or ovum has 23 individual chromosomes rather than 23 pairs of chromosomes. Therefore, when conception occurs the respective chromosomes match up in the zygote, giving a full complement of genetic material.

Autosomes and Sex Chromosomes

Of the 23 pairs of chromosomes in each human cell, 22 pairs match in size and number of genes. These 22 pairs, called autosomes, control the functioning and development of most of the body. The 23rd pair is the sex chromosomes, referred to as the X and Y chromosomes. Normally, females have two X chromosomes (referred to as XX), while males have one X and one Y (referred to as XY). The X and Y chromosomes are unique for two reasons. First, this pair determines the sex of the child. Since a female is XX, then all ova are potentially female because female germ cells each have one X chromosome. On the other hand, since each male is XY, one sperm from each germ cell will be X (a female chromosome) and one will be Y (a male chromosome). Therefore, if the ovum is fertilized by a single X sperm, the child will be female, and if it is fertilized by a single Y sperm, the child will be male. Second, since the X chromosome is larger than the Y chromosome, a male will inherit genes from his mother on her X for which there is no counterpart on the Y from his father. The implications of this imbalance will be discussed under the section on sex-linked inheritance.

Genetic Uniqueness

Even though each child in a family receives 23 chromosomes from each of the parents, it is highly unlikely that any two children will be exactly alike except in the case where they develop from the same fertilized ovum. These twins, termed monozygotic because they develop from the same zygote that happens to subdivide into two separate groups of cells, share the exact same hereditary influences and processes, for example, gender, appearance, susceptibility to disease, growth patterns, and so on. Therefore, these twins are theoretically identical.

Fraternal (dizygotic) twins, on the other hand, develop from two separately fertilized ova and may have no genetic similarity with each other. The reasons for this dissimilarity are varied. First, when the chromosomes divide during meiosis, there is no telling which chromosome of a pair will go into which germ cell. Hence, there are about eight million possible combinations of chromosomes that could occur for each germ cell. Second, during gamete production, chromosome pairs occasionally exchange portions of their genetic material before they separate, a process called crossing-over. Finally, when the genes from the sperm and ovum unite, they form combinations that are not present in the parents. Therefore, any set of parents can produce more than 65 trillion genetically different offspring (which is more than all of the people who have ever lived on the planet).

Genetic Interaction

If the genes on the chromosomes from both the mother and father are the same for a particular trait, then the genotype (the genetic potential inherited from the parents) will equal the phenotype (the actual expression of that inheritance). For example, eye color is a two-gene trait, meaning that only two genes are required to produce an individual's eye color. If a child inherited a gene for brown eye color from both the mother and father, then the child's genotype would equal his phenotype.

However, many traits are not so easily determined. In the first place, many human traits are polygenetic, meaning that many genes are required to determine the nature of that trait. Intelligence and skin color are good examples of polygenetic inheritance: each one requires the interaction of many different genes on many different chromosomes. It is likely that all complex human characteristics are at least in part the result of polygenetic inheritance.

In the second place, for those traits that utilize only two genes, there has to be a mechanism to determine what the phenotype will be when the two gene messages are different. There are three such mechanisms, all of which revolve around the concept of one gene being dominant (having a stronger influence) over another (called recessive).

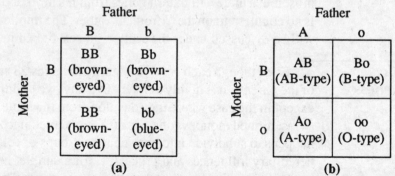

Table 4.1   (a) shows genotype possibilities and phenotype outcomes for all possible outcomes of eyecolor (brown vs. blue) where brown (B) is dominant over blue (b) and both parents have a recessive blue gene. (b) shows all possible bloodtype outcomes for co-dominance inheritance where A and B are both dominant and o is recessive.

STRAIGHT DOMINANT/RECESSIVE GENOTYPE

In this case, the influence of one gene will always be dominant over the influence of another. Whenever the dominant gene is present in the geno-type, its influence will be expressed in the phenotype regardless of the presence of the recessive gene. For example, brown eye color (B) is considered dominant over blue eye color (b). Therefore, a person will have blue eyes only if he or she has a "bb" genotype, meaning that the person acquired a "b" gene from Mom and a "b" gene from Dad. A mixture of either "BB" or "Bb" will produce brown eye color. Following this line of thinking, it is not possible for two blue-eyed parents to have a brown-eyed child because both parents must have a genotype of "bb" and their germ cells will have only "b" genes in them. On the other hand, it is definitely possible for two brown-eyed parents to have a blue-eyed child if their genotypes are both of the "Bb" type. They would then have some germ cells containing "B" genes and some containing "b" genes. (Table 4.1(a) shows this same example with all possible genotypes and phenotypes noted.)

CO-DOMINANCE OR COMBINING GENETIC INFLUENCES

This mechanism is found where more than one genetic influence is dominant. The best example is blood typing where types A and B are dominant and o is recessive. In this instance, wherever A and o or B and o interact, A and B, respectively, will dominate o as in a normal dominant/recessive interaction. Likewise, the only way to obtain a type o child is for o germ cells from each parent to combine at conception. However, should an A gene from one parent combine with a B gene from the other parent, then both influences will be present in the blood type AB, which is neither A nor B and is a distinct type of its own. Table 4.1(b) demonstrates this interaction between a parent who is Ao and one who is Bo for both genotypes and phenotypes.

INTERMEDIATE EXPRESSION

This mechanism does not seem to utilize either dominant or recessive qualities to any strong degree and may be a way of explaining how poly-genetic inheritance works. Essentially, all the genes involved in the specific trait combine to produce a working average of all the influences present. An example of this may be height: if a very tall man fathers a child with a very short woman, it is unlikely that the child will be one or the other. It is more likely that the child will be closer to the average height between the two parents. Indeed, there are probably many more genes that provide subtle influences to the overall phenotype.

A SPECIAL CASE: SEX-LINKED INHERITANCE

From the above discussion one can easily see that recessive genes can apparently show their influence only when they are present on both chromosomes of a pair. That is the case most of the time. However, as mentioned in the section on sex chromosomes males do not have a complete complement of genetic material on their Y chromosome to match the amount on the X chromosome. Therefore, wherever there is a gene on the X that has no matched locus on the Y, then the X chromosome gene will be both the genotype and phenotype; that is, the single X gene will be expressed. If that gene is normally a recessive gene in females (meaning that two of them would be needed for expression of the trait), it will act as though it is a dominant gene in males (meaning that it alone will express the trait). This will be of particular importance in the area of sex-linked inheritance of genetic disorders.

HEREDITARY ABNORMALITIES

Chromosomal or genetic defects are apparently quite common at the time of fertilization in more than half of all zygotes. Most of these are aborted early, often before the woman knows she is pregnant. The majority of the rest either die or are aborted later in the pregnancy. What remains, about 3 to 5 percent (or about 100,000 to 150,000 annually in the United States), are born with either a clear chromosomal abnormality, a specific genetically based disease or some genetically influenced malformation.

Chromosomal Problems: Autosomal and Gamete

AUTOSOMAL

Occasionally in the meiosis process an extra autosome is put into a germ cell so that 23 instead of 22 autosomes exist. At conception, the extra autosome attaches itself to one of the other completed pairs, usually to chromosome pair 8, 13, 14, 15, 18, 21 or 22. This results in conditions known as trisomy-8, trisomy-13, trisomy-14, and so on, respectively. Most of these die shortly after birth, except for trisomy-21, which is the main cause of Down's syndrome. These children exhibit facial characteristics of the eyes and nose that resemble those of people originating from Mongolia (thereby the mistaken description of a Down's syndrome child as mongoloid). They usually have heart problems and are slower physically and mentally in their development throughout life. Their life expectancy is shorter, probably because the extra chromosome makes them more vulnerable to disease and normal bodily deterioration through aging.

SEX-CHROMOSOME (GAMETE)

Most of the chromosomal anomalies occur with the sex chromosomes and involve multiple duplication of either the X or Y chromosome. Males, who normally would have an XY chromosome combination in the 23d pair, might be born with either multiple X (XXY) or multiple Y (XYY) chromosomes or both (XXYY). Females, on the other hand, who would normally have an XX chromosome combination, might be born with only one X (XO), or three, four or five (XXX, XXXX, XXXXX). In most cases, these problems occur no more than 1 in 1,000 births of either sex. A main characteristic of all of the sex chromosome problems is that if the children survive they almost invariably have some type of decreased or impaired mental functioning, a learning disability or a language skill problem.

Fragile-X Syndrome. This occurs when what appears to be a normal X chromosome in either a male (XY) or female (XX) is fragile or weak and may actually break apart. When it occurs in females, the side effects appear minimal, probably because of the influence of the normal X chromosome that remains. In the male, however, the fragile-X is strongly associated with the appearance of mental retardation, hyperactivity, autism, and a number of physical abnormalities. As mentioned in the discussion of the sex-linked inheritance, the occurrence of these problems in the male with fragile-X may well be due to the lack of corresponding genetic material on the Y chromosome to counteract or normalize the genetic message.

CAUSES OF CHROMOSOMAL PROBLEMS

The occurrence of these problems significantly increases with the age of one or both parents. Aging of the parent may not actually be the causative factor, but rather the age of the gametes/reproductive system. First, because women are born with all the gametes they will ever have, as the woman ages so does each remaining gamete. It is possible that as the gamete ages, the chromosomal material deteriorates. This could explain the rise in chromosomal abnormalities seen in older women as well as the same sorts of problems seen in women at an earlier age; that is, each gamete may age at a different rate. Second, since there is also a strong relationship between the age of the father and the occurrence of chromosomal problems, the male reproductive system may actually malfunction in the meiosis process with increasing age. It is possible that malformed sperm are produced with increasing regularity as the male ages. Finally, because people seem to decrease sexual activity as they age, and because sperm may deteriorate as time passes, the length of time between periods of intercourse may cause deformed sperm to be released when sex does occur.

Single Gene Defects

While the above chromosomal problems are relatively rare, the number of genetic diseases or malformations caused by one or two genes is not. At present, there appear to be about five thousand gene-related problems that can be transmitted from parents to children. Most of these problems are recessive, meaning that both genes for the disease must be present in order for the disease to be present (e.g., cystic fibrosis, sickle cell anemia, cleft palate, club feet). A few of these diseases are dominant (e.g., Huntington's chorea) and are therefore caused by the presence of a single gene for the disease. Finally, some of these genes are carried as recessive genes on the X chromosome and are subject to the sex-linked inheritance problem mentioned earlier. That is, a recessive gene for a particular disease (e.g., hemophilia, color blindness) on the X chromosome will only be expressed in females if there is a corresponding gene for the disease on the other X chromosome. However, that recessive gene on the X chromosome in a male may be expressed (just like a dominant gene) because of the lack of corresponding genes on the Y chromosome.

It should be noted at the end of this discussion about problems resulting from chromosomal or genetic influence that they are actually very uncommon. Although it is believed that each person carries at least four genes for some hereditary disorder, the vast majority of people are born with no outward expression of a genetic abnormality.

HEREDITY AND ENVIRONMENT: WEIGHING THE RELATIVE EFFECTS

What has been presented weighs very heavy on the nature side of the nature/nurture argument (see chapter 1 for a history of this discussion). However, as the following will demonstrate (as well as much of the other text), environmental influences can help or hinder genetic influences. This means that we should always expect to see some behavior or developmental process as the product of a variety of genetic and environmental factors; that is, that it is multifactorial. We will examine this with regard to both the physical and psychological sides of development.

Physical

Physical characteristics can be strongly influenced by factors in the environment. The following examples help demonstrate this point. First, the age at which children attain puberty is genetically programed; however, it has dramatically changed over the last hundred years in most industrialized societies. A century ago boys attained puberty usually between the ages of 15 and 17, and girls around the age of 15. Today, boys enter puberty usually between ages 11 and 13, while girls enter between ages 10 and 12. Given the centuries of time it takes for a genetic change to become commonplace in all of the population, a hereditary explanation of this phenomenon is highly unlikely. What is more likely is that the change has occurred because of better nutrition and medical care over the last hundred years. Hence, as people were better able to meet their nutritional and medical needs, those factors became less influential in determining the onset of puberty. Genetic and gender factors became more influential. Therefore, environmental influences can be used to allow genetic influences to emerge.

For the second example, phenylketonuria (PKU) is a recessive inherited disorder that results in a person's inability to oxidize the amino acid phenylalanine, which is found in many protein sources. By-products formed by this incomplete oxidation subsequently build up, causing central nervous system damage with resultant mental retardation. However, early infant detection can result in controlling PKU by simply removing phenylalanine from the diet. In this case, environmental influences can prevent the emergence of a genetically programed disease. There are many more instances, but these two examples demonstrate how factors in the environment can interact with factors in the genetic code of an individual.

Psychological

Because psychological factors are often seen as being the direct result of environmental influences, techniques have been developed for determining the genetic influences, if any, on behavior. The first technique uses identical (monozygotic) and fraternal (dizygotic) twins. If identical twins (who have the exact same set of genes) share a trait and fraternal twins (who share only half the same genes) don't, then it is likely that genes influence the occurrence of that trait. The second technique uses children who have been adopted as well as their adoptive and biological parents. On any particular trait, a strong relationship between the adopted child and the biological parents suggests a genetic explanation for the trait; a strong relationship between the adopted child and the adoptive parents suggests an environmental explanation for the trait. The third technique is actually a combination of the first two: the study of identical twins who have been separated at birth and raised in different families. Regardless of the technique used or the researcher involved, one major conclusion seems evident from all the research conducted: whatever the characteristic or trait studied, genes affect it. For example, when we look at intelligence we find that identical twins have IQ (intelligence quotient) scores that are more alike than those of fraternal twins. Likewise, there is often a stronger relationship between the IQ scores of an adopted child and his or her biological parents than with the adoptive parents. Finally, identical twins separated at birth and raised in different environments have closer IQ scores than fraternal twins raised in the same environment.

However, this does not mean that genetic influences are the sole determining factor of intelligence. For example, a genetic explanation for intelligence would predict that identical twins born in an intellectually impoverished environment (one where they would get little stimulation and interaction from adults except for survival needs) and separated at birth would have equivalent IQ scores regardless of what type of environment the children went into. Such does not appear to be the case. If one of the twins is adopted into an environment in which he or she receives individual attention, environmental stimulation, and personal encouragement from adults, while the other twin stays in the impoverished environment, then their IQ scores may have little relationship to each other. This fact has often been used to support early education/intervention programs such as Head Start. Basically, if we let the environment encourage intellectual growth, then we have the ability to achieve our genetic intellectual potential.

SPECIAL ISSUES IN CONCEPTION AND HEREDITY

Eugenics

As early as 1883, Sir Francis Galton proposed the idea of eugenics, or selective breeding, of humans much the same way that race horses are bred for particular traits. In this way, the better traits of society could be kept and the worst traits of society could be eliminated. A major problem became who or what would determine the traits to be kept versus those to be discarded. This was taken to its extreme during World War II when the Nazi army would steal babies—from the countries that they overran—who appeared to have the physical characteristics of the "pure stock" that Hitler wanted to run the world. In addition, special breeding houses were established where SS soldiers selected for their light features, height, and physique could mate with females who had such physical characteristics as blond hair and blue eyes. To weed out the undesirable traits, anyone who was mentally ill, who had a genetic disorder or who was otherwise deemed inferior was murdered.

Eugenics is conducted in a fashion today under the auspices of family planning, genetic counseling, and abortion. This does not mean that individuals are conducting genetic programs similar to those of the Nazis. The purposes are often more personal and family oriented: should a couple adopt someone else's child if the likelihood is high that the child will either die young or live a very restricted life? should a couple decide to abort a child if diagnostic tests reveal the same sort of choices? Either way, the decision to not have a child, or to abort one that is on the way, sometimes involves the removal of an individual because of a defect the individual has and the desire to ultimately have a child that is more genetically "correct."

At conception, the union of a male sperm and a female ovum brings together an individual's genetic blueprint for his or her entire life. The basic unit of genetic transmission (i.e., the gene) is composed of DNA coded to provide information for a particular trait for that individual. Genes are located on all 46 chromosomes. Twenty-two pairs of these chromosomes (autosomes) determine most of the bodily characteristics, whereas the 23d pair (sex chromosomes) determines the sex of the individual. The messages that genes carry make up the genotype of the individual, but what is actually expressed to the outside world makes up the phenotype. When these two "types" do not match, it is usually because one gene is dominant over another (a recessive one) or because somehow the gene messages "average" out.

Genetic errors can occur because of improper chromosome division during meiosis when the sex cells are formed, or because of specific genes for specific kinds of disease or malformation. Either way, the occurrence of genetic errors is small even though it is believed that every human carries at least four genes for some hereditary disorder.

At any point in development, every behavior or developmental process is most likely the result of an interaction of heredity and environmental influences. For example, the age at onset of puberty (heredity) has declined over the past hundred years because of better nutrition and medical care (environment). Likewise, IQ scores, which theoretically reflect the influence of heredity on intelligence, can be improved or reduced depending on the child's family environment.

Eugenics, the selective breeding of humans and animals, has been proposed in the past for societies to help them deal with the problem of genetic defects. As a societal process, it is not popular, yet individual couples practice a form of eugenics with the use of family planning, genetic counseling, and abortion.

Selected Readings

Dillon, L. S. (1987). *The gene: Its structure, function, and evolution.* NY: Plenum.

Emory, A. E. H. (1983). *Elements of medical genetics.* Edinburgh: Churchill Livingstone.

Koweles, R. V. (1985). *Genetics, society, and decisions.* Columbus, OH: Merrill Lynch.

Maxson, L. R., and C. H. Daugherty. (1985). *Genetics: A human perspective.* Dubuque, IA: Wm. C. Brown.

McKusick, V. A. (1986). *Mendelian inheritance in man.* 7th ed. Baltimore: Johns Hopkins University Press.

Packard, V. (1977). *The people shapers.* Boston: Little, Brown.

Patterson, D. (1987). The causes of Down's syndrome. *Scientific American* 257.

Rosen, R., and L. R. Rosen. (1981). *Human sexuality*. NY: Knopf.

Sutton, H. E. (1980). *An introduction to human genetics*. 3d ed. Philadelphia: Saunders.

Watson, J. D., and F. H. C. Crick. (1953). Molecular structure of nucleic acid: A structure for deoxyribose nucleic acid. *Nature* 171.

Wheale, P. R., and R. M. McNally. (1988). *Genetic engineering: Catastrophe or utopia*. NY: St. Martin's Press.

5

Prenatal Development

D_evelopment of the child is initially examined from the child's viewpoint. The three stages of pregnancy (germinal, embryo, and fetal) are outlined along with their major characteristics. This is followed by a lengthy discussion on the problem of birth defects (congenital problems)._

Congenital problems are usually the result of some disease, drug, environmental hazard or some factor in the maternal makeup that the placenta is unable to prevent from transmitting to the fetus. Methods of assessing the risk for congenital problems encompass looking at the dose-response curve in conjunction with the mother's nutrition and the child's critical periods in development. The father's role is also examined as a possible causative factor in the incidence of some abnormalities.

Emotional change seems to be the major component in the parents' view of prenatal development. This change includes developing an attachment to the fetus, treating it as an individual, and a willingness to take the responsibility for its upbringing. Essential to the parents' view of prenatal development is an understanding of genetic counseling, prenatal diagnostic techniques, and the issue of abortion.

FROM THE CHILD'S POINT OF VIEW

A child's life begins at the moment of conception, the point at which a male sperm unites with a female ovum. The journey for that life from a single-celled zygote (the fertilized ovum) to a newborn baby takes about forty weeks (counted from the first day of the last menstrual cycle) and is divided into three time periods, each of which is responsible for different aspects of prenatal development.

Period of the Ovum (or Germinal Period)

This segment of the pregnancy is the shortest, lasting from conception, which usually takes place within the fallopian tubes, through to implantation of the blastocyst in the wall of the uterus, approximately two weeks. The blastocyst is a fluid-filled sphere consisting of approximately 150 cells that have already begun the process of differentiation, aligning themselves into layers relative to the body organs and systems that will eventually develop. The outer, or upper, layer of cells is called the ectoderm; from it the skin, teeth, hair, nails, sensory organs, and the nervous system will develop. The inner, or lower, layer of cells is called the endoderm; from it the majority of internal body organs (digestive system, liver, pancreas, salivary glands, and respiratory system) will develop. Later a middle layer called the mesoderm will form the basis of the skeletal, reproductive, excretory, circulatory, and muscular systems. Finally, the implantation process occurs when the trophoblast (the outer layer of cells of the blastocyst) produces "threads," which burrow into the lining of the uterus for the purpose of obtaining nourishment from the mother. At that point, the blastocyst initiates hormonal changes that signal the body of the mother that a pregnancy has begun.

Period of the Embryo

This segment lasts from the end of the second week of the pregnancy (when implantation occurs) until about the end of the eighth week. More specifically, this period ends when solid bone cells begin to replace softer cartilage. Growth during this period is marked by certain general characteristics.

PATTERNS IN DEVELOPMENT

From this point onward through the pregnancy and for some time following the birth of the child, physical development will follow two basic patterns.

Cephalo-caudal. Literally, this means "head to tail." That is, those structures or systems that are closer to the head will begin development sooner than those that are farther away. For example, the heart begins to beat (circulatory system) long before there is any outward appearance of genitals (reproductive system). After birth, the same general pattern determines that an infant can control its head and neck long before it is able to stand and walk.

Proximo-distal. Literally, this means "near to far." That is, those structures or systems that are closer to the spine (representing the midline of the body) will usually develop before those that are farther away. For example, the heart, eyes, and nose will usually begin development before the hands and fingers because the former group is closer to the midline. This same pattern will also govern development within many systems. For example, the human tongue has four basic taste sensations (bitter, sour, salt, and sweet) that run from the back of the tongue (proximo) to the tip (distal), respectively. Of importance is the fact that these four sensations appear in that order (proximo to distal) over the course of the last month of the pregnancy.

DEVELOPMENT OF THE UMBILICAL CORD AND THE PLACENTA

Recall that implantation involves "threads" from the trophoblast burying themselves into the lining of the uterus. These threads subsequently develop into the placenta and umbilical cord during the period of the embryo. The purpose of these structures is simple: they provide a mechanism for the embryo to acquire oxygen and food molecules *for* cell metabolism while at the same time eliminating waste molecules *from* cell metabolism. When the child is in the germinal period, these acquisition and elimination processes can be done through simple cellular exchange because the child consists of so few cells. That is, oxygen and food molecules can easily pass through the ectoderm to the endoderm, and waste molecules can pass through in the opposite direction. As the embryo becomes more complex, the placenta serves to make that acquisition and elimination exchange from the embryo's developing blood stream and circulatory system to the mother's blood stream and circulatory system.

This exchange is done without mixing any of the mother's or embryo's blood. The reason for this is also simple: if the blood supplies mixed, then the mother's immune system would respond to the "invader" in much the same way that it would to a disease. The mother's immune system would attempt to destroy the embryo. The placenta serves as a barrier allowing only molecules of relatively small size to pass from parent to child. However, this placental barrier is not perfect, as we will discuss later in this chapter.

CRITICAL AND SENSITIVE PERIODS IN ORGAN DEVELOPMENT

Fig. 5.1 is a graphic presentation of the differentiation that occurs during the period of the embryo. In essence, the appearance of the embryo is transformed from almost reptilian early in the period to distinctly human by the end of the period. In order for that transformation to occur, all of the major body systems must essentially be "turned on" during this time so that they can begin their respective roles in the transformation, or development, process. When each system is activated, it undergoes an initial period of rapid growth and change that may last anywhere from two weeks (as in the case of tooth development) to five weeks (as in the case of ear development). This initial time of rapid growth, commonly referred to as the critical period for that system, is followed by a longer time of sustained growth and change, commonly referred to as the sensitive period for that system, that may last many weeks or even months or years, as in the case of the central nervous

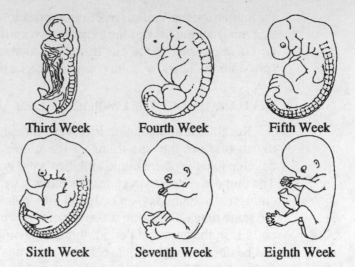

Third Week   Fourth Week   Fifth Week

Sixth Week   Seventh Week   Eighth Week

Fig 5.1   Development of the human embryo from the third through the eighth week after conception.

system, which continues to change well into the years that follow the birth of an infant.

The importance to the embryo of these critical and sensitive periods in organ and system development is simply this: all major body systems begin their critical periods during the time span that encompasses the period of the embryo, and most of them end during that same time span. This will be of crucial importance as we look at the negative effects that can result when events from the environment occur during an organ's or a system's critical period.

Period of the Fetus

Referring to Table 5.1, one could easily deduce that all major body and organ systems are in place and functioning to some degree by the end of the period of the embryo. Such would be a correct deduction. Hence, the period of the fetus amounts to a refinement of all the systems in preparation for the birth that will eventually occur.

Table 5.1 briefly summarizes the major accomplishments that occur in development during the period of the fetus. Of special importance is something that is usually referred to as the age of viability. After about twenty-four weeks of gestation the brain starts to show activity similar to that of a newborn whereas before that time brain wave activity is essentially flat, not unlike in someone who is brain dead. This accomplishment may be necessary for the regulation of body functions for attainment of the age of viability, that is, that time at which, should the infant be born, it has some chance of survival. Usually somewhere between the ages of twenty-two and twenty-six weeks a child may survive if it is born. More than likely, survival

Gestational Age	Major New Developments
12 weeks	Sex of child can be determined; muscles develop more extensively; eyelids and lips are present; feet have toes and hands have fingers.
16 weeks	First fetal movement is usually felt by the mother at about this time; bones begin to develop; fairly complete ear is formed.
20 weeks	Hair growth begins; child looks very human at this age, and thumb sucking may be seen.
24 weeks	Eyes are completely formed (but closed); fingernails, sweat glands, and taste buds are all formed; some fat is deposited beneath skin. The infant is capable of breathing if born prematurely at this stage, but survival rate is low for infants born this small.
28 weeks	Nervous system and blood and breathing systems are all well enough developed to support life; premature infants born at this stage have poor sleep/wake cycles and irregular breathing, however.
29–38 weeks	Interconnections between individual nerve cells (neurons) develop rapidly; weight is added; general "finishing" of body systems takes place

Table 5.1   Major Milestones of Fetal Development

will involve the use of extraordinary medical measures because many of the infant's systems are not mature enough to work properly.

In any event, the fetal period runs from about the ninth week (or beginning of the third month) through birth. At the twelfth week, we mark the end of the first trimester (first three months of a normal nine month pregnancy). The child at this point resembles a human, even though the head is disproportionately large. The muscle system is well developed, as demonstrated by spontaneous leg, arm, finger, and toe movements as well as rotation of the fetus, even though the mother may not know that any of this is occurring. The onset of these behaviors marks what some developmentalists believe to be the beginning of true, even though reflexive, behaviors. In addition, the sex of the child can be determined, the kidneys begin to function, the heart can be heard, and the nervous system is becoming larger.

The second trimester (months four through six) sees the child grow in length to almost one foot. The "quickening" (the point at which the mother first notices the child's movements) will occur during this time, and the fetus will increase its movements over this trimester. Apparent sleep and wake cycles begin along with such behaviors as hiccuping, thumb sucking, and doing somersaults during the later part of the trimester. At the end of this trimester the age of viability occurs. The primary reason for the death of an infant born at this time is the immaturity of the lungs; they will not be efficient at transmitting oxygen from the outside air into the blood stream until the third trimester.

The third trimester (months seven through nine) sees an emphasis on weight gain and body growth. As the infant gets larger, however, the amount of activity may decrease somewhat because there is less room for the infant to

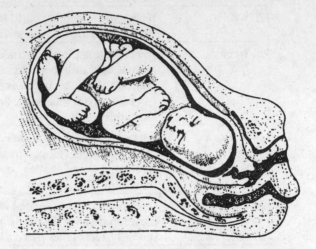

Fig. 5.2   A full-term fetus has little room to move around and is therefore generally less active.

move around. This state of affairs can most clearly be seen in Figure 5.2 which shows a full-term fetus within the uterus and how cramped that child is. As time passes, the fetus's internal organs mature and the brain's control over their functions improves to such an extent that survivability improves almost daily.

Congenital Problems

In chapter 4 we saw that it is possible for the genetic information from either the mother or father to influence a child's development negatively. This could be done through specific genes for diseases or deformities or through a chromosomal aberration that occurs during cell division. Either way, these types of problems are generally referred to as genetic because they are hereditary in origin. A whole different set of problems, however, can occur that have virtually nothing to do with heredity. Diseases, substances ingested (either voluntarily or involuntarily) by the mother, environmental hazards, and even some supposedly miscellaneous factors of the mother's life can cause congenital problems. This happens partly because the placental barrier, mentioned earlier, is not perfect. While it allows important nutrients and oxygen to reach the fetus, it allows viruses, micro-organisms and some chemicals to reach the fetus as well. Whereas we may refer to genetic problems as hereditary ("nature") in origin, congenital problems are considered environmental ("nurture") in origin.

DISEASES

Although many diseases that a mother contracts cannot pass the placental barrier, others—most notably those of viral origin—can. The following is only a partial list of the diseases that may have little effect on the mother, assuming that she undergoes medical treatment, but can have a devastating effect on the fetus: rubella (German measles), rubeola (red measles), syphilis, gonorrhea, diphtheria, influenza, typhoid, chicken pox, cytomegalovirus (a herpes virus), herpes simplex-2 (genital herpes), and toxoplasmosis. Of these, a small handful seem to occur with the greatest frequency.

Rubella. German measles lasts only a couple of days with a rash and a low-grade fever in an adult who contracts it. However, exposure of the embryo to the virus during the first eight weeks of the pregnancy may result in congenital eye cataracts, heart deformities, brain damage, and/or deafness. Exposure during the second trimester may result in less severe effects, such as mild hearing loss and slowed general development. Since rubella is preventable through vaccination, the risk can be reduced by regularly immunizing children against the disease. If a woman was not vaccinated in childhood, vaccination can occur in adulthood with no problem except that it should occur at least three months before the woman attempts to become pregnant.

Cytomegalovirus (CMV). This is a common herpes virus that can infect the female genital tract. More than 80 percent of women in the United States carry antibodies for this virus, indicating exposure during some time in their lives. It is believed that about 3 percent of the female population may have ongoing infections at any point in time. This virus can attack the brain and nervous system, causing microcephaly (an abnormally small head) or deafness.

Herpes simplex-2. This form of the herpes virus family is commonly found around the genitals, hence its nickname of "genital" herpes. The usual time of transmission to the fetus appears to be during very late pregnancy or delivery. That is, if a woman is suffering from an outbreak of skin sores from the virus at or around the delivery date, the fetus may be exposed by direct contact with the sores or the virus being shed from them. The greatest likelihood of contact appears to be through the birth canal during delivery. Not only are the skin sores themselves a problem, but exposure may also result in meningoencephalitis (inflammation of the brain and spinal cord). Major treatment for prevention of exposure is to deliver the fetus through the abdomen (caesarean delivery).

Toxoplasmosis. This disease is caused by a parasite that is found in uncooked meat and cat feces. The disease is barely noticeable in adults but can cause blindness and brain damage in the fetus. A blood test early in the pregnancy can determine if the mother-to-be is immune or not. If not, then simply staying away from rare meat and cat litter boxes can avoid this problem.

AIDS. Acquired Immune Deficiency Syndrome (caused by HIV, the human immunodeficiency virus) was not included in the earlier list because it will ultimately affect the mother. This virus can be transmitted to the fetus and result in death of the infant sometime usually within the first four to five years of life. The importance of this problem is demonstrated by the fact that heterosexual young women of child-bearing age are now the fastest-growing group testing positive for HIV. Often they are unaware of their medical condition until their newborn child tests positive for HIV. AIDS currently is the number one deadly teratogenic (producing a congenital defect) disease known.

DRUG (CHEMICAL) EXPOSURE

As mentioned above, the placenta cannot screen out all possible harmful disease pathogens from exposure to the fetus. In like manner, it cannot screen out other substances (chemicals) that may be within the mother's blood (e.g. prescription and nonprescription drugs, vitamins, alcohol, caffeine, and so on) and that could also detrimentally effect fetal development. This fact is obviously known for substances that include warning notices to the effect that they should be taken only under a doctor's supervision if the person is pregnant. To date, knowledge of the congenital problems caused by different chemical substances is known through experiments with animals that attempt to establish a cause-effect relationship, and through studies with humans that attempt to demonstrate a correlational relationship. (See chapter 2 for a discussion of the correlation and experiment methodologies.) The first inform us as to the amount of a substance (called the dose) that causes a specific problem (called the response), and the second allow us to predict the size or type of response that may occur given knowledge of the amount of exposure. Some specific examples are given below.

Nicotine (Smoking). Smoking during pregnancy puts nicotine and carbon monoxide into the mother's bloodstream. The first is a vasoconstrictor, constricting the capillaries in the mother's body, resulting in reduced blood flow and therefore less oxygen to the fetus. The second occurs because hemoglobin, the substance in blood that carries oxygen, is more attracted to carbon monoxide. Hence, the available hemoglobin begins to carry more carbon monoxide and less oxygen to the fetus. The result is that a smoking mother deprives the fetus of needed oxygen for normal brain development.

The research on nicotine appears to indicate a strong relationship between dose and response. For example, women who smoke one pack per day have a 60 percent chance of delivering at thirty-three weeks and of having a low birth weight baby (see chapter 6 for a discussion of the complications of low birth weight). Increasing the amount of cigarettes smoked also increases the likelihood of an even shorter pregnancy, miscarriage or subsequent possible death of the child from sudden infant death syndrome (SIDS) (see chapter 10 for a discussion of SIDS). Similar dose-response results are seen for women who are exposed to second-hand smoke either at work or at home.

Alcohol. Alcohol has been shown to cause similar restriction of blood flow to the fetus (thereby reducing oxygen flow as does nicotine) as well as destruction of brain, muscle, and liver cells. For alcohol, however, as opposed to nicotine, a specific medical/psychological deformity has been defined to describe the various problems and symptoms of infants who are exposed to alcohol in the uterus: fetal alcohol syndrome (FAS). Generally, FAS includes any combination of the following: facial and limb deformities; stunted growth; reduced brain size and mental capacity or ability; defects in the functioning or structure of internal organs such as the heart and liver; and the presence of behaviors that negatively influence the psychosocial development of the child (reduced attention span, difficult temperament, repetitive autistic-like body motions).

Pregnant women are advised to abstain from all alcohol during the pregnancy because research indicates the possibility that either small daily doses of alcohol or one large binge during those nine months can result in FAS. No "safe" amount of alcohol has ever been determined. If a mother-to-be ingests alcohol and nicotine together during the pregnancy, the likelihood of a growth- or mentally retarded infant is usually higher than if she ingests either of the two separately.

Other Drugs. Many other drugs, both legal and illegal, are known or are suspected to cause problems for the developing fetus. Some examples include: aspirin (inhibits blood clotting and prolongs labor); contraceptive jellies and foams (usually taken while the mother is unaware that she is pregnant and related to higher miscarriage rates); cocaine (causes extreme fragility in the infant); birth control pills (cause congenital heart disease); and tetracycline (cause tooth discoloration and stunted or defective bone growth). In any event, the timing and amount of exposure will significantly influence whether there will be an effect and what kind and how much of an effect there will be. It is probably safe to say that generally exposure to any chemical during pregnancy makes an infant more susceptible to a general problem. Ultimately, one needs to weigh the needed effects of a particular drug against the possible harmful effects on the fetus.

ENVIRONMENTAL HAZARDS

In large part because of the interest generated by declining bird populations throughout the world in the early 1960s, people began to examine possible congenital problems resulting from exposure to different environmental hazards. That is, when pesticides in the food chain were discovered to cause eggshell thinning in different bird species, developmentalists began to ask whether they could cause birth defects in humans. For example, women exposed to the high levels of radiation around Hiroshima and Nagasaki following the atomic bomb explosions over those cities consistently showed higher numbers of miscarriages and mutations. Likewise, minimata disease (named for the industrial town in Japan where the problem was found to occur frequently) is a syndrome marked by cerebral palsy and severe physical defects resulting from maternal consumption of mercury during pregnancy. Maternal lead exposure is known to cause decreased enzyme production and increased learning and psychological problems in children who are prenatally exposed. Even excessive heat (as one might get from a hot tub or jacuzzi) for fifteen minutes is sufficient to cause nervous system damage in the fetus.

MISCELLANEOUS MATERNAL FACTORS

A variety of factors related to the mother's lifestyle, psychology, and general health, besides the diseases mentioned above, are suspected of causing birth defects.

Stress. Maternal stress levels have been implicated in milder but noticeable effects in newborns. Since stress produces an increase in adrenaline (a vasoconstrictor) output, it is possible that long-term stress levels reduce oxygen intake by the fetus. Maternal stress levels during the first trimester have been shown to be predictive of irritability and difficult temperaments in infants at six to eight months of age. Likewise, women with increased or long-term stress levels show a greater propensity for complications during the labor and delivery process.

Number of Pregnancies. Because of a variety of religious, cultural, economic, and personal reasons, many people choose to have large families, meaning more than four children. However, the likelihood of birth defects appears to increase for each pregnancy after the fourth one. The prevailing hypothesis is that each pregnancy reduces some capacity in the mother to have, foster, and biologically protect a developing fetus. Granted, the mother's body can recover after each pregnancy, but it never quite returns to its pre-pregnancy level. Hence, past the fourth pregnancy, the placental barrier becomes less protective.

Age. An increased risk of problems exists if the mother is over the age of 30 or under the age of 18. Over 30, the primary risk appears to be delivery complications (longer labor, stillbirth, and an increased risk of maternal death). In addition, the risk for a Down's syndrome child (see chapter 4) increases dramatically from age 30 onward. The cause of this problem may stem from the fact that a woman's ova, which she will cycle, are all present at birth; by age 30, an individual ovum is also 30 years old. If an individual ovum deteriorates over the years and is subsequently fertilized, the chances are increased for some abnormality.

For those under the age of 18, the likelihood of a low-birth-weight infant, stillbirth or other delivery difficulty increases, and moreso the younger the mother. The reason may stem from the competition for nutrients that the fetus would have with the mother who, as a developing teenager, is also requiring a vast assortment of nutrients to complete her own development. Generally speaking, this analysis is borne out by the fact that the incidence of abnormalities increases sharply below the age of 15.

For both the younger and the older mother, problems are more pronounced if the mother is from a lower socioeconomic segment of the society. Basically, if there is less money available for adequate prenatal care and maternal nutrition, the likelihood of abnormalities increases. For both of these groups, if adequate nutrition and care are made available, the rate of abnormalities declines to about that of women between the ages of 20 and 30, the prime childbearing years.

Assessing the Risk of Congenital Problems

As one can see from the discussions above, three factors appear important in determining the risk of having a child born with a congenital problem or of having some form of labor or birthing problem. First is the dose-response curve. Generally speaking, the larger the dose (exposure) of a given substance, the greater the response (detrimental effect). This can be seen most dramatically with FAS. It also raises the question on the other end of the continuum of whether there is such a thing as a "no-effect" dose of any particular substance. That is, as in the case with alcohol, is there a minimum amount that a person can ingest during pregnancy for which no detrimental effect will occur? Because the answer to this question is unknown for most substances, doctors usually advise mothers to abstain from ingesting any product that is not essential to a normal, healthy diet and medical regimen, and to take any other substance only under direct supervision of a physician.

The second factor is the concept of the critical period, which relates to the timing of exposure. For example, rubella is most destructive to the fetus if it is exposed during the embryonic period. Since the period of the embryo is the time during which most critical periods begin, it is the time when the dose-response curve should have its greatest meaning. That is, a small dose of a substance will more likely have a detrimental effect during a critical period in development than when the critical period is over. For example, the drug thalidomide, which was once used to prevent morning sickness in women early in their pregnancies (weeks 4 to 8), was subsequently found to cause limb abnormalities because the critical periods for arm and leg development are during weeks 4 through 8. Exposure to thalidomide for morning sickness after week 8 of the pregnancy was unlikely to cause limb abnormalities.

The third factor is the nutritional level of the mother. Nearly all normal nutrient requirements are raised by at least 10 percent during a pregnancy, with calcium needs rising to 50 percent above normal. This means that a normal diet for a nonpregnant woman is likely to be an insufficient diet for a pregnant woman. As malnutrition increases, the likelihood of stillbirth, low birth weight, infant mortality during the first year, and slowed brain development increases. Since it is a safe assumption that good nutrition is directly related to good health and development of the fetus, thereby reaching critical periods and maturational landmarks at the appropriate times, it is probably also safe to assume that poor nutrition slows development, thereby setting the stage for a worsening of the dose-response curve/critical period relationship. That is, poor nutrition may slow up development, thereby lengthening the critical periods and/or lowering the dose needed to cause a maximum response.

One final note should be mentioned regarding the role that the father may play in the occurrence of congenital problems. At a supportive level, it would be more difficult for a mother to abstain from alcohol consumption, for example, if the father continued to drink throughout the pregnancy. Likewise, a fetus exposed to secondhand cigarette smoke from the father's smoking probably suffers the same kind of oxygen depletion as when the mother smokes directly. It seems easier for the mother to quit a particular behavior for the duration of the pregnancy if the father gives needed emotional support by quitting the behavior also. At a causative level, some data exist implicating changes in male sperm because of exposure to different chemicals and the occurrence of different problems. For example, men who were soldiers during the Vietnam War and who were exposed to the defoliant Agent Orange have a higher incidence of birth defects in their children than do any other group of men. Also, evidence exists that molecules of cocaine attach themselves to the sperm in a man's testicles. The implication of this is that if a sperm containing cocaine molecules fertilizes the ovum, then the molecule may remain active during the initial critical periods in development, potentially causing birth defects.

Learning Abilities and Activities of the Prenatal Child

Although references to the abilities of the prenatal child will be made in chapters 6 and 7, it is important to lay the groundwork for those discussions. Only one sensory system, hearing, appears to be fully functional before birth. Fetuses as young as thirteen weeks have displayed a "startle" reaction to the sound of a bell near the mother's abdomen. Other researchers have recorded increased heart rate and muscular activity in response to sounds from the twenty-ninth week forward. Likewise, some fetal discrimination of sounds as measured by different reactions to a range of tones is apparent during the last ten weeks of the pregnancy.

By means of a pacifier that can be sucked two ways, scientists have tested infants' choice between two stimuli. In these tests newborns have demonstrated a preference for sounds that they repeatedly heard during the last weeks of the pregnancy. This indicates at least a rudimentary fetal learning ability, that is, classical conditioning.

One can also examine behavioral activity differences between fetuses and predict general behavior patterns for the first year after birth. There are three types of fetal activity: sharp kicking/punching, slow squirming/writhing, and sharp, convulsive (spasm) type movements. Different fetuses exhibit different patterns of each of these movements, and to some extent that the patterns can reliably be used to predict the amount of activity and restlessness after birth. More active fetuses are usually more active babies and are more advanced in their motor development than less active fetuses.

FROM THE PARENTS' POINT OF VIEW

Whereas the child's preparation for birth is largely physical, the parents' is largely emotional. Upon discovering that a woman is pregnant, the parents begin making the emotional adjustment and develop an attachment to the fetus. Women feel this attachment as an intimate presence for which they are responsible. Men on the other hand often define this attachment with a sense of pride for the fetus and identification with the mother. Some men identify with their wives so strongly they actually experience some of the same physical changes of the pregnancy (weight gain, oral cravings, and so on). This attachment expands over time to include talking to the fetus, picking the "right" name, and paying close attention to fetal activity patterns.

Somewhere in the development process, the parents begin accepting their relationship with the fetus by viewing their child-to-be as an individual and by their willingness to take the long-term responsibility for raising and caring for their child. With this acceptance comes a realization that they will soon take on the roles they dreaded as children: they will become parents. Often this means that parents-to-be rethink their images of their own parents, accepting them as people who did the best they could or knew how. Ultimately, parents-to-be complete their preparation by accepting the identity of independence needed for care giving, thereby resolving their own dependency issues with their parents. This last change often results as a direct by-product of the parents' beginning preparation for the birth of their child: childbirth classes, acquiring furniture and clothes, preparation of the child's room, and talking with other parents-to-be.

SPECIAL ISSUES IN PRENATAL DEVELOPMENT

Prenatal Diagnostic Techniques

A discussion of techniques for diagnosing a problem prenatally should begin with the use of genetic counseling. This is a preventive measure usually undertaken before becoming pregnant by people who have a family history of genetic disorders, infertility or miscarriages, or who are closely related genetically, or who will be older parents. Through the taking of a detailed family history, genetic counselors can often determine the likelihood of a child having a particular recessive, dominant or sex-linked disorder (see chapter 4 for a discussion of these patterns of genetic inheritance). When those determinations are made, parents can then decide whether to become pregnant or to consider adoption.

Should they decide to begin the process of becoming pregnant, a number of techniques are available to measure the normalcy of the pregnancy. These range from very simple urine analyses and blood pressure screenings (which measure how well the mother's body is handling the pregnancy) to complicated procedures that can look for specific physical abnormalities or genetic disorders. For example, sonograms (outlining the shape of the fetus with sound waves) can reveal physical deformities, some diseases, and microcephaly (abnormally small head size). Because this technique can also help determine the sex of the fetus, estimate fetal age, and determine the fetal growth rate, it is the most common technique used. Amniocentesis, on the other hand, is a complicated procedure that cannot be performed until the pregnancy is about half concluded. By removing a sample of the amniotic fluid, which contains some sloughed-off cells, a detailed examination for chromosomal and genetic problems can be undertaken. Although the analysis is both detailed and informing, the timing leaves a major problem for the parents to face should a disabling genetic or congenital abnormality exist. That is, by the time amniocentesis can provide reliable information the time for ending a pregnancy may have already passed. Because of this disadvantage, many now choose to undergo chorionic villi sampling (CVS), which involves taking a sample of the placental membrane surrounding the fetus. The information obtained through CVS is about the same as that provided by amniocentesis, but it can be acquired in the ninth week of pregnancy.

Abortion

The philosophical, political, religious, and even personal feelings toward abortion are beyond the scope of this book. However, a discussion of abortion as it pertains to ending fetal development is not. A miscarriage or spontaneous abortion usually occurs as a biologically protective event, meaning that it happens early in a pregnancy to remove a fetus that probably could not survive outside the womb. The assumption behind this event is that somehow Mother Nature continually "checks" the fetus, removing it when viability is unlikely. An induced abortion, on the other hand, is usually done at the decision of the mother or of the mother and father. This procedure may occur as a result of the prenatal diagnostic techniques, the cause of pregnancy (rape or incest), socioeconomic conditions (no money or an already large family), personal reasons (not wanting the pregnancy at that time) or any combination of these. Often some psychological discomfort (guilt or mild depression), which can be handled usually through support groups or short-term psychotherapy, accompanies the abortion.

A pregnancy can be divided into three periods: germinal (the first two weeks), embryo (week three through week eight), and fetal (week nine on). The germinal period is noted for fertilization, beginning cell differentiation, and implantation into the wall of the uterus. The embryo period is critical to normal development because nearly all body systems begin rapid development and are then sensitive to outside interference. During this time physical development follows the cephalocaudal (head to tail) and proximodistal (inside out) principles. In addition, the placenta and umbilical cord develop, thus providing a route for the fetus to acquire nutrients and eliminate waste products.

Whereas the embryonic period sets individual body systems in motion, the fetal period refines them. This means that the fetus puts on weight, grows in size, and generally fills out the body design established during the embryonic period. The fetus attains the age of viability around the twenty-fourth week, meaning that survival outside the womb is possible given extensive medical intervention. Generally speaking, however, the longer the wait the better the chance of survival.

Congenital problems (those commonly called birth defects) differ from genetic defects; the later are inherited while the former occur as a result of fetal exposure to some disease, substance, environmental hazard or maternal factor that upsets the normal development of a particular body system. Disease causes of congenital problems are usually viral in nature and can therefore cross the placental barrier whereas bacteria usually cannot. Drugs and other chemicals can also cross into the placenta, making them potentially dangerous to the fetus. Nicotine and alcohol are two very common drugs that cross the placental barrier and can cause dose-related effects, meaning the higher the dose, the worse the effect. Some factors concerning the psychology, health or family history of the mother may also affect the occurrence of similar problems. Generally speaking, exposure to any substance or disease organism makes the infant more susceptible to a general problem.

In order to assess the risk of a particular congenital abnormality, one must be aware of the dose-response curve, the timing of the exposure (critical period or not), and the nutritional status of the mother. This last factor is important because it may set the stage for the onset of the critical period, slow physical development, and/or lower the dose required to obtain a maximum effect. Presently the emphasis on congenital problems is on the maternal environment; some evidence exists, however, that may implicate the father as a possible causative factor in these problems.

As mentioned in later chapters, the fetus (during the last two trimesters) can demonstrate some hearing acuity and discrimination ability. The fetus may also establish some sound preferences during the last ten weeks before birth. Potentially, one can predict the general behavior of the infant during the first year after birth by monitoring the amount, kinds, and frequency of activity in utero. In general, the rate of activity of the fetus relates to the speed of motor development.

Prenatal development from the parents' point of view involves emotional changes as opposed to the physical changes that incorporate the child's orientation. Essentially, parents usually come to terms with their own upbringing as well as accept responsibility for the care of this child. They will often attach themselves to the fetus long before birth.

A number of techniques can be used to determine if any genetic or congenital problems exist. The most common (sonogram) is not the most thorough (amniocentesis). Either way, these techniques are used if one has a family history of genetic problems or if there is a need to monitor the fetus for the development of a birth defect. Should a problem be present but not be severe enough for nature to abort the fetus (miscarriage), an induced abortion can be done if it is within the first couple of months of the pregnancy. In both cases, a period of depression and grief is very common.

Selected Readings

Abel, E. L. (1984). *Fetal alcohol syndrome and fetal alcohol effects.* New York: Plenum.

Behrman, R. E., and V. C. Vaughan III. (1983). *Pediatrics.* Philadelphia: Saunders.

Butler, R. N. and J. Golding. (1986). *From birth to five: A study of the health and behaviour of Britain's 5-year-olds.* Oxford: Pergamon.

Grant, J. 1986. *The state of the world's children.* Oxford, England: Oxford University Press.

Heinonen, O. P., D. Slone, and S. Shapiro. (1977). *Birth defects and drugs in pregnancy.* Littleton, MA: Publishing Sciences Group.

Kopp, C. B. and S. R. Kaler. (1989). Risk in infancy: Origins and implications. *American Psychologist,* 44.

Moore, K. L. (1988). *The developing human: Clinically oriented embryology.* 4th ed. Philadelphia: Saunders.

Schardein, J. L. (1976). *Drugs as teratogens.* Cleveland: CRC Press.

6

Birth and the Neonate

An examination of the human birth process and the resulting neonate begins with a look at the specific physical and psychological characteristics of birthing. The birth process is followed through the three stages of birth with emphasis on the differences between and importance of dilation and effacement. A general description of the neonate includes a rundown of the physiological conditions and physical appearance at the time of birth as well as of the scales used to measure infant viability. Included is additional information on the behavioral repertoire of the neonate: reflexes, motor skills, cognitive functioning, and social abilities.

Various problems that can occur at the time of birth are discussed including loss of oxygen to the fetus and breech (or transverse) positioning, both of which could result in caesarean delivery. A discussion of low-birth-weight infants (especially preterm and small-for-date) is presented with emphasis on causes as well as short- and long-term consequences.

The birth experience is examined from both the baby's point of view and that of the parents. The later includes alternatives to medicated hospital deliveries along with parents' reaction to the birthing experience. Although it is the female that carries the baby and gives birth, the father's role appears significant as a coach. Once the infant has arrived, the parents' and sibling's initial responses can be indicative of the nature of the relationship that will develop. This is important because it leads into the emotional attachment that the other household members will have with the infant.

Finally, in an overview of the birth process, some factors stand out: the possibility of a stillbirth (i.e., death of the infant); the effects of medications on the infant that may have been used for the mother's comfort; a com-

parison of breast vs. bottle feeding; and the importance of crying, along with the parental response to it.

PHYSICAL AND PSYCHOLOGICAL CHARACTERISTICS OF BIRTH

The precise mechanism that causes the birth process to begin is unknown. Possibly it happens by some sort of timing mechanism in the fetus, or one in the mother or a combination of mechanisms between the two. There is evidence suggesting that fetal urine stimulates the actions of some maternal hormones, causing the beginning of the birth process. In any event, the process usually begins in a first pregnancy with something called the "lightening," that is, when the fetus turns and begins its headfirst descent into the birth canal. At that point, some of the pressure on the stomach and diaphragm is relieved, resulting in easier breathing for the pregnant woman.

The actual birthing process (i.e., labor and delivery) is divided into three stages, the first of which has two purposes: dilation and effacement of the cervix. The purpose of dilation is to open the entrance to the birth canal (like opening the lens of a camera) to approximately ten centimeters (about four inches) in width. Dilation provides a passageway out of the uterus for the head and body. Effacement, on the other hand, makes the cervix more pliable so that it will not impede the birth.

In the early phase of stage one, during which dilation goes to about five centimeters, contractions are far apart and mildly uncomfortable. In the later phase of stage one, during which dilation goes from five to eight centimeters, contractions are closer together and more intense. Contractions are very strong and spaced closest together during the last, shortest, and most painful phase of stage one labor, the transition phase. Labor is painful for most women because the human skull has enlarged over time through the process of evolution. To navigate through the opening in the woman's pelvis, the head (due to its large size) must first pass through the birth canal sideways and then turn facedown.

The second stage of labor is the actual birth of the child and lasts anywhere from thirty minutes to two hours. This stage, commonly called the expulsion stage, begins when the baby's head first appears (crowning). It is completed when the baby's head moves through the stretched cervix, into the birth canal, and out of the mother's body. Delivery is generally head first. Some infants are born feet first, commonly called the breech position. This stage is commonly felt to be less stressful and painful because the mother can be more involved in the delivery process; that is, active maternal pushing usually expells the infant from the uterus. The third stage of delivery is when the placenta, sometimes called the afterbirth, is delivered from the uterus.

With reference to the overall process, the pains of childbirth are directly related to the opening of the cervix. Once the cervix is fully open, the painful part of the delivery process diminishes drastically. Subsequent births, if any, will be progressively easier and labors shorter as the body responds more efficiently to the entire labor process and opening the cervix becomes much easier.

NEWBORN CHARACTERISTICS

A newborn infant is commonly referred to as a neonate. During the first two to four weeks of life, referred to as the neonatal period, the infant makes the transition from intrauterine life (supported solely by the mother) to an independent existence. The infant becomes responsible for all life support functions including circulation, respiration, and digestion.

Because all of these life-support systems were conducted through the placenta during prenatal life, the birth process serves to "kick start" all of those systems to life. For example, at birth the infant's heart takes over responsibility for blood circulation. The neonatal heartbeat is usually accelerated and regular for the first days, while blood pressure stabilizes about the tenth day. The infant's respiratory system usually starts when the infant hits the air, although a few need a small slap or minor skin stimulation to begin breathing. The gastrointestinal system also starts digesting food and eliminating wastes shortly after birth. About 50 percent of all babies develop physiological jaundice, where the skin and eyeballs look slightly yellow due to immaturity of the liver. It is not a serious condition and can be remedied by putting an infant near fluorescent or ultraviolet light.

Size and Shape

An average neonate is approximately 20 inches long and weighs approximately 7½ pounds. Generally, 95 percent of full term births weigh from 5½ to 10 pounds and measure from 18 to 22 inches in length. Newborns are covered with very fine hair called lanugo (which falls off after the first few days) and a thick secretion called vernix. Supplied by the mother, vernix is a thick liquid that protects the skin of the fetus and eases birth by "greasing" the fetus. Soft spots on the top of the head (fontanels) are between the bones of the skull. They allow the bones to move during birth, thereby allowing the head to fit through the smaller space of the birth canal. The bones reshape within about two weeks and cover over the fontanels in about a year and a half.

Neonates look wrinkled and somewhat fat, with disproportionately large heads. Largeness of the head follows from the cephalocaudal principle. Not until later years will the proportion of head size to overall body size become more like that of an adult. Newborns generally have flat noses and virtually no chin, making suckling from a mother's breast much easier.

Neonate Assessment Scales

To make sure the infant is physically capable and that no unseen problems exist, all infants are tested after delivery with the Apgar scale, developed by Dr. Virginia Apgar in the early 1950s. With this scale, an infant receives a rating from 0 to 2 on each of five different subscales. (Table 6.1 presents a summary of what each rating of 0 to 2 represents on each of the subscales.) An overall total score of 7 or better indicates a normal infant at birth (i.e., medical intervention is not needed), which occurs for about 90 percent of normal births. A score of 4 to 7 indicates the baby may need help to establish consistent breathing and should be watched for a period of time. A score below 4 means the infant is in immediate danger and needs life-saving treatment. The test is usually done at one minute and again at five minutes after delivery.

Sign*	0	1	2
Appearance (color)	Blue, pale	Body pink, extremities blue	Entirely pink
Pulse (heart rate)	Absent	Slow (below 100)	Rapid (over 100)
Grimace (reflex irritability)	No response	Grimace	Coughing, sneezing, crying
Activity (muscle tone)	Limp	Weak, inactive	Strong, active
Respiration (breathing)	Absent	Irregular, slow	Good, crying
*Each sign is rated in terms of absence or presence from 0 to 2; the highest overall score is 10. Adapted from Apgar, 1953.			

Table 6.1   Apgar Scale

Checks are also done for any structural or physical deformities that may be present, such as spinal defects or cleft palate. In addition, silver nitrate, or tetracycline, is usually dropped into the newborn's eyes, thereby preventing infection from bacteria possibly picked up while passing through the birth canal.

Whereas the Apgar measures an infant's medical condition at birth, the Brazelton Neonatal Behavioral Assessment Scale measures an infant's neurological and behavioral repertoire on the third day of life and then again some days later. It tests four distinct areas: social behavior (interactive behaviors in the home); motor behaviors (reflexes and muscle activity); control of physiology (e.g., the baby's ability to quiet himself); and a stress response (e.g., a startle reaction). Essentially, the Brazelton serves two purposes: (1) as an index of neurological integrity after birth; and (2) as a measurement of infant development at birth. High Brazelton scores indicate a neurologically well developed infant. Low Brazelton scores may indicate a sluggish infant who needs help in responding to social situations, or possible brain damage.

Reflex	Eliciting Stimulus	Response	Developmental Duration
Babinski	Gentle stroke along sole of foot from heel to toe.	Toes fan out; big toe flexes.	Disappears by end of first year.
Moro	Sudden loss of support.	Arms extended, then brought toward each other; lower extremities extended.	Disappears in about 6 months.
Palmar grasp	Rod or finger pressed against infant's palm.	Object grasped.	Disappears in 3 to 4 months.
Rooting	Object lightly brushes infant's cheek.	Baby turns toward object and attempts to suck.	Disappears in 3 to 4 months.
Sucking	Finger or nipple inserted 2 inches into mouth.	Rhythmic sucking.	Disappears in 3 to 4 months.
Walking	Baby is held upright and soles of feet are placed on hard surface; baby is tipped slightly forward.	Infant steps forward as if walking.	Disappears in 3 to 4 months.

Table 6.2   Some Neonatal Reflexes

Reflexes at Birth and Motor Skills

Most full-term newborns come equipped with a variety of reflexes for use in dealing efficiently with stimuli present in their environment. Some reflexes are necessary for survival (e.g., rooting and sucking reflexes), while the importance of others is unclear and may have been lost in evolution. (Table 6.2 presents the important characteristics of some of these neonatal reflexes.) Reflexes are probably genetic in origin and include a timing mechanism that allows them to fade away after a period of time. In some cases, the recurrence of reflexes after the normal cutoff time may indicate persistent neurological problems. For example, the Babinski reflex (where the toes fan out and the big toe flexes following gentle stroking of the foot) indicates good neurological development in an infant. However, in an adult, the same reflex may reflect some brain damage. The grasping reflex, which is strongest at birth and weakens over time, usually disappears by three months of age. Presence of the reflex after four or five months may indicate some brain damage.

Theories attempting to explain why infant reflexes seem to disappear abound. Possibly a genetic timing mechanism governs reflexes so that each one exists for only the period of time it is needed and then is "programed" to dissipate. Another theory states that reflexes allow an infant to interact appropriately with the environment while the cortex develops. As cortical development progresses, reflexes can be overridden and in effect suppressed. This interpretation, however, does not explain why some reflexes persist while others do not. A third theory postulates that reflexes disappear quickly after birth because they had more utility within the womb than outside of it. For example, the stepping reflex (movement of the feet up and down as though walking), which appears useless at birth, may be important to keep the fetus continually moving so that it does not adhere to the uterine wall. A final explanation posits that these reflexes do not disappear at all; that is, they are hidden because of the normal growth of the infant. For example, the walking reflex, which appears to disappear by three to four months of age, may be involved with the stepping reflex. As infants get larger and heavier, these reflexes become more difficult to display. However, an infant's kicking while lying on its back may be the expression of those reflexes. In that event, the reflexes may last through at least the first year. That is, the underlying mechanism has not disappeared, but rather a lack of muscle strength has made expression of that particular reflex or motor development impossible.

The motor skills of newborns, outside of reflexes, are very limited. Generally, they can move their heads and rotate their eyes to follow an object moving in front of them. Coordinated arm, leg, hand or foot movements for any purpose are virtually unknown. It is also unknown whether observed neonatal movements are an attempt to explore the world or simply automatic reflexive movements in response to environmental sounds or sights. In general, most movements appear uncoordinated and undirected toward any sort of locomotor ability.

Learning, Cognitive, and Social Abilities at Birth

Probably because of constant exposure to the mother's voice before birth, neonates seem to quickly associate it with the face of the person from whom it comes. This association is a good example of classical conditioning (see chapter 3 on theories). Historically, demonstrating operant learning has been easy when using infants of three to four weeks of age but difficult to demonstrate in the neonate. Current conditioning techniques, on the other hand, appear to be usable shortly after birth. For example, the sucking response and head turning have both been successfully increased when using the sound of the mother's voice or heartbeat as reinforcement for those behaviors.

In understanding how the ability to learn and associate develops, Piaget's concept of schemas or schematic learning is helpful. That is, the neonate may be organizing its early experiences into combinations it is familiar with, for example, hearing a mother's footsteps and then turning its head in the direction of the footfalls if it is the mother. In any event, what is known about the learning and association capabilities of the neonate indicates that cognitive functioning is ongoing from birth.

With regard to a newborn's social abilities at birth, one that appears to be reflexive in nature is the ability of a newborn, even hours old, to imitate the facial expressions or the facial movements of an adult. These facial expressions include sticking out the tongue, pursing the lips, and opening the mouth. An infant can also imitate the opening and closing of a hand. Initially, developmentalists did not believe that a newborn infant could make the connection between the gestures it saw in another and making those gestures itself, particularly since it had never been able to see itself in a mirror. The current view is that this is simply a reflex, another wired-in behavior that requires no thought or understanding.

Reflexive imitation is rarely seen in babies over six weeks of age. Another kind of imitation occurs several months later, but this seems to be under a great deal more control, and the early imitation reflex does not appear to lead to the later kind of imitation. This reflex may serve a social relationship function, that is, help set up a social relationship with a caregiver. Other social abilities that are present at birth include looking, turning the head in response to a voice (as though searching for its source), and an attraction to faces, which helps initiate reciprocal interest from the adults the infant is looking at.

BIRTHING PROBLEMS AND SOLUTIONS

Low-Birth-Weight Infants

Following a full 38-week pregnancy, the average normal birth weight is 7½ pounds for males and 7 pounds for females. As the range of normal birth weights falls between 5½ and 10 pounds, any infant born weighing less than 5½ pounds is considered low birth weight. These infants account for approximately 7 percent of all births in the United States. An infant born weighing less than 3⅓ pounds, approximately 1.2 percent of all births in the United States, is considered very low birth weight.

At one time, all low-birth-weight infants were considered premature. However, they are now subdivided into two groups: preterm (meaning they are born before the regular 38-week gestation length is completed but are developing normally); and small-for-date (meaning they completed the full gestation period but weigh less than 5½ pounds). The small-for-date group probably suffered a significant prenatal problem (e.g., malnutrition or constriction of blood flow from the mother), whereas the preterm group, because it is early, lacks weight normally put on during the third trimester. Birth weight is important because it is considered a good predictor of infant mortality; that is, low-birth-weight infants are in greater risk than normal infants.

Many maternal factors result in low birth weight, including cigarette smoking; malnutrition (during the third trimester); age (specifically if the mother is less than 18 or more than 35); constriction of blood flow (from drug usage); a multiple pregnancy (twins, triplets, and quadruplets are born earlier); race (more black women have low-birth-weight infants than white women); and economics. As a causative factor, the economic condition the mother is experiencing appears to be one of the greatest causes for low-birth-weight infants. If the mother is poor, she is less likely to have received prenatal care for herself and the infant; hence, she would be more likely to give birth to a low-birth-weight infant.

For both preterm and small-for-date infants, one must make sure their weight increases before they leave the hospital or intensive care facility. For the preterm infant, however, some of its reflexes may be immature at the moment of birth since it was growing normally and just delivered early. For example, the breathing and sucking reflexes (needed so the infant can breath, swallow, and suck in a coordinated fashion) may not be mature enough; the more premature an infant, the greater the likelihood of choking and possible asphyxiation.

In any event, low birth weight appears to be a good predictor of infant mortality, although with recent improvements in medical knowledge as many as 80 percent of low-birth-weight infants over 1,000 grams (approximately two pounds) at birth survive. As for long-term consequences, preterm infants who weigh more than 4 pounds at birth and are normal-sized for their length of gestation generally catch up to their full-gestation-length peers within the first couple of years. This is true especially if they are raised or cared for by adults who provide a great deal of stimulation and social contact and do not reject them. Very-low-birth-weight infants, as well as many small-for-date infants, show higher rates of long-term problems, including lower IQs, smaller size, and learning disabilities in school.

Another consequence of low birth weight for infants is that they are usually required to stay within an isolate in a nursery for an extended period of time. In such a case it is not uncommon for them to receive less stimulation and contact from parents or other adults, which could influence the parent-infant relationship. As this relationship will be important for providing stimulation to the child throughout development, this may be an important consideration. Low-birth-weight children reared in middle class or highly stimulating environments do better than those raised in poor environments. Generally, low birth weight is a risk factor for slow development, but, unless it's a symptom of some genetic disorder or congenital problem, the deficits related to it appear to be capable of being overcome.

Stressful Births

The birth process is a stressful event for both mother and infant. On the mother's side, anything increasing the length of the labor or delivery increases the amount of stress. For example, if the fetus's head is larger than the birth canal or the baby's body position is not headfirst with the front of the infant facing the mother's spine, the labor will be lengthened. The longer the labor and the greater the amount of stress experienced, the more likely a nonvaginal birth (i.e., a caesarean) will occur. Approximately 23 percent of all births in the United States are done by caesarean section. Basically, the mother's abdomen is opened surgically, and the baby is removed. The surgical incision is then closed, just as with any other procedure requiring an incision. Where the baby's position is irregular, as in a breech (bottom or feet first) or transverse (sideways) position, it is possible to rotate the infant from the outside, assuming that the condition is found early enough in the labor.

Although a birth that is stressful for the mother is usually seen as undesirable, a certain amount of stress is generally required for the infant. For example, during the birth process, the fetus is forced through a very small canal and is intermittently deprived of oxygen, not unlike an adult holding his or her breath. During this time the baby secretes the hormones adrenaline and noradrenaline, which help the child transfer from a liquid environment to an air environment. Adrenaline opens up the lungs, dries out the bronchial cavities, and helps the baby attempt to make the direct switch to an air environment. Likewise, noradrenaline slows the heartbeat, enabling the fetus to withstand some oxygen deprivation. Therefore, even though the birth process is stressful, it serves to help make the transition from a liquid environment to an air environment easier to survive. When infants are born by caesarean, they do not go through that lung preparation and change process, which may explain why it is not uncommon to find that caesarean infants often have respiratory problems.

Even though some amount of oxygen deprivation is normal in the birth process, when it lasts for a long time (such as when the umbilical cord is pinched or the placenta is detached from the uteral wall or the infant's head is damaged so that there is hemorrhaging), insufficient oxygen may be getting to the infant's brain (a condition called anoxia). Prolonged anoxia can cause brain damage, cerebral palsy or even death, especially if the fetus is undernourished or premature. To avoid this problem, some form of fetal monitoring usually occurs; a sensing device is often fitted around the woman's midsection, enabling measurement of fetal heart rate as well as strength and frequency of uterine contractions.

BIRTH EXPERIENCE

Birth—Trauma for Baby?

A misconception about the birth experience is that it is very traumatic for the baby. That may not necessarily be the case, because it is easy to comfort an infant right after birth. Even though a child may start crying shortly after birth, that crying can easily be terminated when the infant is either held by its mother or cradled or wrapped in a towel or blanket and held up next to the beating heart of the mother.

Attitude Toward the Birth Experience

A number of factors can make the physical experience of having a baby easy or difficult. However, the psychological experience can be vastly different. Interestingly, easy births can be seen as something that the parents would never want to experience again, and difficult births, or long labors, can be seen as exhilarating. Many factors seem to be essential in making the psychological experience of childbirth a positive one for the mother and father.

CHILDBIRTH PREPARATION

As recently as forty years ago, most births in North America and Western Europe (in industrialized societies) used general anesthesia with very little preparation or knowledge on the part of the parents as to what was involved in the birthing process or what their responsibilities would be after the child was born. Today most parents-to-be approach childbirth with a desire to reduce their potentially negative feelings as well as to know more about the birth process and the medical techniques involved. A larger number of parents are getting training in the specific biology involved in the birthing process, in the pregnancy process, and in breathing and concentration techniques to reduce birthing pain or overall discomfort.

The most common method of prepared childbirth today is the Lamaze method, which uses information and education as well as training and reorientation about the birth experience. There is often instruction in the anatomy of a baby and in the physiology of childbirth along with training in breathing techniques to help ease pain and reduce fear of the event. The Lamaze method also recommends the use of a partner ("labor coach"), who helps remind the woman to relax, breathe and stay centered on the process without fearing it. The coach also helps in cognitive restructuring, that is, helping the individual concentrate on sensations other than those of the major birth contraction. Finally, the coach acts as a social support. Since the coach attends classes, participates in the delivery, helps in the exercises, and helps direct the mother's concentration during the birth process, coaching improves the mother's sense of worth by reducing her fear of loneliness. The coach is usually the father.

Use of the Lamaze technique has been aided by hospitals and birthing centers allowing the father to be in the birthing room for the birth process. When the mother and father attend the education classes and when the father is an active participant in the labor process, women generally feel less pain, utilize less anesthesia, experience shorter labor, and have more positive feelings about the birth process and themselves. There is a socioeconomic factor in preparing for childbirth, however. People who go through preparation classes are generally middle, not lower, income parents. Therefore, middle income women will usually experience less pain, feel less lonely, and have less confusion about childbirth than lower income women.

Research comparing the birth experiences of first-time mothers indicates that those women who have general anesthesia, and therefore are unconscious during the birth, feel most negative about the whole process as well as about the baby. Those who go through natural childbirth without childbirth preparation classes are generally positive about the baby and negative about the process. Their labors tended to be very difficult. Those who have a general blocking anesthesia—that is, sensation to the lower half of the body is blocked while the woman is awake—feel detached from the entire experience, even though they are moderately neutral about the baby and the birth. Finally, those that have specific childbirth preparation training (e.g., Lamaze training) have short labors and positive reactions to both the birth process and to the babies. Education seems to bind the parents to the overall process by helping their attitudes improve toward the process and the infant, thereby helping the bonding process between parents and the infant.

FIRST GREETING BETWEEN PARENTS AND NEWBORN

Because the emotional impact of the childbirth experience is usually extreme, parents often experience joy, laughter, and delight within the first moments after the birth. They appear intensely interested in having the baby look at them, showing extreme delight if the baby opens its eyes. They may even attempt to stimulate the baby with tentative touching. In general, these parental behaviors are all part of an acquaintanceship pattern whereby the parent initially touches the neonate with the tip of the finger and proceeds to gradual stroking with the full hand. This pattern may be indicative of normal parent-infant relationship development or be at least minimally necessary for a good relationship to exist between them over time.

Some researchers argue that deviations in this pattern signal potential problems in the parents' future interactions with the infant. Specifically, mothers and/or fathers who have little pleasure in seeing the neonate, speak critically of the child's appearance, speak negatively about the child in general, physically turn away, refuse to smile at the neonate or even resort to poking or pinching instead of stroking the newborn have been found more likely to be abusive or neglectful of the child. The emotional experiences of the parents at first encounter with their baby may be indicative of the wide range of possible emotional responses to the presence of the newborn in the home.

PATERNAL PARTICIPATION

The emotions of delight, pride, and relief seem to be experienced by both the mother and father in the overall process; however, little research has been conducted with fathers who are present at the birth of a child. Generally, three arguments are given in favor of the father being present: (1) he can provide psychological support for the mother; (2) he can help control the pain of her experience through coaching; and, (3) he may be more strongly attached to the infant by being present. The first two have evidence supporting them; the third does not.

Coaches appear to help reduce the problems of labor and delivery as well as the duration of the labor and the amount of pain experienced. Therefore, mothers with coaches receive less medication. In addition, many mothers regard the birth as a "peak experience" in their lives if the father is present. With regard to aiding attachment, there seems to be no magical effect between the father and infant resulting from the father's presence. No consistent evidence shows his attendance makes the father a better parent over the long term. In essence, the major effect may be to enhance the marital or love relationship between the mother and the father, but attendance at birth isn't necessary for the father's emerging attachment to the infant.

BIRTH ATTENDANTS

The sensitivity of doctors, nurses, the other parent or even midwives to the parents' psychological needs during the birthing experience can be essential to making it satisfying for both the mother and father. Generally speaking, the parents-to-be are interested in having a birth attendant who is sensitive to birthing as both a psychologically and possibly physically excruciating experience. Therefore, the sensitivity of these attendants can extend past the moment of birth. One study of postnatal depression found the degree of support from attending medical personnel to be more influential on postpartum depression ("baby blues") than any of the physical variables about the birth (e.g., ease of labor, amount of anesthesia or birth complications).

SIBLING EXPERIENCES WITH THE NEW BABY

An infant's older siblings may not be overwhelmingly happy with the prospect of competing with someone else for the parents' affection or attention. The birth of a younger brother or sister is often a stressful event for children already in the family. Preparing the older children can often reduce this stress. That means giving them information about what to expect, helping them understand the changes that will occur, and reassuring them that being big siblings will have positive side effects, like being able to teach the young one or help the mother and father with infant care. This preparation is helpful for the siblings because it is not uncommon for the birth process to be seen as a traumatic event since Mom, and possibly Dad, leaves the home and goes to a hospital. The siblings cannot attend the birth, resulting in their feeling left out. Many hospitals, on the other hand, allow siblings to visit shortly after a birth because they know that planning a trip to see Mom and the new baby can be very reassuring.

Home birthing, which is occurring with greater frequency in the industrialized world, offers greater sibling contact; however, it must be done with care. A three-to-five-year-old sibling may not be able to emotionally handle or even understand all of the blood, pain, and intensity around the birth process. Hence, it may be best for the sibling to be away from the home during the actual labor and delivery. Any changes in routine and surroundings, such as new babysitters or furniture, can be taken care of easily in the months before the birth, thus helping the sibling prepare for and understand the changes involved. Special periods can also be set up when the sibling receives individual time with the parents.

Occasionally, the older sibling regresses (see chapter 3 in the discussion of defense mechanisms) to some childish behavior (e.g., whining, crawling, talking baby talk or wetting the bed for the first time in months or years) in response to the anxiety created by this new member of the family. This behavior is neither abnormal nor unhealthy, assuming that the child returns to normal age-appropriate behavior. With family support, not only can the parents help each other adjust to the arrival of the new child, they can also help the older child adjust to the arrival of this competitor for their attention.

BONDING WITH THE INFANT

The beginnings of the relationship between parent and infant, sometimes called bonding or emotional attachment, will be addressed in greater detail in chapter 9 as part of a larger discussion on the different general types of attachment that can occur (secure and insecure) between a parent and infant. Nonetheless, a great deal of interest exists regarding the events in an infant's early moments, hours or days and their effects on the attachment process.

The question arises because of studies indicating that some animal species imprint, that is, form a bond or permanent attachment with the first organism they contact during some critical period for attachment formation. Often, species that imprint do so with their mothers. This process has obvious survival value as well as importance in learning the social behaviors of that species. For some animal species, the mother and infant must be together for a period of time after birth to allow the mother to clean the infant and to connect the infant socially to its own individual species.

Generally speaking, the higher up the animal kingdom, the longer the critical period for imprinting. For example, imprinting for ducks occurs within the first fifteen minutes after hatching; it takes approximately eight weeks for dogs. One would suspect that if the process is upset in some fashion, then the young will experience significant identity, attachment, and/or behavior problems. Often, removing a dog from its mother before eight weeks of age results in behavior problems; that is, the dog may not know it is a dog. Thus, imprinting appears crucial for understanding the mother-infant bond and the relationship between an animal and its own species.

This raises significant questions about the amount of time a human mother and child spend together in the first days. How much does it influence the relationship between the infant and the parent? Does it make the infant more or less likely to feel wanted or desired? Does it make the mother feel more or less like a mother? In other words, does the amount of time together hamper or facilitate attachment formation between the mother and child?

Humans do not appear to imprint; that is, emotional attachment doesn't hinge on how long the initial relationship or contact lasts. Researchers see events in the early days as just part of the attachment process. This can be seen in cases where an infant is removed from the mother for adoption . The adoptive parents do not need to be present for the first hours, days or even weeks. The bond between the infant and adoptive parents is established through parental care and concern.

Early contact between a mother and infant has been overemphasized and overdramatized in the media. Mothers often feel guilt and sorrow if they can't spend extended time with their infant during the early days of life. While lower animal species require that initial contact for their own individual development, humans do not. Early contact appears more helpful for the mother's emotional stability and reduction of any postpartum depression.

Infants are not passive in this process. They encourage the development of emotional attachments with behaviors like cooing, cuddling, and snuggling. As mentioned earlier, the ability of the neonate to imitate the facial expressions of an adult encourages bonding of the parent to the infant. Crying has a similar effect by eliciting behaviors on the part of adults to provide care. The infants then respond to that care by being soothed, thereby reinforcing the caregivers. Infants can also look you in the eye and exchange gazes and smiles, all of which are powerful hooks for the adults' continued attention and emotional responsiveness to the infants.

SPECIAL ISSUES IN BIRTHING

Stillbirth: Results for Parents

Delivery of a dead child, commonly called stillbirth, combines the union of two major events: birth and death. Regardless of whether the death occurs before or during labor and delivery, parents should be expected, and encouraged, to grieve. They often experience four distinct phases of grief. The first phase is shock and disbelief at the event. Seeing and holding the dead infant as well as an autopsy and a funeral help parents resolve the grief process. The second phase is a yearning for the child. Grief is usually so intense that new parents may try to find the child by beginning another pregnancy almost immediately, thus serving to bury and complicate rather than resolve the grief. The third phase is one of disorganization. It usually lasts about six months and includes depression, apathy, and a devaluation of themselves. The last phase is one of reorganization, that is, an acceptance that the child was born dead followed by re-entrance into society. Basically, the parents accept that the event occurred but life and the living must go on.

Medications Given During Delivery

Despite the interest in natural childbirth discussed above, more than 95 percent of all deliveries in the United States utilize drugs in some form of obstetrical administration. Medications fall into one of three categories: anesthetics (used for caesarean delivery or some sort of spinal block—total or local); sedatives/tranquilizers (used to relieve anxiety on the mother's part, e.g., Valium); and analgesics (used to reduce pain, e.g., Demerol or morphine). Regardless of type, medications are prescribed for a desired effect on the parent.

The question remains as to what sort of effect, physical or psychological, the administration of medications has on an infant. This is important because the amount given to a mother in order to achieve a desired effect is based on her age and weight. The effect can be stronger for the infant, who not only weighs less than the mother but is also still experiencing critical/sensitive periods in development at the time of administration. Since these chemicals also traverse the placental barrier, the infant is almost immediately exposed to them once they hit the bloodstream of the mother. Generally speaking, the more medicated the mother is, the more medicated the infant will be and the longer the time of recovery. Infants who have been medicated in this fashion (compared with nonmedicated infants) are sluggish, suck less vigorously if at all, and interact very little with the environment or the mother. These differences between medicated and nonmedicated infants last for as long as two weeks, depending on the amount of medication. Generally speaking, however, medicated and nonmedicated infants are the same after the first month following birth.

On the other hand, the amount of maternal attachment to an infant can be significantly influenced by the effects of the medication. It is not uncommon to find the mothers of medicated babies spending more time stimulating their infants to suckle. They see their infants as being less adaptable, more intense, and more bothersome. Because medicated infants respond poorly for as long as the first couple of days, their mothers often see the sluggish behavior as a rejection by this infant that they have carried for the past nine months. In addition, compared with mothers who had no medication, mothers who had excessive anesthesia often suffer depression following the birth and report experiencing difficulties in, and getting fewer rewards from, caring for the infant.

Mothers who have been medicated should realize that the infant will not be responsive to them for a period of time and not let that deter their own responsiveness to the infant. Nonresponsiveness between mother and infant creates a cycle of nonresponsive behavior and, therefore, a less optimal environment for the child to grow in. In summary, if medication is needed during labor and/or delivery, as little as possible should be taken. If medication is taken, particularly anesthesia, it is important to remember that the child will also be medicated and will take longer to recover from it.

Breast-feeding Versus Bottle-feeding

The decision to breast-feed or bottle-feed an infant may depend on more things than just the mother-infant relationship. There may be cultural and/or societal influences on breast-feeding, as well as specific hospital procedures. Some hospitals make it difficult for a mother to be near her newborn day and night so that she can nurse the infant whenever it is hungry. Also, in the early weeks of life convenience factors play a factor. If an infant is to be breast-fed, a mother would feed every two to three hours with each feeding lasting at least twenty minutes. For some women, meeting this kind of schedule would be very difficult.

Breast-feeding has three general positive effects on the infant. First, the first "milk" that comes from the breast, called colostrum, includes many of the antibodies that will help the infant fight infections and allergies for at least the first six months of life. This allows the infant's immune system to mature sufficiently to create many of the antibodies to diseases and allergies. The result is that breast-fed infants generally have fewer respiratory and gastrointestinal infections than bottle-fed babies. Second, breast milk is easier to digest than cow's milk or formula. The fat in breast milk is almost entirely absorbed by the baby, whereas only 80 percent of the fat in formula is absorbed. This difference could be very important for the low-birth-weight infant who needs to put on weight as quickly as possible. There is also evidence that the high-cholesterol fats in breast milk influence low cholesterol levels later in life. A third factor to consider for breast-feeding is that there may be slightly higher risk of obesity in bottle-fed babies.

Generally, an infant who is breast-feeding stops sucking when full. The mother also watches for cues that tell her the infant has had enough, because she can't measure the amount of milk being fed. The mother of the bottle-fed baby, on the other hand, may try to get the infant to drink all the milk in the bottle, encouraging the child to eat long after he or she is no longer hungry. Thus bottle-fed babies, at least in some situations, may be overfed.

The physical side effects of breast-feeding seem to argue for it in lieu of bottle-feeding. However, the social, or parent-infant, bonding characteristics of each method are not nearly as explicit. Bottle-fed babies are held, cuddled, caressed, and "loved" as much as are breast-fed babies, and the parents tend to be as sensitive and responsive to their babies as mothers who breast-feed. From the infant's point of view, it does not appear to matter. The infant comes wired to create an attachment to whoever feeds it. That is, the infant is able to focus its eyes only about 8 to 10 inches from its face, meaning it is "legally blind" at birth. Because the face of the person doing the breast- or bottle-feeding would be about 8 to 10 inches from the infant's face, the infant comes to recognize that adult much sooner than other adults in its environment. Breast-feeding may have the advantage of aiding the mother-infant relationship by providing pleasure and reassurance of close physical contact.

Crying and Parental Response

Crying is a major form of communication, expressing distress to the child's caregivers. When distress occurs, it is not uncommon for an adult to pick up a child, console it, pat the child's back or head, and for the child to respond by calming down. Crying also has survival value. It informs the caregiver, parent or other adult of the infant's condition and encourages care on the part of that adult.

Researchers have delineated four different types of cries in the neonate: the birth cry (not often recognized by parents because it is heard so infrequently); the hunger cry; the mad cry; and the pain cry. It is often easy for parents to decipher which of these cries is occurring, based on the environmental cues. For example, the hunger cry is heard often when the infant is hungry, approximately every two to three hours for breast-fed infants. It is rhythmical, following a pattern of crying, silence, air intake, silence, and crying. The mad cry follows the same general pattern only more forcefully. Besides being more forceful than the mad cry, the first crying phase and the first silent period in the pain cry are generally much longer. The pain cry also begins very suddenly without any moaning, which may occur before the hunger or mad cries.

The response of adults to the different cries depends on whether they are parents or not. For example, experienced parents do not always come quickly to the sound of the hunger cry, whereas inexperienced parents will. Both sets of parents may go to a crib to check on a baby following a mad cry but may not be overly concerned. All adults caring for an infant, however, will immediately recognize the pain cry and attempt to console the infant. Without immediate environmental clues as to what the cry may be about, it is not uncommon to find an initial pattern of picking up the child, putting the child on the shoulder, talking to the child, and patting, stroking or rocking. Generally, experience with infants' crying makes adults or care-givers better at quieting infants than those who have little experience.

There is controversy about the effect of picking up a baby when the baby cries, that is, whether it encourages or discourages crying. When parents respond to the needs of the child by picking it up, a stronger bond between the infant and the adult is forged, thereby helping develop a sense of trust and security in the infant. Generally speaking, parents who are sensitive and responsive to the child's signals have children who cry less than those who are less sensitive. The rate of crying may be what is reinforced by the attention.

Studies with newborns indicate that they cry less often than people generally think, usually only about two to eleven percent of the time during the first three days of life. Normal physical development requires at least some crying, because it helps improve the lung capacity of the infant by forcing it to gulp in more air between cries and organizing the workings of the heart and respiratory system. In addition, the actual sound quality of crying can be used by doctors as a diagnostic tool. New studies indicate that small-for-date babies, preterm infants, and babies who suffer some birth trauma or complications during delivery have more piercing, grating or unpleasant cries than physically normal infants. The presence of different cries may be diagnostic for some underlying physical problems with in-dividual infants.

The actual birth of a human baby occurs in three stages: (1) dilation and effacement of the cervix so that the child can pass out of the mother's body; (2) the actual birth; and (3) delivery of the placenta (afterbirth). The longest and most painful stage is the first one, which may be why it is affectionately called labor. Assuming a normal birth, the newborn has behaviors that are mostly involuntary and reflexive in nature. The main body systems that will sustain life are quickly measured with the Apgar scale to determine if medical intervention is needed. Altogether, the strongest behaviors that the newborn comes equipped with are those responsible for feeding (i.e., root-ing, sucking, and swallowing reflexes) and those responsible for fostering attachment (i.e., social abilities and the imitation reflex).

Although a sustained loss of oxygen (anoxia) and a fetus in a difficult birthing position (breech or transverse) are reasons for a caesarean delivery of the infant, these are not the most significant birthing problems that can affect development of the child. Rather, low birth weight (whether the child is premature or small-for-date) can have a greater long-term impact.

The actual birth experience, contrary to popular belief, is highly untraumatic for the infant. The amount of anxiety or trauma for the parents, on the other hand, is often quite high. This can be reduced with sufficient preparation on what to expect as well as by the overall attitude of the parents toward the upcoming arrival of the new baby. In this regard, a father's participation in the birth as a coach is helpful in reducing the amount of psychological stress and physical pain experienced by the mother. The greeting behaviors of the parents on first meeting the child can be indicative of the parents' overall acceptance of their roles as parents and of how welcome the child actually is. Of importance in the family picture is the older siblings' degree of acceptance of the infant. In any event, human infants are very robust in making emotional attachments (bonds) with their caregivers; that is, they are not automatically attached to those around them at birth. Unlike imprinting in animals, human bonding occurs over a long period of time and appears to have little or no relationship to what events occur in the first hours, days or weeks after birth.

Finally, some issues are especially difficult for parents with regard to the birth and subsequent care of an infant. First, stillbirth can be excruciating for the parents. The passage of time and experiencing a normal grief process are the two best remedies. Second, medications given to the mother during labor and delivery may have the desired effect of reducing pain or anxiety, but they also medicate the infant. Sluggish behavior or an unresponsive baby often results, which should be viewed within that context rather than as some sort of rejection of the mother. Third, there is continued debate over the pros and cons of breast- versus bottle-feeding. Whatever the final decision, minimally newborns should get the first "milk" from the breast (colostrum) because it contains antibodies that will protect the infant for the first six months of life from many diseases until its own immune system can take over.

Fourth, crying is the major form of communication available to an infant. Four types of cries have been determined to which adults seem to respond differently, regardless of whether they are the parents or not.

Selected Readings

Apgar, V. (1953). A proposal for a new method of evaluation of the newborn infant. *Current research in anesthesia and analgesia,* 32.

Bower, T. G. R. (1979). *A primer of infant development.* San Francisco: Freeman.

Bowlby, J. (1980). *Attachment and loss. Loss, sadness and depression.* NY: Basic Books.

Dick-Reed, G. (1972). *Childbirth without fear: The original approach to natural childbirth.* NY: Harper & Row.

Harper, R., and I. J. Yoon. (1987). *Handbook of neonatology.* 2d ed. Chicago: Year Book Medical Publishers.

Klaus, M. H., and J. H. Kennell. (1976). *Maternal-infant bonding. The impact of early separation or loss on family development.* St. Louis: Mosby.

Macfarlane, A. (1977). *The psychology of childbirth.* Cambridge, MA: Harvard University Press.

Rank, O. (1929). *The trauma of birth.* NY: Harcourt Brace.

Tanzer, D., and J. L. Block. (1976). *Why natural childbirth? A psychologist's report on the benefits to mothers, fathers, and babies.* NY: Shocken.

7

Infancy and Toddlerhood: Physical Development

*T*his chapter covers physical development for the ages of 0 to 2 with emphasis on changes in size and shape, followed by an examination of the changes in motor abilities during this period. Specific reference is made to the appearance and disappearance of reflexes, the development of gross versus fine motor skills, and how the interactions between heredity and the environment effect motor development.

Basic sensation and perception skills of the infant and toddler are also covered. Beginning with a brief overview of the research techniques involved, all major sensory systems are summarized relative to the infant's capabilities from birth onward. Information is presented showing that infants are able to integrate information from many sensory modalities earlier than most researchers originally thought.

Brain growth and maturation are covered, particularly as they relate to motor, sensory, and perceptual development over this two-year period. Of interest are the states of consciousness early in life, maturation of the sensory and motor areas of the brain, plasticity of the infant brain, and the interactions between heredity and environmental experiences in determining the course of development.

Finally, the role of nutrition in physical development is summarized. Malnutrition and subnutrition are covered with respect to the negative effects of nutritionally poor diets. In addition, normal patterns of feeding from breast or bottle to solid food are reviewed, especially with emphasis on the question of obesity in infants and any long-term relationships to adult obesity.

SIZE AND SHAPE DEVELOPMENT

Physical growth and development during the first few years of life follow the maturational principles outlined in the biological theory of development (chapter 3) and first observed during prenatal development (chapter 5). Basically, physical growth appears to be governed by the cephalocaudal, proximodistal, and mass-to-specificity principles.

The cephalocaudal principle specifically says that development proceeds from the head downward (i.e., head to tail). Accordingly, an infant gains control of its head and arms long before it gains control of its legs and feet. The proximodistal principle states that development occurs from the midline (near the spine) outward toward the extremities. Hence, an infant can control its arms before controlling its hands or its fingers. The mass-to-specificity principle relates exclusively to muscle development; that is, large muscles will develop first, making major gross body movements possible. Specific muscles for fine body movements, such as the use of fingers, will develop later. Therefore, an infant will be able to move its arms before being able to pick up a single piece of paper.

Putting all three principles together, development can be seen to be directional. It begins at birth with an infant who is under complete involuntary control and continues, over a period of time, to a point where the infant has voluntary control. Where initially there is little differentiation in movement, development proceeds to a point where there is very subtle differentiation in movements and where new abilities arise from old abilities.

As stated in chapter 6, newborns measure about 20 inches long and weigh approximately 7 to 7½ pounds. They experience a 5 to 10 percent loss of body weight within the first couple of days. Following this, their bodies adjust to the sucking, swallowing, and digesting reflexes so that they can eat and consistently gain weight from then on. Growth occurs very rapidly, with weight doubling by the fourth month and tripling by the end of the first year. In addition, for each month during the first twelve, an infant gains about one inch. By the end of the first year, the average child weighs about 22 pounds and is about 30 inches long. Growth during the second year proceeds at a slightly slower rate so that by the end of the second year most children weigh about 30 pounds and measure somewhere between 32 and 36 inches. Generally speaking, two-year-olds are about one-fifth of their adult weight and half their adult height.

Weight gain during the first months of life is primarily composed of fat, which provides an insulating layer and a storehouse of energy for those times when the child may be eating little (e.g., during illness or teething). After the first few months, the weight gain can be attributed to both muscles and bones, which were mostly water at birth as to allow the fetus to fit within culture, nutrition, opportunity to practice, and amount of social encouragement may influence how that particular genetic timetable displays itself.

When motor development is being examined, the concept of the "statistical" child should be ever present. That is, most of the bench marks for certain characteristics are statistical averages. For example, there is an average age at which a child will stand, say his or her first word, and so on. These averages are just bench marks to keep in mind as children are growing. Not only will every child's genetics be different, so will his or her environmental experiences.

SENSATION AND PERCEPTION SKILLS

In understanding the sensation and perception skills of infants, it is important to understand how they can tell us what skills they have. Generally, three basic research procedures allow infants to "talk" about their different skills. First is the single stimulus procedure. An infant is initially observed to determine a baseline interest level in its environmental surroundings. A single stimulus is then presented, and measurements are made of any changes in the infant's behavior. Subsequently, the stimulus is withdrawn and behavioral measurements are retaken. In each measurement period, behavioral changes would indicate an ability to discriminate that an environmental change has occurred. Second is the preference procedure. Two stimuli (e.g., two photographs) are presented to an infant simultaneously; any preference the infant shows for one stimulus over the other indicates the infant can discriminate between them. This procedure requires controlling right and left positioning of the stimuli since all infants (even newborns) show a preference for their right side when looking at things early in their lives. Therefore, an infant's preference for something on its right over something on its left may indicate no preference at all. In contrast, an equal preference for a picture on the left over one on the right may indicate more actual preference for the one on the left. Third is the habituation procedure. Basically, one stimulus is presented often enough or long enough so that the infant becomes "bored" with it, and then a second stimulus is presented. If the second stimulus causes an increase in heart rate, blood pressure or visual fixation, we know the infant recognizes the second stimulus as being different from the first. All three of these procedures have been used to determine the sensory and perceptual skills discussed below.

Vision

At birth, an infant can focus approximately eight to ten inches from its face. It can blink at bright lights and follow a moving a light or target but is legally blind according to adult standards. An infant at birth has approximately

the cramped area of the uterus. Subsequently, the muscle fibers become longer, thicker, and a lot less watery. In like fashion, the number of bones increases after birth as well as the calcium content or hardening of the bones (a process called ossification). The ossification process will continue right through adolescence.

In terms of shape, body proportions will change over the first two years. At birth, the head is approximately one-fourth of the overall body size, whereas by the end of the second year it is about one-fifth. Likewise, the infant maintains a fairly chubby-looking appearance for the first year; by the end of the second year, the toddler becomes more slender as weight is more evenly distributed and the child's activity level increases.

Keep in mind that slight gender differences in the growth rate exist. At birth, a female is approximately four to six weeks closer to physical maturity than is a male. By age two, the average female is already over half of her adult height, whereas the male is just attaining half his adult height.

MOTOR ABILITIES

Reflexes

As mentioned in chapter 6, the newborn comes equipped with a variety of reflexes. They can be divided into four general categories: breathing, feeding, body maintenance, and development indicators. The breathing reflexes are those involved with getting the infant an adequate supply of oxygen. Within the first days of life, the infant has to learn to begin coordinating the breathing reflex with those reflexes responsible for fostering feeding in the infant: crying (for indicating hunger and resulting in the presence of the food source); rooting (for finding the nipple and getting it into the mouth); sucking (for getting food into the mouth); and swallowing (for transporting food from the mouth to the stomach). Initially, the breathing and feeding reflexes are totally involuntary, but over time they will come under more voluntary control as the infant learns to coordinate them to allow crying, suckling, and swallowing without gasping, chocking, or struggling for air. The third set of reflexes are those used to maintain body temperature (such as crying, shivering, and tucking the legs), all of which serve to change muscle activity and keep the infant warm.

Unlike the first three sets, the fourth set of reflexes does not appear necessary for survival. Rather, these reflexes appear useful as signs of normal brain and body functioning. They (i.e., the Babinski, walking, grasping, and Moro reflexes as described in Table 6.2) are normally used to test infant neuromuscular capabilities (e.g., as with the Brazleton Neonatal Behavioral Assessment Scale). Most in this last set of reflexes disappear within six months after birth. Some of them are thought to be a vestige of an earlier evolutionary form of development. For example, the grasping reflex is ever present in infant monkeys at birth as they need to grasp the hair of their mothers as they move on the ground or through trees. (See chapter 6 for a further discussion of reflexes as well as Table 6.2.)

Gross vs. Fine Motor Skills

In the development of motor abilities, a distinction is usually made between gross motor skills (those requiring a large muscle mass to enact large body movements) and fine motor skills (those requiring smaller muscles that are utilized in small movements). Jumping, hopping, and skipping are examples of gross motor skills; picking up a penny is an example of a fine motor skill.

Of the two types, gross motor skills may be more influential in development because of their importance in allowing the infant ultimately to separate from its parents. These skills develop in a steady progression, or maturational order, that is fairly consistent across all infants, from the newborn fetal position through the infant's being able walk by itself. Some individual differences exist. For example, the creeping stage may be accomplished as early as five months or as late as twelve months. Some infants crawl on their hands and knees; others walk on all fours, like a bear. Generally speaking, the time from when they stand alone to about six months after they walk alone is the age at which we usually refer to infants as toddlers. This is because their heads and stomachs are relatively large and heavy, forcing them to spread out their legs for stability. This stance makes them bow-legged in order to maintain a sense of equilibrium. As they start to walk, they fall frequently; but since they don't have far to fall, they are generally unhurt. By the age of two, most children walk and run fairly well, even though they may still place their feet wide apart for balance.

Fine motor skills follow the proximodistal pattern of development. By the age of six months, most babies can hold onto objects that are dangled in front of them; however, because they are still slightly reflexive, infants have a difficult time letting go of an object. By eight to 10 months of age, they can adjust their reach, catching objects tossed toward them. Another skill easily mastered is picking up small objects with the fingers. Even though they initially use a whole hand (the ulnar grasp), somewhere between nine and 14 months of age they are able to use the thumb and forefinger (the pincer grasp). At this point, infants enjoy picking up small objects such as pieces of rice, cereal or even bits of fuzz from the carpet.

Genetic (Maturational) Influence

At this point, it is important to understand the principle of motor primacy (the principle of readiness). In physical development, the principle of motor primacy states that an infant cannot do a particular skill until the body has matured sufficiently to promote that skill. Stemming from the biological

theory of growth, this relates to maturation and the timing of the onset of individual skills. The principle of motor primacy says that an infant at four months who can sit with support would have been unable to do that at two months because the necessary bone structure, muscle development, and sense of balance would not have been present. The same can be said for an infant able to walk alone at approximately 15 months. That is, the infant requires sufficient strength in the legs, bones, and muscles; proportional body weight; a sense of balance; and the ability to stand unaided prior to being able to walk alone.

ENVIRONMENTAL INFLUENCES

With the principle of motor primacy, a clear interaction between genetics (biology and maturation) and the environment can be observed: that environmental influences can impact on when and how a particular behavior may occur. Three main environmental effects influence the rate at which maturation occurs: practice, nutrition (diet), and illness. When practice of a skill does not occur or when opportunities to practice are restricted, a child's motor development can be retarded. For example, lack of practice can result in slowed development of universal skills, like crawling or walking, where a small amount of practice might be needed to keep everything working as it is supposed to. For complex combinations of motor skills (e.g., kicking or throwing objects), practice may be essential for that skill to develop at all. Additional evidence suggests that practice stimulates brain development. Therefore, brain development may make motor skills possible and better while practicing the skills may influence brain development.

Dietary environmental influences are seen most dramatically with severe malnutrition. If it occurs during the last trimester of pregnancy and/or the first two to three years after birth, malnutrition slows physical and motor development. A child's illness pattern can also influence motor development. Generally speaking, the earlier in life that an illness, or malnutrition, occurs, the more lasting the effect and the less successful the child will be in catching up to fully normal development. This assumes that the illness is a major debilitating or chronic disease. Yet, even less severe illnesses or medical problems can slow development. For example, a broken arm on a two-year-old will slow development of skills for which that arm was essential.

STATISTICAL VS. PARTICULAR CHILD

The rate at which a child develops and displays certain behaviors is probably an interaction between inherited genetic qualities and environmental factors. Each infant will have its own particular inner timetable, which may be faster or slower than that of another infant. Also, an infant's family,

20/600 vision, meaning that it can see at 20 feet what a normal adult with 20/20 vision can see at 600 feet. Acuity develops quickly, however, with focusing distance equivalent to that of an adult by about six months of age.

The preference procedure has demonstrated that infants less than two days old have definite likes and dislikes with regard to visual patterns: curved over straight lines; colors over black and white; complex over simple patterns; three-dimensional over two-dimensional objects; pictures of faces over pictures of other things; and new sights over familiar ones. These preferences aid discrimination in the ability to identify people. For example, babies can recognize their mothers' faces by about one month of age.

In the development of pattern recognition, infants show a two-step process. First, up to about eight weeks of age, an infant looks more at the edges of an object rather than at its appearance or internal features. In effect, infants look for a contrast between light and dark (an edge) and will then trace that contrast, outlining the newly found object. They will also follow moving objects with their eyes because of the high contrast. Essentially, the infant is looking to see where something is in the environment.

Second, from eight weeks onward, infants are interested in what something is more so than in where it is. In other words, the identity rather than location of an object becomes important. For example, an infant will examine the individual parts or pieces of a picture and will prefer pictures consisting of two or three objects over pictures of single objects.

This shift from interest in the "where" to the "what" of an object helps infants pay attention to detail. At three months of age, infants can pick out their parents from other people by examining facial features and, at five to six months, they can differentiate emotional expressions on their parents' faces. The ability to discern detail is important in social referencing, that is, being able to read emotions on the faces of others in order to decide what emotions or behaviors are appropriate in a given situation. The ability to differentiate emotional expressions is clearly seen at six months of age, when infants show a preference for happy faces over sad or angry faces.

COLOR VISION

Four-day-old infants are able to discriminate red from green and can see red, green, and yellow. However, they apparently cannot see the color blue until three months of age. It is not known if neonates see colors the same way older people do. All we know is that they can discriminate these colors from one another.

DEPTH PERCEPTION

There is conflicting evidence regarding the development of depth perception. Some studies, for example, show two-week-old infants demonstrating some perception of objects coming toward their faces (by flinching).

The main test for depth perception uses an apparatus, called a visual cliff, in which a stand is constructed about four feet above the floor and divided in half, each side covered with glass. Under the first side is a checkerboard pattern placed up against the glass (i.e., "shallow"). On the opposite side the checkerboard pattern is on the floor so it appears to be a drop-off or cliff (i.e., "deep"). Six-month-old infants show a definite preference for the shallow side of the visual cliff as opposed to the deep side by their willingness to cross the former and not the latter; but two-month-old infants show an increased heart rate if they are placed on the glass over the deep side, indicating they perceive a difference between the shallow and deep sides. Testing for fear of the deep side shows no reaction of an emotional nature until at least six months of age.

Hearing

Auditory acuity is better than visual acuity in newborns. They can hear the range of pitch and loudness of an adult human voice; adults have better hearing for quiet and low-pitched sounds than newborns do. Newborns and infants can also detect where a sound is coming from, but this ability is much more rudimentary in the newborn. That is, newborns are limited to just turning their heads in the general direction of a loud noise. However, most six-month-old infants can accurately determine the location of softer sounds. One-month-old infants can discriminate between the sounds of *p* and *b* and *d* and *t*.

Much of the auditory acuity that is present at birth may result from development of auditory sensitivity before birth. For example, at birth a newborn can usually discriminate between the sounds of the mother and another female. However, the same is not true for discrimination between the sounds of the father and another male. These results are easily understood when you consider that the fetus was listening to the mother's voice for much of each day during the last three months of the pregnancy when the ears and auditory system in the brain were developing. Additional evidence that infants pay attention to patterns of sound comes from a 1986 study in which mothers read the Dr. Seuss book *The Cat in the Hat* out loud once a day during the final weeks of pregnancy. After birth, infants preferred the sound of the mother's voice reading *The Cat in the Hat* to any other story. This indicated that fetuses pay attention to and discriminate between complex sounds before birth.

All of this may be particularly important for a point that will be developed in chapter 8 on cognitive development. Infants who are consistently spoken to from birth (and possibly even before birth) with a wide variety of language will develop language themselves more rapidly. In addition, the early preference infants show for their mothers' voices may help initiate the attachment process (bonding) between a mother and an infant because the infant has been listening to the mother's voice while still in the womb.

Olfaction

The sense of smell appears well developed in a newborn. This is commonly tested using a stabilimeter, which measures an infant's breathing rate, heart rate, blood pressure, and changes in the electrical potential of the skin's surface. When any new smell passes under an infant's nose, these bodily reactions are measured by the stabilimeter. With this methodology, infants have been found to detect the same odors that adults can as well as not detect the same ones that adults cannot. Quick development of the sense of smell appears related to the growing mother-infant attachment; that is, one-week-old babies can tell the difference between their mothers' smells and those of other women. This finding, however, appears true only for breast-fed babies, who spend a great deal of time with their noses against their mothers' bare skin and near their armpits. Young infants, on the other hand, do not appear to be able to detect their fathers by sense of smell.

It is important to note that bottle-fed babies can recognize odors of breast-feeding females. They can detect a different aroma on a pad worn by a nursing mother than on a pad worn by a non-nursing mother and will prefer to smell the pad worn by the nursing mother. It may be that nursing females produce some sort of generally attractive odor for infants that helps bonding or makes them more distinguishable from the scents of other mothers.

Taste

The sense of taste is largely based on the sense of smell since both smell and taste together produce the taste sensation, or the psychological reaction to food. Using the same stabilimeter technology, infants have been shown to respond to the four taste sensations (sweet, sour, salt, and bitter) that adults respond to with a particular attraction for sweet-tasting substances.

Another way of testing taste sensations or capabilities in newborns is to see how quickly they will suckle on a particular nipple. An infant sucking and receiving a sweet solution through a nipple will suck faster if the sweetness is increased and slower if the sweetness is stopped. However, even though infants dislike sour or bitter solutions, they appear unable to slow down drinking these liquids, apparently because the reflexes for sucking and swallowing are so strong. Discrimination of the taste sensation for salt is difficult to test. Occasionally infants have a difficult time telling the difference between salty fluids and plain water.

Touch

Work with touch centers upon the grasping, Babinski, and rooting reflexes. Essentially, full-term newborns are sensitive to both strong and mild tactile stimulation. They are also sensitive to pain as a response to touch. In general, sensitivity is greatest around the mouth, face, hands, soles of the feet, and abdomen, and least on other parts of the body. Little research on touch perception, however, has been accomplished because of difficulty in separating the emotional context of where the touching occurs on the infant's body from the actual physical response to the touch itself. One gender difference is apparent: female infants appear more sensitive to touch than males, a result that also appears true among adults.

Sensory and Perceptual Integration

All sensory systems seem to be functioning at birth and quickly become more refined with experience and maturation. Infants also seem to coordinate all of these senses, one with another, thus developing perceptual skills and cognitive abilities very early.

Specifically, research indicates that infants can "cross-connect" information from one sensory modality to another. In one experiment, infants sat in a chair and viewed a film of an angry-looking woman on one side of the chair and a happy-looking woman on the other. When a tape of an angry voice was played, they looked at the film of the angry woman and when a tape of a happy voice was played, they looked at the film of the happy woman. Similarly, other research has shown that four-month-old infants will look at a film of an animal bouncing in synchrony to an auditory beat that is being played, as opposed to looking at a film of another animal bouncing at a different beat from what they are hearing.

This ability to connect information across two modalities is called intermodal perception. It appears to exist for vision to hearing, vision to touch, and with regard to some types of comprehension. For example, one study used seven-month-old infants who were shown two slides: one of two objects and one of three objects. At the same time, they heard the sound of a drum beaten either two or three times. The duration of the drum beats from start to finish was the same regardless of whether two or three beats sounded. When the infants heard two beats, they looked at the slide that had two objects, and when they heard three, they looked at the slide that had three objects. This appears to indicate some rudimentary understanding of a mathematical concept. Some cognitive theorists once believed this sort of intermodal perception, or integration of sensory information, was not possible in early infancy. According to them, infants would develop knowledge about the world within each modality separately but not be able to combine that knowledge until a much older age. Such a supposition does not appear to be the case. (See chapter 8 for a further discussion on this issue.)

Some general characterization of the sensory and perceptual skills of infants seems to be possible. First, young infants and newborns appear to be "captured" by particular toys or objects in their environment, meaning that their attention is glued to a particular object. Usually by the end of the first year, however, they can systematically and intentionally explore objects that are presented to them, thus reducing the control exerted by one particular object. Second, individual infants will pay attention to an increasing variety of aspects of an object over time. As infants age, the pattern of information appears more important than the specific properties of some stimulus. As noted earlier, newborns initially pay attention to the edges or movement of objects, whereas older infants pay attention to object texture, color, shape, and density, as well as movement and edges. Lastly, as infants age, they become better able to ignore irrelevant information presented to them and to pay attention to changing stimulus patterns as well as to things that change between objects. Thus, they pay attention to constancies of objects.

BRAIN GROWTH AND MATURATION

The brain of the neonate looks very similar to the adult brain, with some major differences. First, the infant brain is not totally functional. The hind-brain (or medulla), which sits atop the spinal cord, and the mid-brain are the most functional portions of the brain at birth. The medulla governs all basic bodily functions necessary for infant survival, such as suckling, breathing, heart rate, body temperature, and muscle tone; the mid-brain governs behaviors like attention, sleeping, wakefulness, and elimination. All of the mid-brain and medulla functions happen to be behaviors that the newborn does well. The least functional portion of the brain, the fore-brain, includes much of the cortex that is involved in perception, body movement, thinking, language, and association, that is, higher-order human functions.

Second, for the first couple of years after birth, the infant brain is much smaller than it will be in the adult. Even though all the necessary brain cells (neurons) for the adult brain are present at birth, they are not fully grown, connected or myelinated. In effect, it is smaller because it has not matured. The infant brain is only about 25 percent of its adult weight at birth, but increases to about 75 percent of its adult weight and size by age two. The main growth appears to be in the number and density of dendrites (i.e., those parts of neurons that receive information from other neurons). This dendritic branching process ceases at about age two, at which point the brain literally "prunes" itself much the same way gardeners prune trees of unneeded branches. The same thing occurs at the neuronal level, reducing the number of connections between dendrites and other neurons (synapses). Apparently, by removing unneeded synapses, maximum efficiency can be achieved for brain functioning throughout childhood. Another pruning process of synapses occurs during adolescence, finalizing brain structure and functioning for adulthood.

Lastly, the brain gains weight by adding myelin around individual neurons. This fatty substance serves two functions. First, it insulates the signals that individual neurons carry from interference by signals from other neurons. Second, it makes the neurons work faster. The myelinization process continues from birth onward through the end of adolescence. As more myelin is added to neurons in the brain, there is an increase in brain function and control. Specifically, a direct relationship exists between the amount of myelin present and the amount of control. Likewise, as myelin increases, distractibility decreases, attention becomes more controlled, and the amount of voluntary behavior increases. To demonstrate the importance of myelin in nervous system functioning, consider that multiple sclerosis is a disease that causes a breakdown in the myelin around individual neurons. As the disease progresses, adults lose motor control as well as thinking and perceptual abilities; in effect, they regress to a level of capabilities similar to those of infants, who have little myelin in their brains.

The brain of a newborn or infant contains the motor, sensory, auditory, and visual cortex areas. Respectively, these areas control movement of the infant, sensory input, auditory input, and visual input. Myelinization appears faster for sensory than for the motor sections of the brain. This probably serves a survival function, enabling the infant to get information needed to negotiate the environment safely. What we see, then, is that many of the sensation and perceptions skills required for correct locomotor activity are present before the locomotor skills mature.

Hereditary and Environmental Interactions

In terms of brain development, an apparent interaction exists between an individual's hereditary make-up and the environmental experience. Work with rats in the early 1970s showed that growing up in an environment that provided a lot of stimulation resulted in more synaptic connections and heavier brains than did growing up in a fairly unstimulating environment. This also appears to be true for humans. The wiring of the brain, which we get from heredity, is present at birth and allows development of certain specific genetically programed capacities. The environment, however, helps fine-tune those capacities through the connective networks (synapses) so the relative processes can function better. For example, the brain development that allows seeing, hearing, touching, and olfaction to occur can be fine-tuned through visual, auditory, tactile, and olfaction stimuli (experiences) in the first months of life. Biological events can interact with the environment, influencing what kinds of experiences can occur, which in turn can influence further brain development.

Plasticity of the Brain

Besides being highly redundant (meaning that many neurological systems, or neurons, exist to do the same functions), many processes in the infant brain can be carried on by a wide variety of brain areas. This defines the concept of plasticity. Essentially, the newborn or infant brain is highly flexible in terms of where a particular function may ultimately be located, even though genetic programing for specific functions to reside at specific locations exists. A brain disease or tumor could hamper development of a certain area of the motor cortex in an infant's brain. However, other sections of the motor cortex could easily take over those functions without any observable loss of control to the infant. This factor of plasticity is lost between the ages of seven and ten, at which point damage to a motor section would cause permanent motor deficits.

Early States of Consciousness

Important functions of the neonatal brain are regulating the physiological conditions the infant will be exposed to and making sure sufficient rest is acquired to handle the stimulation it will receive. Some of this rest is called REM (rapid eye movement) sleep. Adults and children who can speak report dreams when they are awakened during REM sleep. Adults spend about 20 percent of their time in REM sleep. However, almost 50 percent of a full-term infant's sleep is spent in REM, with premature infants spending even more time in REM sleep. For example, infants who are born as early as 30 weeks' gestation show 80 percent REM sleep; those between 33 and 35 weeks' gestation show 67 percent REM sleep; and those born between 35 and 38 weeks' gestation show 58 percent of their sleep time in REM sleep. The amount of REM sleep decreases after birth; for example, three-month-olds spend 40 percent of their sleep time in REM.

Development and maturation of the brain over time can be outwardly viewed in the changing states of consciousness an infant progresses through daily. For the first month, infants spend more than three-fourths of each day in either active or deep sleep (see Table 7.1). A smaller amount of each day is spent in an active (awake), quiet (awake) or crying/fussy state. Over the first month, the amount of time spent awake increases while the amount of time spent asleep decreases. Infants repeatedly cycle through all five of these states over the course of a day. For the neonate each cycle lasts from one and a half to two hours: from deep sleep to light sleep, to fussing and hunger, to alert wakefulness, to becoming drowsy and quiet, and finally back into deep sleep. With time, the brain develops sufficiently to put together a couple of these cycles so it does not have to come to full wakefulness, which means the baby can sleep through the night.

Infants appear to respond best to social interaction from adults during the quiet awake state, which is usually after feeding, and sometimes in the active awake state, although stimulation in this state needs to be much quieter. The implication is that the amount of alertness an infant shows affects the opportunity for social stimulation from adults. If more opportunity exists, then interaction will occur during alert or awake periods. Generally, neonates spend between six and eight hours awake. By age two, infants spend from ten to twelve hours awake. Between ages two and thirteen, children continue to spend less time asleep until they can handle as little as eight hours of total sleep a night.

State	Characteristics	Average Number of Hours Spent in State	
		At birth	At 1 month
Deep sleep	Eyes are shut, breathing regular, little movement, occasional startle reaction.	16 to 18	14 to 16
Active sleep	Eyes are shut, breathing irregular, no major body movement, occasional twitches.		
Quiet awake	Eyes open, breathing regular, no major body movement.	6 to 8	8 to 10
Active awake	Eyes open, breathing irregular, movements in head, trunk, arms, and legs.		
Crying and fussing	Eyes entirely or slightly shut, large varied movements while crying or fussing.		

Table 7.1   The Basic States of Infant Sleep and Wakefulness

NUTRITION

Because the growth rate is so phenomenal during the first few months after birth, infants eat as often as every three or four hours, day and night. The schedule, however, is less important than is the quality and quantity of the infant's nutritional intake, because adequate nutrition helps physical growth as well as brain development and skill mastery. Keep in mind that an infant's nutritional needs are vastly different from those of an adult and they can all be met with breast milk as opposed to bottled milk. (See chapter 6 for a discussion on breast- versus bottle-feeding.) A mother's milk appears to be natural food for human infants and meets all the nutritional requirements except for vitamin D, which is synthesized through exposure to sunlight. Breast milk also contains antibodies for certain diseases, and allergies occur less frequently in breast-fed infants. Breast-feeding helps mothers' bodies return to a normal state following pregnancy and, in a passive way, helps mothers lose weight because energy is required to produce milk. On the other hand, breast-feeding may cause bone loss around the spine and hips, although the loss appears reversible.

With regard to bottle-feeding, a major problem, called nursing bottle mouth, can occur when children are routinely put to bed with a bottle. Sugar from the formula may stay within the child's mouth when a bottle is used to help the child go to sleep. This sugar promotes tooth decay and can contribute to early tooth loss.

Usually breast or bottled milk is the exclusive food for the first six months, at which point an infant can move to soft solid foods (cereals) or fruits (bananas). As first foods, vegetables, meat, fish, and eggs can provide correct nutrition as long as they are ground up (the infant will not have the coordination or teeth to chew the food).

Of importance in the discussion of nutrition and feeding is the question of obesity, which seems to be the chief nutritional problem of children in the United States, as well as in most Western industrialized societies. Most infants are chubby, having excessive fat until at least nine months of age. This occurs because infants need a storehouse of energy during times when they either do not want, or actively refuse, to eat; for example, during teething and illness. However, no strong relationship between the size of the infant before age two and any measure of obesity in adulthood appears to exist. Infant chubbiness at four or six months is no predictor of obesity when the child is older. On the contrary, when the toddler moves into the preschool years, activity increases and much of what was baby fat burns off, leaving a more slender child.

Malnutrition

A strong relationship appears to clearly exist between an infant's nutritional intake and later developmental problems. A bad diet for the first two or three years of life will significantly alter the size of the brain, myelinization of the brain, and the number of dendrites and synapses of individual neurons. This alteration appears to be permanent, decreasing physical and motor development significantly. Marasmus and kwashiorkor, both severe protein/calorie deficiencies occurring in infancy and toddlerhood, respectively, cause an infant's abdomen, face, and legs to swell. This creates an appearance of being well fed, whereas the infant is actually showing severe signs of a protein and/or calorie deficiency.

These two problems are more common in developing countries where mothers do not breast-feed as long. Usually, an infant is breast-fed for the first few months. Breast-feeding is often abandoned, since the mother believes bottle-feeding to be easier. If she does not have the money to buy enough milk, then the formula, which would normally be good, is diluted with water. The infant does not get the same caloric or protein intake it would normally get. In Chile, for example, infants are four times, and in Egypt five times, more likely to die from these types of severe malnutrition. For infants who are chronically malnourished in infancy, severe physical and intellectual problems can be carried into adulthood. These types of malnutrition problems are not so common in developed countries. However, cases exist where severe malnutrition occurs because the caregivers are so overwhelmed with physical and emotional stresses that they ignore the infants' feeding needs.

Subnutrition

There is a middle ground between malnutrition and good nutrition in which a child might be exposed to subnutrition. An issue revolves around the concept of mild malnutrition. If it exists, detection may be difficult, especially as studies of this matter have not been well documented. Specifically, how poorly nourished must an infant be before the effects of malnourishment are seen? An infant's diet may meet only the minimal nutritional requirements, affecting energy levels and interactions with adults and the environment. Usually, cases of subnutrition are first diagnosed by the child's total weight; that is, when the child's weight is in the bottom tenth of the usual weight range for healthy children of that same age, sex, and height. The second criterion has to do with weight gain. An infant's not gaining weight from one month to the next during the first two years indicates subnutrition is occurring.

As with severe malnutrition, subnutrition (or undernutrition) appears to be the result of a number of emotional as well as family factors. It is not uncommon to find well-nourished infants who suddenly show a lack of weight gain on a month-to-month basis because they have entered into day care, a new baby has arrived in the home or, as might be the case in families of military personnel, the father or the mother might leave for an extended deployment. The effects of subnutrition, with respect to cognitive ability, may be marginal if a concomitant amount of stimulation in the environment is present. Even when subnutrition occurs during a period of rapid brain growth, intellectual abilities show resiliency and can recover. Studies in Mexico, Kenya, Barbados, Europe, and North America show, however, that early undernutrition coupled with an environment having minimal stimulation from family members or school leads to long-term learning impairment, decreased ability to concentrate, and/or decreased language skills. These deficits can last throughout childhood and adolescence.

*P*hysical development during the first two years of life follows the basic maturational, cephalocaudal, and proximodistal principles. In addition, growth is very rapid, resulting in an infant who is nearly one-half its adult height and one-fifth its adult weight by age two. Much of the initial weight acquired is in the form of fat that is subsequently used as an energy and calorie source during times of illness and teething.

The main characteristic of the development of motor abilities in this age range is a shift from complete involuntary control at birth to near total voluntary control by age two. Very quickly, however, infants learn how to *manipulate individual reflexes and control interactions among multiple reflexes. For example, the rate of suckling will vary depending on the flavor of the substance ingested; and a variety of reflexes work together in order to keep an infant from ingesting food into its lungs and choking. The principle of differentiation is involved in the development of gross and fine motor skills. Essentially, large motor movements (gross) appear sooner that small ones (fine).*

For all of motor development it is important to remember the principle of motor primacy; that is, a behavior will be impossible to reproduce until the physical structures necessary for the behavior have matured. Hence, new behaviors become possible as maturation occurs. The environment, however, can slow that process or improve the skill of a behavior through practice.

The sensory and perceptual skills of an infant are nearly complete at birth for what appears to be their initial primary purpose, that is, aiding the attachment of an infant to its primary caregiver. This developmental aspect reflects the brain's predisposition to developing sensory areas before motor skills.

Finally, nutrition plays a crucial role in healthy development. Whether an infant is breast- or bottle-fed, solid foods can usually begin around six months of age. Although most children appear fat during early infancy, this is probably a survival technique. That is, infants put on considerable weight during the first few months to tide them over the times when they may be ill or teething and will eat little or not at all. Poor nutrition, on the other hand, can cause major long-term physical and mental defects (from malnutrition) or subtle learning problems (from subnutrition).

Selected Readings

Bril, B. (1986). *Themes in motor development.* Dordrecht, Netherlands: Martinus Nijhoff Publishers.

Clark, J. E., and S. J. Phillips. (1985). *Motor development: Current selected research.* Princeton, NJ: Princeton Book Co.

Eichorn, D. H. (1979). *Handbook of infant development.* NY: Wiley.

Grant, J. (1986). *The state of the world's children.* Oxford, England: Oxford University Press.

Lowrey, G. H. (1986). *Growth and development of children.* Chicago: Year Book Medical Publishers.

Rallison, M. L. (1986). *Growth disorders in infants, children, and adolescents.* NY: Wiley.

Tanner, J. M. (1978). *Fetus into man: Physical growth from conception to maturity.* Cambridge, MA: Harvard University Press.

8

Infancy and Toddlerhood: Cognitive Development

*T*his chapter covers the cognitive development of children from birth to the end of the second year. Special emphasis will be given to the approach of Jean Piaget and his overview of cognition, from the involuntary reflexes that are present at birth to the ability of infants to construct language and symbols. Piaget's six stages of sensorimotor intelligence are presented in detail, demonstrating not only the development of object permanence but also voluntary control by the infant of his or her intellectual interactions with the environment.

Psychometric and information-processing views of infant intelligence are presented briefly because they offer differing viewpoints on intelligence and memory functioning that Piaget did not directly cover. Additionally, a perceptual approach to understanding cognition is presented, which incorporates possible inborn mechanisms that may encourage cognitive development.

Finally, since the first two years incorporate the most dramatic changes in language development, this ability is also examined in some detail. Emphasis is placed on the steps of language acquisition as well as the theories that attempt to explain why and how these steps occur. The importance of parental interaction with children in learning language is also covered.

APPROACHES TO VIEWING COGNITIVE DEVELOPMENT

Piaget

According to Piaget, there are four chief characteristics of the sensorimotor stage that are present at birth: the infant responds to its surroundings primarily with sensory and motor actions; the infant focuses on the present (i.e., there is no past and it is unaware of the future); the infant does not plan; and the infant has no mental image or word that represents objects. Over the course of the first two years, however, goal orientation, planning, organized voluntary mental imagery, and an object concept develop. Piaget determined that there are six stages of sensorimotor intelligence in the first two years of a baby's life that accounted for these changes in thinking abilities. (See also chapter 3 for a brief overview of Piaget's concepts regarding cognitive development.)

STAGE ONE

Newborn infants (birth to one month) have innate reflexes such as sucking, grasping, looking, and listening that represent the schemas with which newborns approach the world. Nearly everything that comes near a baby's mouth is sucked, everything placed in the center of its palm is grasped, and everything within focus is stared at. Since reflexes are instinctive (involuntary) responses to outside stimulation, an infant gains more knowledge about the world as it continues to utilize them. Gradually an infant will come to initiate and repeat these reflex exercises without a stimulus; that is, they come under voluntary control of the infant. Piaget believed the infant progressed from being a passive observer to being an initiator of these activities.

Of importance is the observation that infants in this stage appear to show no object permanence. This means that when an object (presumably a person, also) leaves the infant's field of view, the infant responds as though the object no longer exists. There is no looking for the object, nor is there any apparent sign of distress at the object's disappearance.

STAGE TWO

In this stage (1–4 months), the first acquired (learned) adaptations appear. Up to this point, infants existed with very rudimentary and involuntary reflexes. Now they begin to learn how to adapt those reflexes under their own control to their environment. Reflexive sucking techniques needed to receive nourishment from their mother's breasts become modified for use with a pacifier. In addition, they begin distinguishing between things that can and cannot be suckled (e.g., fuzzy blanket, wooden block).

Infants also begin coordinating two sensory actions. Prior to this stage, an infant could suck a thumb if it accidentally came in contact with its mouth; now, however, the baby can control its motor skills enough to purposefully place a thumb in its mouth. This behavior of purposeful thumb sucking is an example of a primary circular reaction. Circular reactions are basic repetitive acts associated with the baby's body that previously were accomplished by accident. They usually occur when an infant performs an action that triggers a reaction, causing the baby to repeat the initial action (very similar in design to the learning concept of reinforcement from chapter 3). For example, when an infant sucks its thumb, it feels good, allowing not only instant gratification but promoting continuation of the action. Because most of these circular reactions involve some body part, this stage is often referred to as the "self-investigation" stage. Finally, there still appears to be no object permanence. Yet, because the baby adapts and responds differently to the presence of returned objects that were previously in the child's field of view, memories on how to react to them must have remained after the object was removed.

STAGE THREE

Piaget called the stage 3 phase (4–8 months) the "procedures for making interesting sights last" stage. Others have referred to this stage as the "secondary circular reactions" or the "coordination and reaching out" stage. By stage 3, infants have learned to experience the workings of their own bodies through primary circular reactions. Now they learn to perform an action in order to get an external reaction from another source (person or thing), which encourages them to repeat the first action. This is referred to as a secondary circular reaction. For example, a rattle becomes a tool for a baby to shake and get an instant enjoyable response (the rattle sound), which encourages more shaking. Any object that makes noise is now a favorite of stage 3 babies. Likewise, it is easy to understand why vocalization increases: the baby makes a sound and the parent responds, encouraging the child to answer. Regardless of the fact that babies realize some action they perform resulted in some response, they have no clue as to why or how it happened.

At the end of stage 3, object permanence becomes more apparent. An 8-month-old will look for a toy if only a part of it can be seen. A favorite teddy bear mostly covered by a blanket except for one arm will be recognized and wanted; however, if it is completely hidden, the child will act as if it no longer existed.

STAGE FOUR

The fourth stage (8–12 months) seems to mark a significant change in the development of intelligent behavior. Infants anticipate events that will bring about something they want or need, and they know how to initiate those events. An example is a 10-month-old hearing its bath water being drawn. It might be very excited in anticipation of bathtime. Likewise, dragging out bath toys may mean the infant is encouraging a bath to be drawn.

Infants begin to coordinate several actions together in order to bring about something they want. They remember and utilize previously learned strategies (like sucking, hitting or grasping) in new circumstances. In addition, they begin coordinating several actions together sequentially to bring about a desired goal. For example, an 11-month-old may see a ball partially hidden behind a pillow across the room, crawl over to the ball, push the insignificant pillow aside, and attain the goal—the ball. In this situation, perseverance becomes important and purposefulness becomes apparent: the baby first wants the ball and then must keep that decision in mind while going over to it and removing the obstacle blocking it, thereby producing the desired results: playing with the ball. These goal-directed behaviors may frustrate parents at the same time, as when a 10-month-old sees another child's toy while visiting friends and is determined to take it home, even to the point of rejecting its own favorite toys. The behavior is goal-directed toward getting the other baby's toy. Likewise, a child may spit out broccoli at feeding time because it does not want to eat broccoli—again, goal-directed behavior.

Finally, stage 4 infants realize that objects exist even if they are completely out of sight. However, they will actively search for the object where it has been most often found in the past. If you hide a ball under one blanket (A) repeatedly and then hide it under a second blanket (B) even while the infant is watching, the child will begin the search under A and not B. Researchers refer to this as the AB error and believe it to be a coordination problem between knowledge and action. That is, the placement of the ball under B will register surprise (as measured by increased attention toward that blanket), indicating knowledge of where the ball has moved to, but the memory of past events will appear to override that knowledge, causing the child to look under blanket A.

STAGE FIVE

Stage 5 (12–18 months) is referred to as the "active exploration and experimentation" stage. Activities at this stage could best be described by the word *novelty* because most behaviors revolve around attempts to try something new and exciting. Piaget labeled stage 5 infants little scientists who "experiment in order to see."

Your 13-month-old son is contentedly sitting in his playpen enjoying his favorite toys. The telephone rings and you leave the room to answer it. When you return a couple of minutes later you find your son has thrown all the toys out of the playpen. You replace the toys and leave the room, but this time you watch him. He methodically takes each toy and repeats his previous behavior of throwing everything outside the playpen, but you notice that he varies the height at which he releases each object and the intensity of the throw, and he throws them in different directions. You are witnessing a child exhibiting tertiary circular reactions, that is, discovering innovative ways of doing things through experimentation. Unlike the previous two circular reactions, primary and secondary, where an infant uses repetitive actions to reach its goal, tertiary reactions involve new experimentation. The baby intentionally accommodated his actions to find new answers. He varied the height, velocity, and direction of his throws to find out what would happen to different toys: how would they sound when they hit the floor? would they bounce off the floor or just lie there? what would they look like? For little scientists, trial and error seems to be an effective way of learning about their world and objects within it. Because this stage can try the patience of even the most understanding parent, it is important to keep in mind that exploration is a sign of developing intelligence rather than stubbornness or difficult behavior.

Object permanence is in place during this stage. If stage 5 babies drop their bottles outside their cribs, they know the bottles still exist even though they cannot see them. They can locate toys put under a blanket while they watch and they do not make the AB error. If the toy is placed under a different blanket while a child watches, he or she will be able to find it. Although object permanence is now a reality, infants at this age still have a problem with imagining movement they do not see. If a father hides a small toy in his hand and places it under a blanket and then withdraws his hand without the toy in it, the child will look in his hand and will be both surprised and unable to locate the toy. He or she will not know to look under the blanket.

The old saying "think before you act" is not representative of infants in this age range. They are unaware of the consequences of their actions. This is the last cognitive substage without mental representation of exterior events, or what we refer to as thought.

STAGE SIX

Until now infants have had to rely on their reflexes, assimilating and accommodating new schemas, adapting and anticipating new events, as well as experimentation through trial and error in order to interact and be a part of their world. With the beginning of stage 6 (18–24 months) children can use mental combinations to arrive at a solutions. Toddlers using mental combinations are able to think through a simple task without having to physically perform it first. In order to be able to do this, a child visualizes the situation without having seen it. This is referred to by Piaget as mental representation. The infant in stage 5 who could not locate the toy when it was invisibly displaced would now in stage 6 be capable of using mental representation and coming to the conclusion that if the toy was not in the hand, then it must still be under the blanket.

Due to the fact that toddlers are now able to create images through mental examination, they can also reproduce behavior they have previously seen. Piaget's daughter, Jacqueline, witnessed a neighbor's child throwing a temper tantrum in his playpen. She had never seen this type of behavior before. The next day Jacqueline had her own tantrum. Jacqueline remembered what she had witnessed the day before. She was using deferred imitation, a delayed acting out of something that occurred in the past.

Pretending is a strong indicator that a child is in stage 6 development. The 18-to-24-month-old will spend many hours playing tea party with stuffed animals as invited guests, or cowboys and Indians with all the neighborhood children. A common characteristic of behaviors in this stage is the progression from sensorimotor thought to "the more contemplative, reflective, symbol-manipulating activity" that we call cognition.

During this final stage, an infant's mental representations allow him to imagine where an object might be. Hence, a stage 6 child no longer has to see something to know it exists. Object permanence is complete. One way to interpret this stage is to see it as a transition between the sensorimotor stage and the symbol using of the preoperational stage (see chapter 12 for a discussion of cognitive development in the 2-to-6-year-old).

Current Evaluation of Piaget's Work

Piaget's theory of sensorimotor cognitive development has been widely accepted by experts in the child development field. His analysis of the cognitive growth of children was excellent, but many feel it was incomplete and underestimated the intelligence of infants. Some psychologists have claimed that the familiarity of the testing environment and the motivation of the infant could significantly influence experiments examining the cognitive development of infants.

Familiarity appears to be an important factor in testing for cognitive development. If the experimenter is familiar, children will be more at ease than if a stranger conducts the studies. Likewise, if children are at home or somewhere they are accustomed to, this familiarity may also influence the results. Lastly, the familiarity an infant has with the tested item may also be significant. In an object permanence experiment, if the object being hidden is a favorite toy of the child, then motivation to look for it will be greater than if it is unknown or unwanted.

Almost everything we do requires some degree of motivation. The same is probably true of infants. Therefore, as Piaget's critics argue, when he administered a test and did not get the expected results, instead of concluding the infant was not cognitively ready for the next stage, the researcher should conclude that the baby may not have been in the mood to do the test because of insufficient motivation.

Finally, motor coordination goes along with cognitive development. A baby may see a task being performed, but if it doesn't have the physical abilities needed to achieve that task it won't be successful. This may be important, for example, in understanding the AB error.

Alternative Approachs to Cognitive Development

PSYCHOMETRIC

At the beginning of the twentieth century there was serious overcrowding in the schools. School administrators in Paris decided to alleviate the problem by not schooling children they felt would not benefit from an education. They asked psychologist Alfred Binet to design a test that would give a numerical score to intelligence and thereby identify those children. Although Binet was focusing on identifying children who were unlikely to take advantage of an academic education. Tests of intelligence are now designed to identify children with special strengths who will benefit from a more enriched environment. Three factors that people who think of intelligence psychometrically (meaning in a number-related measurement, i.e., the higher the number, the more intelligence you have) keep in mind are: the different components that make up intelligence; the amounts of these elements a person has; and using these factors to foresee or predict a person's intelligence.

Mental level was a term employed by Binet to symbolize a child's test score. Today we refer to it as mental age (MA). Binet grouped children who performed similarly on certain items in a given test. These "normal" children were used as a group representing the test takers whose scores were norms, or averages, and were referred to as the standardization sample. Their test scores were used as a comparison guide for future test scores.

Later, an equation to measure IQ (intelligence quotient) was devised. This allowed the translation of mental age into a number that could be used for people in all age ranges. IQ represented the ratio of a person's mental age (MA) to his or her chronological age (CA) multiplied by 100. The equation looks like this:

$$IQ = \frac{MA}{CA} \times 100$$

In theory , if the MA was the same as the CA, the person would be said to have average intelligence, i.e., 100. There are, however, various factors that have a direct impact on a person's IQ. Genetics, environment, race, and sex all play an important part in influencing our cognitive development.

Generally, psychometric tests on infants have proven to be poor indicators of later intelligence, especially for the baby possessing motor disabilities. Binet's test (the Stanford Binet) is unreliable for anyone under the age of six. The WISC (Wechsler Intelligence Scale for Children), another popular IQ test, shows poor reliability below the age of three. Finally, the Bayley Scales of Infant Development, a standardized test of infant's intelligence, gives a better description of the child's intelligence at the time of the test than a prediction of the child's later intellectual abilities.

INFORMATION PROCESSING

Some psychologists, believing that Piaget's theory is too restrictive, have begun monitoring infant intelligence through the information-processing approach. The underlying rationale is to get an understanding of how intelligence works. Essentially, an analogy is drawn between the thinking process and the steps a computer must follow to accomplish its program. That is, our manner of processing information is not unlike that of a computer, with its input and output capabilities and the capacity to manipulate symbols.

This avenue of research has provided a way to measure the intelligence of an infant between 3 months and 3 years of age. A child is allowed to sit on the mother's lap and watch several "puppet" shows. Over the testing period the child views five episodes designed to create expectations; then the child is surprised by a change in the expected pattern of events. Electrodes attached to the infant's chest monitor heart rate. When the child sees the unexpected happen, heart rate increases. The testers analyze the reaction time and the level of increase. After developing norms for children of different ages, researchers have been able to assess intelligence without the need for motor control on the infant's part. To date, this technique is in its infancy but it is serving as a way to open the study of intelligence in younger children more than any of the psychometric techniques are able to do.

Another avenue of study looks at the development of visual-recognition memory, or how long an infant remembers a visual stimulus. Three techniques used to examine an infant's ability to remember are habituation-dishabituation (described under techniques for examining perception in infants in chapter 7), paired comparison, and operant conditioning. In the paired comparison method an infant is shown one visual stimulus (picture) for a couple of minutes and then is shown two test pictures at once: the original just viewed and a new one. Usually the infant spends more time looking at the new picture; how long the memory of the original lasts can be measured by varying the time between original and test presentations. In the operant conditioning procedure, infants can bring a picture into focus by sucking on a nipple that doesn't produce food; the picture itself is reinforcing the motor response of sucking. As infants get used to a picture, they suck less frequently and vigorously. Then a new picture is introduced. If the infant now increases its sucking it is likely because he remembers the original picture.

Together these techniques have presented evidence that infants born five weeks premature have a memory capacity lasting five minutes for stimuli that are very different. If the stimuli are very similar, then infants need to be older to discriminate between them; however, it does appear that at the very minimum, five-month-old babies can remember a visual pattern or picture for as long as two weeks. These tests are also showing value for predicting later intelligence because a relationship has been demonstrated between an infant's preference for novel visual stimuli and scores in elementary school vocabulary tests. The study of recognition memory in infants has also allowed psychologists to identify retarded children at a very young age, and in doing so, to direct them toward the training most beneficial for them.

The information-processing approach cannot stand alone in studying the development of infant intelligence. It provides useful data that help in ascertaining how cognitive functions work and how those workings change over the course of time. In that way this approach complements the psychometric and Piagetian views.

PERCEPTUAL DEVELOPMENT AS IT RELATES TO COGNITIVE DEVELOPMENT

Affordances, Intermodal, and Cross-modal Perception

Believing that the way we individually "see" or perceive our environment influences our cognitive development and vice versa, Eleanor and James Gibson have fostered much of the current work on perception and cognition. They support the theory that perception is not automatic; it is instead a cognitive wonder that enables each person to interact in his or her own unique way to a variety of perceptual experiences.

In the Gibsons' opinion, all objects have many affordances; that is, they "afford," or offer, varied opportunities to relate. There are three things that need to be considered when studying the affordances a person perceives in reference to a given object: first, the individual's past experiences; second, the person's present needs; and third, how much this person knows about what the object can offer. For example, an apple can be perceived differently by every person that looks at it. A farmer's wife sees a plump, juicy apple just perfect for her next apple pie. Her neighbor sees the same appealing apple as a blue ribbon entry in this year's county fair. And a baby sees this object as a fun toy to roll around the floor. They all see the same apple, but their affordances are all uniquely different, which leads us to believe that the affordances are within ourselves, not in the objects we perceive.

From a baby's point of view, one affordance that is crucial to his or her development of perception of the world is graspability, that is, whether an object is the correct size, shape, and texture for grasping as well as within reach. Babies perceive graspability long before their manual dexterity has developed. When three-month-olds look at objects, some graspable, some not, they touch the ones that are within reach and easiest for them to grasp.

They perceive which ones they can reach and hold before they actually extend their hands to touch the object.

Likewise a baby will almost instinctively grasp for the nose, ears, jewelry or glasses of a person holding him or her and not for the eyes or mouth because those things are perceived as being embedded. A baby also understands the affordability of objects that can be sucked, make noise, move about, and so on. They can differentiate between the affordance similarities in dissimilar objects (a rattle, a teething ring, and a nose can all be grasped) and affordance differences in like objects (furry animals the same color, size and shape as plastic ones are usually squeezed while the later ones are sucked).

Intermodal perception (the ability to assimilate information from two sensory modalities) is a further demonstration of the cognitive abilities of infants and children (see chapter 7 for a discussion of the data showing intermodal perception abilities in infants). Experiments have been conducted in which an infant listens to a sound track while simultaneously watching two puppets jumping up and down. The beat of the music is synchronized with one of the puppets. After watching the baby follow the puppets with its gaze, the experimenters concluded that the baby watched the puppet that was in sync with the music more than the one that was not in sync.

The original experiment was modified to prove babies genuinely match the correct sound with the appropriate film or picture and not just instinctively respond to the music and movement of the puppets. The results showed the infants were actually making a correlation between the sound track and the puppet moving in harmony together. After many different attempts to clarify why babies are able to properly link a particular sound with a particular picture, researchers have concluded that babies have the ability to receive a stimulus through one sensory modality and integrate it with a second sensory modality in order to arrive at their perception of the world.

If you have ever talked on the telephone to a stranger and tried to imagine what this person looked like, you were using an ability called cross-modal perception. This enables us to visualize what some things may look, taste, sound or feel like without actually seeing, tasting, hearing or feeling the objects. Infants have very basic cross-modal perception abilities, but they are evident. One-month-old babies can use this perceptual ability for their sense of touch, not with their hands as older babies might, but with their tongues. One-month-olds were encouraged to suck for a minute on either a rigid or flexible object they had never seen. A pair of black-gloved hands then showed the different objects to the babies and by monitoring their gaze, experimenters could surmise that babies did, in fact, recognize the object they had been sucking.

At 2½ months, an infant can apply its new-found perception abilities in a slightly different way. Instead of sucking on an object, the baby is allowed to handle an object that is kept out of sight. Then two objects are introduced. With careful monitoring of the duration and direction of the infant's gaze, it was concluded that babies recognized the object they had been manipulating. Consequently, even a very young child has the capability of sucking or feeling an object he or she cannot see and still deriving some understanding about what it looks like or how it operates.

Perception and Classification

This tells us that infants must have some way of categorizing things they come in contact with: whether they are soft, hard, round, flat, flexible, stiff, and so on. At this early age, these categories are probably nameless, but they do exist and help the baby put things in similar groups.

One hypothesis is that we are all predisposed to perceive the world in certain ways; that is, we are born with the concepts of suckability, graspability, squeezeability. All that is needed are the environmental experiences to classify things in these categories. Possibly our neurological composition permits us to see certain traits about things around us. A study was conducted allowing three-month-olds to scrutinize several squares and one parallelogram. They looked at the squares for two seconds and at the parallelogram for seven seconds, indicating they realized the squareness of the first shapes as opposed to the nonsquareness of the last one. When they were again shown the same shapes standing (thereby resembling diamonds), there was no difference in observation time because a diamond would be a diamond even if it was shaped a little differently. In another study, four-month-olds were shown geometric shapes of several sizes with the smaller one above the larger. After habituation, the shapes were reversed, with the larger one above the smaller. Renewed interest led researchers to believe the babies could tell something had changed, possibly the variance of the shapes. Compiling the evidence from experiments on infants' perceptions, researchers are drawing the conclusion that infants may have an inborn ability to classify things in their own special categories.

Perception and Gender Expectancies

Gender may also be intuitively classified. From a very early age children seem to be able to distinguish a male from a female. As early as three months, a baby can become habituated to a series of pictures of very different-looking men. When a female's picture is introduced, the baby becomes more alert. A six-month-old, while looking at a picture of a male and female and listening to their voices, can gradually link the male with the masculine voice and the female with the feminine voice.

A one-year-old shows a more advanced grasp of gender differences. One-year-olds gravitate toward members of the same sex even if there seems to be no outward appearance of male or female gender. In one experiment, they were allowed to watch a video of a child playing. The child was dressed in the opposite sex's clothes and was playing with nonstereotypical toys. For example, a little girl was dressed in pants and a shirt and was playing with a drum, while a little boy was in a dress playing with a doll. The one-year-old viewers always watched the children of the same sex with more interest and intent, regardless of all other variables.

In another experiment, children were all dressed in jumpsuits with reflective tape placed on their shoulders, elbows, wrists, hips, knees, and ankles. They were then filmed in special lighting conditions revealing only the reflective bands when they moved. Girls were seen to be taking shorter steps, swinging their hips more and having more fluid motion. Boys bent from the waist when picking up a toy, while girls bent from the knees. When other children were allowed to watch these films, they could separate the girls from the boys by their movements alone.

There are varied opinions as to the validity of the concept of perception in infants. Some believe babies have an innate ability to categorize the things around them. Others feel that it is the maturing of the senses that allows infants to perceive their environment. But with numerous studies completed, it appears there is something cognitive happening inside a child's brain long before adult-level thought is possible.

LANGUAGE DEVELOPMENT

Steps in Language Development

TYPES OF CRIES

To understand the changes in cognitive development occurring over the first two years is to understand the changes occurring in language development, and vice versa. As noted in chapter 6, the initial birth cry of an infant is probably reflexive in nature. After that, three distinct cries can be found within the first month: hunger, pain, and mad cries. However, after the first month, infants expand their vocalizations.

COOING AND BABBLING

Next comes cooing: this is a vowel language consisting of single syllable vowel sounds, occasionally with soft consonants like *m* or *n*. This stage lasts until the third or fourth month when babbling begins: putting together vowels and hard consonant sounds. Babbling lasts until somewhere between 9 and 12 months of age, at which point the infant will make more of an attempt to mimic individual words. It is important to note that where the cooing sounds are vowels and sound just like that, babbling sounds a lot like words. An infant in the babbling stage can be in a nearby room and a parent will believe the infant is talking.

It is unclear whether babbling means anything to an infant or if it is simply random sounds. The research effort to find meaning in babbling sounds has not provided clear interpretations. Babbling may serve a self-stimulation function or improve the ability to understand more language or simply provide practice for the infant. In any event, since babbling generally increases with the presence of other people, it likely has a social function.

HOLOPHRASES AND TELEGRAPHIC SPEECH

Somewhere between 10 and 15 months, infants begin speaking in holo-phrases: one-word sentences. Sometimes these words are "expressive," meaning the infant begins using words involved in some sort of social interaction ("hug," "Daddy"), or they may be "referential," meaning the infant's early language is composed of simply naming objects ("apple," "chair"). Because they are usually one word, the parent or caretaker may not necessarily understand the nuances of what a word means to a particular child. At about 18 months infants begin using telegraphic speech: two-word sentences that give considerably more meaning but can also be vague to the caretakers. Soon after entering the telegraphic speech stage, infants begin applying some basic grammar rules, and communication becomes easier. For example, word order becomes important so the parent or caretaker can understand meaning. "Go bye" may mean the infant wants to leave or it may be a response to someone else who is leaving, both of which would be different than in the holophrase stage in which infants might say "bye," and one would be unable to tell whether that was being said about themselves or someone else. At about the point where an infant uses two-word sentences at least half the time, the infant will move into three-word sentences.

Theories of Language Acquisition: Learning versus Biological

The theories to explain how and under what circumstances language develops have generally fallen into one of two camps. The biological camp assumes a biological or genetic mechanism in all humans that makes it possible for speech to occur. The learning camp assumes speech occurs solely because of the simple rules and principles of learning and reinforcement. The best example of the biological approach would be the theoretical supposition of a Language Acquisition Device (LAD), which has been presented by Noam Chomsky. According to this view, an area of the brain is responsible for language acquisition, making it possible for all humans to learn language. This approach assumes the correct stimulus must be present in order for the LAD to be activated; that is, hearing other people speak.

Infants are born with a genetically programed ability to speak and make some communication, which explains the reflexive cries associated with some particular stimuli, e.g. hunger and pain. But these are all reflexive in nature. The LAD which is effectively turned on at or shortly after birth, helps infants take note of the nuances of language occurring around them. As language occurs, it is registered in the LAD and the infant begins to mimic what has been heard; the LAD could explain why infants babble when they are put to bed at night, as though they are speaking to someone. What they are doing is mimicking, trying to repeat and rehearsing the language they have heard during the day so they can make it sound the way an adult speaks it. According to the LAD approach, the best way for a child to gain an adequate understanding of grammar and language in both solitary and social situations is to hear a number of people talk. Thus, the biological approach assumes that if the correct stimulus is there, that is, language in the environment, the child will develop language capabilities.

As with other applications of biological theory in physical and maturational development, there is also a critical period for language development. This critical period appears to last up to the age of three or four. During this time, if an infant hears a great deal of language, it will learn to speak and speak clearly. However, if the infant is in a language-deprived environment, the infant will not learn a great deal of language, nor will the infant be able to speak well.

The biological approach is in contrast to the two different learning theories that are believed to work together for understanding the acquisition of language. The first is the general reinforcement and learning theory approach (see chapter 3 for a review of reinforcement and social learning theories). According to standard learning theory, an infant learns language through classical conditioning, associating the sounds and words with objects or actions. Through repeated association, the infant comes to understand that a specific word means a particular action or object. With repeated practice of the word, the infant is able to express it and therefore able to make the association stronger. Operant conditioning is strongly involved in learning new words as well as in learning to speak. When an infant coos, babbles or cries, adults or parents present reinforce the vocalizations by giving attention to the infant for each sound. With each attempt at vocalization and each reinforcement from an adult, the infant improves the quality of the vocalizations through the process of operant conditioning. Over time, as the infant gets more reinforcement, the vocalizations more closely approximate actual language.

The second part of the learning theory approach for understanding language acquisition assumes that infants model the language spoken by the adults in the environment, particularly the mother and father. This modeling may include an attempt to imitate the sounds, the muscle and mouth movements, and possibly some of the hand movements that go along with individual words or sounds they hear. The reasons for modeling are simple: they would gain reinforcement (attention) from doing it; they could identify better with a particular adult; and they could see their communication skills with adults improve. In any event, the two aspects of learning theory complement each other; an infant probably attempts to imitate the sounds and the mouth movements it hears and sees adults make, resulting in continual reinforcement from the same adults.

Learning and biological theories probably work together to allow language acquisition: a biological mechanism makes it possible for language to be acquired through learning techniques. Evidence for language skills being learned through reinforcement techniques by way of a biological mechanism comes from many studies with children who have been abused or who have grown up in environmentally unstimulating environments: children who are not spoken to or have very little contact with language until after the age of five or six do not acquire language with any great skill at all, regardless of the learning, reinforcement or modeling techniques used. In other words, there may indeed be a biological mechanism that is turned on and that has a critical period during which reinforcement techniques will work best for an infant to acquire language skills. Outside of that window, the language skills an infant acquires through learning techniques do not appear to be adequate.

Interactions of Parents with Children in Acquisition of Language

In understanding the relationship parents have with children and the development of language, it is important to look at normal adult behavior. Generally speaking, when adults have a conversation, one person speaks while another person listens. In addition, when the second person speaks, the first person listens. This skill of turn taking is responsible for much of what we consider normal social interaction on the communication or language level. That interaction, with turn taking as its basis, is something nearly every individual learns long before he or she is ever able to speak. It begins with a process called mutual monitoring. Basically, infants monitor the actions of the mouth and the face, along with the movements of the hands, so they can see what is going on with the caretaker who is holding and talking to them. Likewise, adults monitor the infant for nonverbal cues about language and attempts to speak. This occurs from birth onward. When an infant makes a face or sound, the parent will often stand, watch or listen. When the sound or action is complete, or nearly complete, the parent will reinforce the child by saying, "Good girl" or "Good boy," or by repeating what the infant is saying. The adult is trying to have a conversation with this little person. While the adult is taking his or her turn, the infant is gazing at the mouth, listening to the sounds, and in effect monitoring the adult so that it can acquire the skills necessary to make those sounds and do those movements. In theory, then, infants begin learning language within the first week after their birth every time they have contact with an adult who interacts, talks, reads, sings or in one way or another has some sort of verbal communication with them.

Some of what is learned here before full communication occurs is a nonverbal pre-language communication. From parents, infants learn about smiling, gesturing, eye contact, and many of the nonverbal interactions that bring about communication from the parent to the infant. By watching the gestures or looks on the infant's face as well as the facial contortions it makes, parents learn to tell when it wants to speak or participate.

In this interaction process, infants will learn not only all of the basic sound units, grammar, and semantics, but they will also learn about putting words together in the right sentence as well as about using the proper words in order to get a message across. One facet of parental involvement is something called motherese. As a language skill the parents use when talking to infants, it is characterized by higher frequency and short sentences and it is spoken in a very calm fashion so the infant will listen and pay attention to it. Sometimes motherese is a simple repetition of things the infant is saying. More often, however, motherese is an expansion of things the infant is saying presented in a format that apparently feels less threatening to the infant. In sum, language development is most likely a mixture of learning, reinforcement, and biological maturation processes, as well as important environmental and social interactions with parents (caregivers) in the environment.

Jean Piaget described the first two years of cognitive development as consisting of sensorimotor intelligence: what an infant learns and understands about the world is defined largely by the sensory and motor experiences that occur. Piaget subdivided this two-year period into six stepwise substages, beginning with a basic reflexive and involuntary interaction with the environment and ending with an ability to make internal mental combinations about events that are not occurring. That is, substage 1 is demonstrated by little purposeful interaction with the world whereas substage 6 is almost completely characterized by purposeful and voluntary interactions. Although Piaget's assessment of the cognitive abilities of infants appears correct in terms of order of occurrence, recent research indicates that these abilities may show themselves much earlier than Piaget predicted.

Psychometric approaches to understanding this area are difficult to use because of the lack of reliable testing materials for use with infants below the age of three. However, the information-processing approach has presented data that not only demonstrate a functioning memory in even premature infants but also the possibility of predicting later intelligence (psychometric) abilities based on these early memory capacities. Both of these approaches appear to fill in gaps of actual brain functioning, which Piaget did not address.

Eleanor and James Gibson have presented a different model for cognitive development, one based on perception. Essentially, perception is not automatic but is rather a cognitive process that each person uses to uniquely interact with the environment. Every object has affordances, or different possible perceptions, depending on past experiences, present needs, and knowledge about the object. This means that infants are born with some basic perpetual processes, allowing the acquisition of information that will influence future perceptions. Infants also show an ability to make perceptions across modalities, demonstrating advancing cognitive properties.

Language begins with four basic cries that appear to communicate basic needs. These are followed by cooing, babbling, holophrases, and telegraphic speech over the first 18 months of life. Although cooing appears to consist of predominantly vowel sounds with little or no meaning, babbling may reflect attempts to imitate adult speech patterns as seen by the increased amount of babbling that occurs when adults are present. Holophrases are one-word sentences that are difficult for adults to interpret but with the advent of telegraphic speech (two-word sentences) and some basic communication rules (word order) interpretation becomes easier.

Language ability may be related to a biological mechanism with a critical period lasting until about age six. During this period, language can be easily acquired following the basic principles of conditioning, reinforcement, and modeling. Parental or caregiver involvement encourages the development of communication skills between infants and adults as well as language ability and vocabulary in infants.

Selected Readings

Bowerman, M. (1982). *Language acquisition: The state of the art.* Cambridge, England: Cambridge University Press.

Braine, M. D. S., and B. Rumain. (1983). *Handbook of child psychology, Vol. 3, cognitive development.* NY: Wiley.

Chomsky, N. (1968). *Language and mind.* NY: Harcourt, Brace and World.

Gibson, J. J. (1979). *The ecological approach to visual perception.* Boston: Houghton Mifflin.

Lenneberg, E. H. (1967). *Biological foundations of language.* NY: Wiley.

Piaget, J. (1952). *The origins of intelligence in children.* M. Cook (trans.). NY: International Universities Press.

Sternberg, R. J. (1988). Intellectual development: Psychometric and information-processing approaches. In *Developmental psychology: An advanced textbook,* 2d ed. Eds. M. H. Bornstein and M. E. Lamb. Hillsdale, NJ: Erlbaum.

9

Infancy and Toddlerhood: Psychosocial Development

*L*ooking at the psychosocial development of the child from birth to age two, this chapter begins by examining the general time frame of emotional development over the period. Particular emphasis is placed on the importance of social referencing (learning about the environment from observing the reactions of other people) and the development of self-awareness.

Personality development is covered both from theoretical and biological viewpoints. That is, the first two years will form a basis for later personality changes and interactions with the environment. Hence, an understanding of the general theoretical influences on as well as of the biological temperamental beginnings of personality is important.

Finally, this chapter will provide an overview of both the styles of parent-child interaction and the importance of the attachment between a child and his or her parents. Factors influencing the attachment process are also reviewed.

SOCIAL/EMOTIONAL DEVELOPMENT

General Considerations

To comprehend human emotional development, it is important to see that emotions serve three basic purposes: motivation, communication, and understanding of the social environment. First, emotions provide a strength of response or motivation to our logical decisions. For example, the desire for love and happiness will motivate us to seek a relationship or marriage with someone who can return those feelings, above and beyond a simpler decision based on height, weight, hair color, and so on. Second, emotions provide a form of communication about ideas; these emotions may include more information than language alone. Clutching the arms of the chair when watching a scary movie may communicate fright better than a verbal expression of fear. Finally, observing the emotional responses of others within the environment helps us understand not only the behavioral expectations of that environmental situation but also the appropriateness of our actions. This last factor describes the concept of social referencing. That is, children and adults look at the emotional responses of people to learn which behaviors work and which ones do not in a particular situation. By watching their parents' reactions at the dinner table, for example, children learn that throwing food on the floor meets with disapproving looks but that dropping food by accident is met with compassion and understanding for their attempts to feed themselves. To examine emotional development, then, is to view it in large part within the context of social interactions.

Time Frame of Particular Emotions

Initially, neonates appear to display emotions across one dimension, that is, pleasantness to unpleasantness. This is generally thought to be portrayed through the presence or absence of distress (crying). As mentioned in chapter 6, a neonate's early language repertoire consists of cries of hunger, pain, and anger—all of which communicate distress.

This form of emotional expression expands quickly over the first six months to include: fear (as when surprised or experiencing a loss of physical support); sadness (demonstrating sensitivity, as when a child cries in response to other infants crying); attention (as seen in the visual tracking of some object); and smiling (in response to physical pleasure at first and then in response to adults at about six weeks of age). Since emotions expand as the result of overall maturation, they become broader and more varied over the next 18 months. They become easier to distinguish and more pronounced. Stranger anxiety, for example, is a fear that begins around the age of six to eight months, peaking around 12 months, and that occurs whenever a new person enters the child's environment. It is thought this anxiety is caused by attachment to the parents, because it becomes present around the same time the infant establishes object permanence. However, familiarity influences the degree of stranger anxiety experienced; that is, infants need time to get used to new people. Separation anxiety (which begins at about 8 to 9 months and peaks at 14 months) is also common during this time. It is precipitated by unpredicted separations from the parents. However, if the parents separate from the child on a regular basis (as in going to work every day), the child gets used to the periods of separation and demonstrates less fear.

Social Referencing

The process of learning about what emotions fit given environmental situations becomes important to the child. The reason for this importance is rather simple and will remain so for the first few years of life: the child is confronted with new situations, people, stimuli, and so on, almost daily. Because this newness is consistently frightening, the child will turn to the people who are most trusted (parents) for reassurance and information about how to deal with these new experiences. We see over the first year the development of the process of social referencing. When a child is unsure of a particular situation, he or she looks to the caregiver or some trusted adult figure for the appropriate way to handle the situation. He or she forms a judgment based on the caregiver's expression, and follows that lead.

Self-awareness

One other important aspect of social or emotional development is the awareness of the self as different from other children and adults. Referred to as self-awareness, it can be demonstrated to exist at the end of the first year. The child develops a sense of "me," becoming newly conscious of others. This allows for the development of new emotions, such as affection, jealousy, defiance, and shame. The onset of self-awareness brings with it a rise in the amount of conflict between a child and all other persons in the child's environment. This happens as a direct result of wanting to get one's own desires, wants, and needs met. Parents start to hear their children saying "No!" as a response to any direct request that the children oppose, like getting ready for bed or eating broccoli.

PERSONALITY DEVELOPMENT

(Before reading this section, it may be worthwhile to review the general theoretical approaches to development covered in chapter 3. Refer also to Table 3.1.)

Psychoanalytic Theories

SIGMUND FREUD

Freud theorized that personality development in the first two years consists of channeling the instinctual libidinal energies through two different stages. The first is the oral stage. Here the mouth serves as the primary source of stimulation, pleasure, nourishment, and gratification. Since virtually all children put everything they can within their mouths during the first year, Freud saw these behaviors as an attempt to satisfy the "oral" cravings that develop because of the active energy instinct. A child who gets fed when it wants and is left unrestricted (within safety limits) to explore the world with its mouth will pass through this stage successfully.

The second stage is the anal stage, during which the focus of the instinctual energy shifts from the oral cavity to the anus, through stimulation of the bowels. In this stage, the child exerts more self-control and experiences the feelings of more power over the environment. That is, along with the development of walking and talking, giving the child more freedom of movement and communication, comes a feeling of increased power over his or her life. Since this time also finds the child learning to be toilet trained, this activity becomes the focal point of this new found power. Allowing a child to toilet train himself or to do so with minimal pressure coupled with supportive encouragement from the parents helps the child maneuver this stage successfully.

Fixation. According to Freud, parental influence is crucial to the successful completion of these two stages. Should a parent wean a child too soon or force a child to nurse long after it wants to stop will cause long-term behavioral problems. For the oral stage, early weaning could result in overeating, bulimia, smoking, constant snacking or constant nail biting. These problems could occur because the need to have something within the mouth was not naturally fulfilled. Likewise, forcing a child to nurse after it wants and is ready to stop could result in childish behavior that lasts well into adulthood.

In like manner, the anal stage can have its problems: an anal-retentive or anal-expulsive personality. The former results from excessive pressure to become toilet trained tied with a strong desire to comply with that pressure and remain "clean." This causes compulsive organization or cleanliness. The latter results from the child's rebellion against all the pressure over toilet training. That child's adult behavior would be demonstrated by excessive messiness, lack of organization, and clutter in all aspects of life.

According to Freud, these problems result when the libidinal energy is blocked in its normal course of biological development. Whenever that block occurs, the individual becomes "fixated" at that particular stage. In effect, emotional and personality development stops at that stage. A forty-year-old man, for example, who was weaned too early as an infant would need to have something in or around his mouth much of the time: smoking, eating, biting his nails, chewing gum, and so on.

From a therapeutic point of view, Freud presents a negative outlook on life. That is, you can never get rid of these fixations; rather, the most you can expect is to learn to cope with the problem. It is not possible to go back and "cure" fixations within Freud's personality framework.

ERIK ERIKSON

According to Erikson, personality development happens as a direct interaction between an individual and the social context within which the individual lives. He assumes every person is faced with different developmental crises from the environment in which he or she matures. For Erikson, then, the first crisis is to learn a sense of trust about one's ability to have one's needs met versus a belief that one's needs and wants will never be met. Actually, a balance between these two forces is what a child should come away with in order to achieve a good sense of self. That is, trusting that one's needs can ultimately be met fosters the development of hope while a healthy sense of mistrust fosters the development of patience and discrimination. Babies develop security that their needs (being fed and kept dry and warm) will be met by sameness and consistency in parental behavior.

Erikson's second crisis begins after the first year and involves a sense of competition between a child's efforts at self-control (autonomy) versus a parent's efforts at maintaining control over the child (shame and doubt). This is a time period (ages 1 to 3) when children begin walking, talking, building things, and knocking them down. That is, advancing biological maturation allows children to learn that they do not need big people to carry them places or get things for them. In effect, they learn that they can do a variety of things for themselves without the aid of adults. Caregivers (parents), on the other hand, need to balance permissiveness (allowing children to explore and learn) with restrictiveness (for the children's safety and the parents' peace of mind). For example, when children first move from a crib to a bed, they become ecstatic with the new-found freedom to get out of bed whenever they want. Parents need to balance letting children explore this freedom with requiring a sufficient amount of sleep at night. Too much permissiveness and children tend to not learn controls on their own behavior; too much restrictiveness and children tend to feel unable to succeed, causing them to feel shame and doubt about their abilities.

Fixation. Erikson also holds that children can fixate on a particular developmental level if they do not acquire an adequate balance between the opposing forces in the crisis. For example, an adult can be very dependent on others for even the most routine tasks (e.g., balancing a checkbook) because of doubt concerning his or her own abilities. However, Erikson assumes a positive outcome through therapy. Essentially, Erikson says that as an adult one can work through those same issues to change one's outlook on the present and to remove the fixation.

Learning Theory

Learning theory takes the approach that through classical and operant conditioning, as well as modeling and observation, children acquire those aspects of personality that result in reinforcement. For example, if a child is comforted by his or her mother when the child is upset, that same child is more likely to comfort someone else who is upset, developing a good sense of compassion. Likewise, a child who receives attention (i.e., reinforcement) only when a rule is broken is likely to grow up breaking the law repeatedly to receive attention. During the age range of birth to two years, children are careful observers of adults: watching what adults do that gets reinforcement as well as what they themselves do that results in reinforcement.

Cognitive Theory

Lastly, cognitive theorists assume that the schemas that children develop and expand on from birth also include schemas about how people interact and function in social environments. Through assimilation and accommodation, the infants' schemas about parents and parental behaviors are observed. They then attempt to use those schemas by assimilating their own behaviors into the equation. If a child sees a parent using a fork and spoon without the aid of another adult (the adult is feeding himself), the child will attempt to assimilate that same behavior into his or her own repertoire. If a frustrated parent spanks a child for some misbehavior, the child will assimilate that behavior into his or her schemas and hit Mom and Dad when the child is frustrated with them.

Importance of Temperament to Personality Development

Temperament is a basic underlying quality of personality that appears to be genetic or inherited. For most children, one of three basic temperament styles is present at birth and will form the core of the child's personality between the ages of one and three. The three categories are easy, slow-to-warm, and difficult. Easy children are happy most of the time, easily follow a regular schedule of eating and sleeping, appear to enjoy (or at least not be upset by) changes in the environment, and sleep through the night. Slow-to-warm children are more reluctant and unsure of new situations but will adjust if allowed to move at their own pace. Difficult children, on the other hand, fear strangers, react very strongly to any changes in the environment, do not have a regular schedule, and express their emotions more strongly than the other two groups.

Evidence for a genetic explanation of temperament as opposed to some very early experiences with parents comes from an analysis of the amounts of kicking fetuses do. Fetuses who kick often and vigorously and are otherwise very active during the last two months of the pregnancy are often babies who turn out to have difficult temperaments. The opposite is true for children with easy temperaments. Slow-to-warm children usually fall in the middle between the two extremes. After birth, temperament is usually determined through a variety of measurements: activity levels (difficults are most active); regular cycles of activity (easies are the most regular); approach-withdrawal in new situations (easies will approach more, difficults will withdraw more); adaptability (difficults do not tolerate environmental changes); intensity of reaction (easies will generally have a less intense emotional reaction); and distractibility (difficults are more highly distractible). Many of these characteristics are easily visible within the first two to three months.

Because of the apparent inborn nature of temperament, parents likely have less influence on temperament during the first few months than during later months. For example, with patience and tolerance for a difficult child's unyielding mood swings and distractibility, this child's temperament can soften over time even to the point of becoming an easy temperament. Likewise, parents who treat an easy child poorly or who experience a variety of traumatic events during the first couple of years (separation, divorce, loss of jobs, and so on) may find their child's temperament becoming difficult.

Miscellaneous Factors Influencing Personality Development

GENDER OF THE CHILD

Gender can influence personality development indirectly because boy and girl babies are often treated differently. Regardless of the gender of the parent or adult interacting with a child, boys often get more rough-and-tumble active play, while girls often are encouraged to play more quietly with dolls or other passive toys. This difference in how children are treated appears to have its roots in very traditional perceptions about male and female behaviors. For example, little girls are read to more often than are little boys, which may lead to the tendency of girls to be better at verbal tasks.

GENDER-RELATED PARENTING BEHAVIORS

Infants and children have modeled for them very different gender-related behaviors, given the normal breakdown of parental caregiving tasks. Mothers are most often the primary caregivers: they change diapers, feed the infant, organize childcare arrangements, and take care of the hurts and "boo-boos" of childhood. Their play behaviors toward their infants are different from those of fathers: fathers engage in more active play. The reason for this is that most of the time fathers spend with their babies is playtime. The father's play is generally more physical, while the mother's is more verbal. Fathers will tend to distinguish more between girl and boy babies and interact with them differently, while mothers tend to treat the infants basically the same.

PARENT-CHILD INTERACTIONS

Differences from Animals

Some species of animals create a strong "parent-child" bond as well as learn about the social and identifying behaviors of their particular species through a biological process called imprinting. In effect, the imprinting process helps those animals acquire the behaviors that will make up their "personalities." Many species of birds, for example, will "attach" themselves to the first moving object they see after hatching. As a biological process, imprinting also appears to have a critical period. That is, if the mother is not available during the time window for imprinting, the hatchlings may imprint with something else. This premise was aptly demonstrated by the ethologist Konrad Lorenz, who was present when geese hatched; the goslings imprinted with him. Later, when the mother of the goslings was presented, they continued to follow Lorenz.

Humans do not appear to have any behaviors even closely approximating imprinting. If they did, then adoption would not be possible. What occurs with humans is called an emotional attachment. That is, children become attached emotionally, not biologically, to the adults who provide care for them. The nature and strength of the attachment or interaction between parent and child will be determined partly by the parenting skills of the adult, partly by the inborn characteristics of the infant, and partly by the infant's stage of development.

Synchrony

Beginning shortly after birth, a period of synchrony is likely to develop between very attentive parents and their children. This means that the parental and child behaviors will often mirror each other with a well-defined rhythm. Parents will time their tickling, playing or talking with the infants' readiness to respond. Likewise, infants stare, vocalize, open their mouths, smile or wiggle and turn in response to the parents' initiative. Synchrony, then, is similar in pattern and style to the turn-taking that is important in language development (see chapter 8). The rhythm of the interaction between parent and child helps the infant learn not only socialization skills during the interaction but also how to fix interactions that may not be going well. When Mommy or Daddy has had a hard day at work and is not initiating interactions, the infant can initiate them and re-establish the synchrony.

Attachment

Toward the end of the first year an emotional bond that will last over time develops between the infant and the parents. The attachment is an internal emotional state one person shares with another. The strength and type of attachment can be seen through attachment behaviors. From the infant's point of view, there are two types of attachment behaviors: proximity seeking and contact maintenance. The former are those that are used to seek out and bring the parent closer to the infant (e.g., following, looking at, climbing onto the lap) while the later are those that should help maintain contact with the parent (e.g., hugging, clinging). Parents demonstrate similar proximity (e.g., keeping a close eye on the infant) and contact (e.g., displays of affection in response to the infant) behaviors.

HOW ATTACHMENT IS STUDIED

The "Strange Situation" is the standardized procedure for measuring the type and strength of attachment. Children are brought into an unfamiliar room where a series of brief separations from, and reunions with, the mother takes place. Some of these separations and reunions are conducted in the presence of a stranger. The behaviors of the child around the mother, or the stranger, or both together, as well as when alone are compared. From these comparisons four general types of attachment have been defined. They are summarized in Table 9.1.

Securely attached	Child shows low to moderate levels of proximity seeking to mother; does not avoid or resist contact if mother initiates it. When reunited with mother after absence, child greets her positively and can be soothed if upset. Clearly prefers mother to stranger.
Insecurely attached: detached/avoidant	Child avoids contact with mother, especially at reunion after an absence. Does not resist mother's efforts to make contact but does not seek much contact. Treats stranger and mother about the same throughout.
Insecurely attached: resistant/ambivalent	Greatly upset when separated from mother, but mother cannot successfully comfort child when she returns. Child both seeks and avoids contact at different times. May show anger toward mother at reunion, and resists both comfort from and contact with stranger.
Insecurely attached: disorganized/disoriented	Dazed behavior, confusion or apprehension. Child may show strong avoidance following strong proximity seeking; may show simultaneously conflicting patterns, such as moving toward mother but keeping gaze averted; may express emotion in a way that seems unrelated to the people present.

Table 9.1   Behavior of Securely Attached and Insecurely Attached Infants in Ainsworth's Strange Situation at 12 Months of Age

There appears to be an interaction between security of attachment and socioeconomic status. That is, securely attached relationships occur between 50 and 70 percent of the time in stable middle-class households; however, they occur as little as 20 percent of the time in poor families or those with histories of abuse or other family problems. Of the insecurely attached relationships, the avoidant group is most common.

HOW SECURE ATTACHMENTS ARE FORMED

From Parent to Child. The attachment process for parents usually begins when they discover they are going to have a child. It incorporates a number of emotional changes and preparations (see chapter 5). The attachment becomes stronger over the course of the pregnancy through such behaviors as choosing names, buying clothes, and attending childbirth classes. By the time the child is born, the parents have been waiting and preparing for it for months. This process of attachment receives a boost if the parents are able to spend time with the baby within the first few hours after birth, although this is not essential.

Although these initial behaviors are important, what occurs over the first year or two will actually have a greater influence on the development and maintainence of a secure attachment. Continual responsiveness to the child's needs, developing a synchrony of interaction, and being emotionally expressive (e.g., smiling and talking more), are important behaviors that represent the degree of commitment the parents have to that attachment. It can be demonstrated that parents have the emotional bond first and then show it through different attachment behaviors.

From Child to Parent. At birth, a child is no more attached to a particular parent than to the doctor who delivers it. The contributions children make to the development of this relationship are in reverse order. Researchers believe the development of attachments in infants goes through a four-step process. In Step 1 (initial preattachment), the child will use and display a wide variety of attachment behaviors during the first three months of age. These behaviors will be directed to any adult caregiver. In Step 2 (discrimination), the child between three and six months old begins to be more discriminating over who gets the proximity behaviors. The child begins to smile readily at the people seen all the time as opposed to strangers. At around six to seven months Step 3 (clear-cut attachment) begins, in which the child prefers one person (usually the mother). Other people can comfort the child if he or she is hurt, but the child will choose to be comforted by this person and will also use this person as a safe base from which to explore the world. Shortly thereafter, Step 4 (multiple attachments) begins, in which the child expands the number of attachments to include siblings, grandparents, and the other parent.

PARENTAL FACTORS IN INSECURE ATTACHMENTS

The interactions forming the foundation of the attachment occur during the first year, which is the same time Erikson theorizes that the child is dealing with the developmental crisis of trust versus mistrust. In both cases, the parents' behavior is crucial in guiding both the development of a secure attachment and the successful learning of a balance between trusting and mistrusting the world. Likewise, parental behaviors can be influential in the creation of insecure attachments. Children who are rated as having insecure/avoidant attachments have parents (especially mothers) who avoid or reject them; the mothers are "psychologically unavailable" and generally dislike any physical contact with the infant. Those children rated insecure/ambivalent have parents who are very inconsistent in their parenting behaviors: sometimes they react warmly and lovingly to the infant and sometimes they reject the infant entirely. In this case, the infant cannot predict when he or she will be loved and when not. Lastly, children rated as insecure/disorganized appear to come from homes where there is a history of abuse.

GENERAL FACTORS INFLUENCING ATTACHMENT DEVELOPMENT

As can be seen, the type of attachment displayed can be an indication of the quality of care the infant receives. When a mother provides excellent care during the early months (i.e., is sensitive and responsive to the child's needs as well as actively encourages the child's growth and development), she is likely to have a securely attached toddler. In a broader context, however, such factors as family stress, father's involvement in child care, the nature of the marital relationship, the temperament of the child, and even the cultural norms for child-rearing behaviors can influence the attachment by changing the patterns of maternal-child interaction. In summary, the attachment that develops can best be seen as an interaction between the mother and child that is influenced by the larger social environment.

LONG-TERM IMPORTANCE OF ATTACHMENTS

The early attachment between an infant and its mother is important because it will serve as the basis for the child's later social relationships. Infants rated as securely attached often become children who are more independent in school, more cognitively and socially competent, more sought out as friends and leaders, less likely to have behavior problems, easier to manage and reason with in a classroom, more empathetic to other children and adults, and more mature and complex in their play behaviors.

This means that the nature of the attachment appears to significantly influence a child's social relationships both inside and outside of the family. Securely attached children show more positive social interactions with other children (such as looking, touching, and imitating) than do insecurely attached children. They are also more likely to comfort a distressed or crying adult or child (a sign of altruistic or prosocial behavior) than are insecurely attached ones.

Environmental Exploration

Just as parental interactions through synchrony in the first months and through attachment by the end of the first year are important in psychosocial development, so is exploration of the environment. As mobility, security, and cognitive functioning improve, children expand their exploratory behaviors. In like fashion, the child's experiences with the environment will provide practice for physical development, greater self-esteem and self-confidence, and improved and advanced intellectual functioning. However, all environments are not created equal: just as some are more stimulating than others, some are more dangerous.

To measure the environmental characteristics that provide the greatest encouragement for child development, the HOME (Home Observation for the Measurement of the Environment) survey was developed. It is a list of characteristics (physical, social, and emotional) that describe the quality of the child's environment. Given the presence (and amount) or absence of these characteristics, one should be able to predict the course of the child's development. There are six subscales: emotional and verbal responsiveness of mother; avoidance of restriction and punishment; organization of physical environment; provision of appropriate play materials; maternal involvement with child; and opportunities for variety in daily stimulation.

Results from the HOME survey are better predictors of later school-age cognitive performance than are traditional intelligence tests given at the same time. This is especially true for the characteristic concerning "appropriate play materials," meaning toys or materials that encourage physical and cognitive development. These do not have to be expensive but could be such things as pots and pans and large cardboard boxes. This factor, along with "variety in daily stimulation," indicates that play behaviors are intimately involved with cognitive functioning and later social adjustment.

Although children have limited emotional expression at birth, they quickly acquire a wide variety of emotions by the end of toddlerhood. Two factors important to the development of an infant's emotional repertoire are social referencing (watching the emotional expressions of others in particular situations) and self-awareness (understanding the "me" concept). The first process is important in learning about the safety and security of different kinds of experiences, and the second is important in beginning a concept of self.

Personality development is explained from a variety of viewpoints. According to Freud, children traverse two stages of development in the first two years (oral and anal). These relate to the areas of the body through which instinctual energy is channeled. In the first stage, a child begins exploring the environment with the mouth. In the second, the child begins to explore the newfound power of locomotion and language and channels this power through control of bowel functions. Freud assumes that if development in one of these stages is arrested in any way, then the individual will become fixated at that personality level of development for the rest of his or her life.

Erikson also postulates a two-stage approach to personality growth. His approach, however, assumes that a child develops his or her personality primarily through social interactions rather than through some inner biological/instinctual urge. In his first stage (trust vs. mistrust), infants learn a sense of self in relation to the world and whether they can have their needs met in that world. In the second stage (autonomy vs. shame and doubt), children learn to balance needs for self-control and for parental control of their behavior. At this point, a parental balance between restrictiveness (primarily for safety reasons) and permissiveness (allowing the child to explore) will allow a child to adequately master this stage.

Learning theory, on the other hand, assumes that our personality characteristics are acquired through standard principles of classical, operant, and social learning theory. In all three theoretical approaches, however, there is knowledge and acceptance of the biological influence of temperament. Present at birth, temperament (either easy, slow-to-warm or difficult) serves as a foundation for personality traits that will later emerge.

One other major influence in psychosocial development is the amount and types of parent-child interactions that occur over the first two years. Initially, synchrony (an interweaving of turn-taking in behaviors) begins a building process that will later encourage the development of a secure attachment relationship. By the end of the first year, infants are attached (securely or insecurely) primarily to their mothers, and the nature of the attachment is determined largely by maternal behaviors toward the child.

Parent-to-child attachment usually begins before birth and is demonstrated by the strength and continuation of attachment behaviors (buying clothes, picking out names, attempting synchrony, and so on) both before and after the baby's arrival. Child-to-parent attachment begins with the display of the attachment behaviors first, followed much later by the development of the emotional attachment. In this sense, what happens in humans is vastly different from what happens in many animal species (imprinting).

Lastly, the second year of life finds the child beginning large-scale exploration of the environment. Adequacy of play materials and a variety of daily stimulation in the child's environment seem to be important to long-term development of physical skills as well as to social interactions and cognitive functioning.

Selected Readings

Ainsworth, M. D. S., M. Blehar, E. Waters, and S. Wall. (1978). *Patterns of attachment.* Hillsdale, NJ: Erlbaum.

Brazelton, T. B., M. Yogman, H. Als, and E. Tronick. (1979). *The child and his family.* NY: Plenum.

Eisenberg, N. (1982). *The development of prosocial behavior.* NY: Academic Press.

Erikson, E. H. (1963). *Childhood and society.* NY: Norton.

Kohnstamm, G. A. (1989). *Temperament in childhood.* Chichester, England: Wiley.

Lamb, M. E. (1981). *The role of the father in child development.* NY: Wiley.

Lerner, J. V., and R. M. Lerner. (1983). *Life-span development and behavior.* NY: Academic.

Lewis, M., and L. Michalson. (1983). *Children's emotions and moods.* NY: Plenum.

10

Infancy and Toddlerhood: Special Issues

*T*his chapter covers many concerns regarding development during infancy and toddlerhood that encompass the physical, cognitive, and psychosocial areas. They are covered in more depth than they have been in earlier chapters. For example, Sudden Infant Death Syndrome (SIDS) is a physical problem of unknown origin that results in the death of the infant. Possible explanations for this problem are discussed.

Similar in-depth discussion covers the question of whether it is possible to enhance a child's intelligence by speeding up the child's passage through Piaget's six substages. The psychosocial relationship between the parents and the child appears to have the greatest effect on the child's cognitive development. This can be seen clearly when a child is deprived of a parent, as through death or divorce.

Finally, a discussion of child abuse as it affects the infant or toddler is presented. This covers aspects of both the victim and the abuser that contribute to the problem. To round out the chapter, the consequences and treatment of abuse are discussed.

SUDDEN INFANT DEATH SYNDROME (SIDS)

SIDS or "crib death" has been written about and studied since biblical times. An apparently healthy baby goes to sleep at its usual time, and some time during that sleep period the parent finds the baby dead. An Old Testament story about King Solomon described a similar death of a child. It was explained: ". . . and this woman's child died in the night, because she over laid it." It was assumed that the infant's death was caused by the mother rolling over and smothering it. (During this historical time, it was commonplace to have infants sleep in the same bed with their mothers.) Some theorists believe this baby was a SIDS victim.

In the United States, approximately 7,000 babies a year die of SIDS, constituting the leading cause of death among infants age one month to one year. The incidence is highest among infants between the ages of two and four months. Although SIDS occurs in families across the socioeconomic spectrum, factors such as low birth weight, poor maternal prenatal care, economic disadvantages, young motherhood, smoking, and the mother having many children with short intervals between pregnancies increase the risk for developing SIDS. The highest SIDS rates are found in babies whose mothers use narcotics or cocaine during pregnancy. SIDS babies tend to have lower Apgar scores at birth and lower birth weights. Black males whose birth weights were low and whose mothers had little or no prenatal care, smoked, and used drugs during their pregnancies are most likely to succumb to crib death. Three-quarters of all infants who die of SIDS are in an economically disadvantaged group.

The cause of SIDS is unknown, and it can strike apparently healthy, normal, happy babies. A number of theories have been advanced to explain crib death. At this point it is a safe assumption that SIDS is the result of a number of disorders rather than one single entity. The only clear assumption about SIDS is that it is caused by a failure in the central nervous system. Other proposed causes include:

Learning Disability. Several researchers have suggested that SIDS may be a type of learning disability. A high proportion of SIDS victims have mild colds at the time of death. Many early reflexes of infants become weak around age two to four months, and the learned response of struggling should, at that time, replace the reflex that the infant had previously used to eliminate a breathing blockage. Because of genetics, or an environmental stress, a SIDS victim may have poorly learned this struggling response. Thus, when a mild cold causes a breathing blockage or the infant rolls over in its bed and places its nose down, it may not have either the reflex or the learned response to clear its breathing passages.

Physiological Problem. Other evidence points to some sort of physical defect in the SIDS victim. SIDS victims frequently show signs of long-term hypoventilation (inadequate respiratory exchange of air). These victims also show higher levels of the brain neurotransmitter called dopamine. High levels of brain dopamine tend to decrease the respiration rate. Also, most SIDS victims show higher levels of infant hemoglobin, which is used initially to transport oxygen to the body tissues. In the normal child, infant hemoglobin is replaced by adult hemoglobin, which is a better carrier of oxygen.

Inherited Problem. Although the incidence of SIDS among identical twins is the same as among fraternal twins, SIDS seems to run in families.

Infant Botulism. Some researchers believe that at least 5 percent of crib deaths are due to infant botulism. Botulism is a toxin produced by a particular bacteria that results in nerve paralysis. Botulism toxin decreases a body's respiratory drive and could cause a fatality.

Excessive Heat. A recent study in England has shown similarities between SIDS victims and heat stroke victims. Infants who have died of SIDS tended to be excessively clothed or covered at the times of their deaths.

Other miscellaneous theories have been advanced as causes of SIDS. These include central nervous system abnormalities, abnormalities in the nerves that regulate the heartbeat, and even abnormalities in the muscles of the tongue.

Although there are certain signs that help doctors predict infants that are at risk for SIDS, not all SIDS victims follow any particular pattern. Apnea monitors have been useful in following a child's breathing rate. The apnea monitor is a device that rings an alarm or buzzer if the baby stops breathing for a preset period of time. The use of a monitor, however, does not guarantee the baby's survival. On occasion, infants who have set off the monitor have died when they were not able to be revived. It is advisable that an infant who is considered to be at risk for SIDS be watched closely.

Losing a child to SIDS has a dramatic impact on the family. When someone is gravely ill for a period of time, the family has a chance to prepare for the death of the individual. SIDS is sudden and unexpected. Parents blame themselves frequently. They suffer self-doubt, emotional pain, and guilt. Marital problems and divorce increase following an experience with SIDS. Support groups are available to help parents of SIDS victims discuss their feelings and help one another. Professional help may also be required to help parents deal with such a sudden and shocking death of their baby.

ENHANCING COMPETENCE AND INTELLIGENCE

A number of factors appear to influence the rate and quality of cognitive development from birth until the age of two: genetics, the amount of stimulation in the environment, the child's attachment to one or both parents, the psychosocial influences of siblings as well as other family members, and the interaction of those family members with that environment. A question often asked of Piaget was: Is it possible to speed up a child's transition through the different cognitive substages and therefore make the child smarter? Because Piaget found that this question usually came from parents and psychologists in the United States, he referred to it as the "American question." If one mobile or one rattle was good and helped the child through the secondary and tertiary circular reactions, they wondered, would three mobiles or three rattles be even better? The essential question was, how much stimulation will push a child through these substages at a faster rate?

The Principle of Readiness

In response to such questions, Piaget was often noncommittal or reluctant to provide any sort of recommendations because he realized the importance of biological maturation to the cognitive process, and you cannot speed up biological maturation. This coincides with the biological theory of the principle of readiness. Piaget believed that the infant's cognitive abilities would be ready when its brain was ready. Therefore, maturation and an interaction with the environment are essential for the child's cognitive development, rather than any sort of formal instruction, programing or tutoring that might be imposed on the developing child.

In theory, this American question could easily be answered. More stimulation, interaction with the child, and better environments for the child should presumably increase the child's intelligence. However, such does not appear to be the case; there appears to be little, if any, correlation between intelligence as determined during the sensorimotor stages and any later cognitive ability.

Over-stimulation

In reality, providing extra stimulation can potentially provide extra problems as well. For example, very early on (under two months) infants may simply turn off overstimulation. The infant will turn away or fall asleep if it becomes overexcited; it will not respond to the stimulation. In addition, if a child is consistently surrounded by an environment that has a high level of stimulation, the child will come to accept that as "normal," thereby missing anything in the environment of a lower level of stimulation. Thus, the stimuli around the child will consistently need to become more and more intense in order to be observed or noticed.

Parental Encouragement

What does seem to be more important for a child's cognitive development is less formal training and more general interaction provided by the parents in the home environment. The research on cognitive development shows the child's parents or parent to be more influential than any object added to the environment. For example, mothers who are more intelligent and competent at dealing with the environment are by their nature "designers" who construct interesting environments for their children. It is important that these mothers encourage their children to actively explore the environment rather than to passively look at materials. It is much more important for the child's intellectual development for him or her to be an active participant rather than a passive observer.

Another factor is that these parents frequently interact with their children at half-minute to one-minute intervals. The parent does not smother the child but is readily available if the child needs help in experiencing an event. Finally, parenting style also seems to be an important factor in cognitive development. It is important for the child to understand that there are limits to his or her behavior relative to the child's intellectual and psychosocial abilities at that particular age. Hence, a parent should not be so permissive as to allow a child to run rampant through the home; neither should the parent be so punitive as to restrict that child's independent intellectual exploration.

There are certain kinds of behaviors that parents can do to encourage cognitive development in children. First, children should not be confined to jump seats, playpens or small rooms. Rather, they should have a considerable amount of physical freedom to explore, get sensory and motor information, and process that information. Second, it is important that parents speak to children directly rather than speak about them or have television or radio do most of the communication. Speaking to the children will help them learn, interact, and understand how communication causes changes in the environment. Speaking will also encourage the child's efforts at communication even when the child is at a prelinguistic stage. Children want an audience, and having one encourages their development. Third, reading to a child helps him or her understand new vocabulary and new concepts. Responding to the sounds that an infant makes by labeling or talking tends to increase that child's vocabulary and overall linguistic development at a much earlier level.

Hindering Development

Though there are many activities that parents can do to encourage cognitive growth in a child, it is important that these activities are both low in intensity and fun. It is not uncommon for parents to become disappointed if their child or infant does not acquire some skill or accomplish some task. That disappointment or anxiety can nonverbally, and verbally, be transmitted to the children. This could hinder the kind of development the parents were seeking in the first place.

Psychosocial Relationship Versus Environment

In summary, the kinds of environments or environmental experiences that will increase a child's cognitive development during the six substages of the sensorimotor period have less to do with characteristics of the environment than with the psychosocial relationship between the child and its parents. A child can easily learn from normal experiences that are present in the home and may not need or benefit from any additional stimulation within the environment. Parenting skills may be the crucial influence on development through the sensorimotor stage. When the parenting skills show improvement and provide the infant with appropriate kinds of stimulation and psychosocial experiences, then the child becomes more responsive, eager, and interactive with the environment.

PARENTAL DEPRIVATION

Institutionalized versus Home-reared Infants

Certain events can disrupt the bond between parent and child. A parent may die, or become divorced, or the child may become hospitalized or institutionalized. In a number of landmark studies in the 1940s, Ren Spitz studied institutionalized babies under age one and compared them with home-reared children. In the homes, children received personal attention from their own mothers (usually unwed teenage girls) or from other mother substitutes. In the institutions, a nurse cared for eight babies. The differences between these children were dramatic. The institutionalized infants were retarded in weight, height, and mental development. The developmental intelligence scores of these infants dropped to the borderline retarded range by the end of the first year of institutionalization, and, by the end of the second year, these babies' scores were in the significantly retarded range. These dramatic results were instrumental in the proposal to use foster homes rather than institutions to care for children who were going through the adoption process.

In response to these findings, there have been a number of studies looking at effects of enriching the environment of institutionalized children. The results have consistently shown that increased stimulation and consistent caretakers produce higher intelligence scores and an increased ability to form interpersonal relationships (such as getting married) in adulthood. A foster grandparent program is an example of one such enrichment program. In this program babies are "adopted" by elderly people and played with, talked to, stimulated, and held. Such warm and loving relationships can compensate for the loss of the natural mother and subsequent damage to the infant's development and emotional well-being. If these babies do not get consistent, warm caretaking, they tend to be more disruptive in school and to seek more attention from adults, compared with those children who are raised at home. They will subsequently grow into adults who are more dependent, more anxious, and have more difficulty finding satisfactory spouses. Even though being with other babies around their own age can increase sociability, children whose bond is disrupted for short or long periods of time tend to show some negative effects.

Stages in Infants' Reactions

Hospital stays can also be disruptive to infants and young children. For infants who are hospitalized during the ages of 15 to 30 months, three stages seem to outline this parental deprivation process: (1) protest stage (an infant expects its mother to return and uses active behaviors such as crying, banging, and rage); (2) despair stage (the baby's movements diminish, it becomes more withdrawn and uses a monotonous, irregular cry); and (3) detachment stage (the infant focuses its attention on various caretakers, such as nurses and nurses' aides, who stimulate it with toys and social interactions). Surprisingly, when the mother returns, the infant may show disinterest and even turn away. Such a disruption can breed an overall mistrust in a child.

The results of parental separation due to divorce, death, day care, and other such separations tend to be mixed, depending on the emotional distress that surrounds the separation. This continues to be a controversy. Studies have concluded that most children attending day care show secure patterns of attachment. The quality of day care appears to be the critical issue, although the adult per child ratio, and the skill and warmth of the caregiver are important for the development of the child. In some situations, high-quality day care can actually enhance the emotional and intellectual development of infants. Babies who are separated from one parent generally do not appear to have their emotional well-being disrupted. Children who have been separated from both parents because of a vacation or illness are less likely to show negative emotional effects as compared with children who have been separated from birth parents due to family emotional problems. Additionally, children who have been introduced to separation earlier, for reasons such as day care or vacations, tend to fare better when they experience later separations.

CHILD ABUSE AND NEGLECT

The term child abuse has generally been defined as the physical assault or sexual abuse of a child by its parent(s) or caregiver. However, the definition of abusive parenting has recently been expanded to include physical assault as well as neglect, emotional and sexual abusive behaviors. Extreme physical abuse experienced by children was first described in 1962 and called the "battered child syndrome." Abused children often suffer cigarette burns, bite marks, welts, bruises, and brain damage, that is, abuse that is sufficient to kill or cripple them.

The second type of child abuse is known as child neglect. With this problem, caregivers or parents fail to provide the child with sufficient food, shelter, safety or health care. Neglect tends to be the most common form of maltreatment. Infants are allowed to starve, freeze to death, become significantly undernourished or are emotionally ignored. Many childhood accidents are the result of parents' lack of supervision of the activities of their children; that is, children may place themselves in dangerous situations without their parents' supervision.

The third type of child abuse (emotional abuse or psychological maltreatment) is found in parents who constantly humiliate or criticize a child, show coldness toward him or her or place impossible or unreasonable demands on a child. Such mistreatment tends to destroy a child's self-esteem and damage the child's capacity for interpersonal relationships. Of all the different types of abuse, emotional abuse is the most difficult to define and legally quantify.

Finally, sexual abuse, including incest, has received much attention recently. Such abuse can vary from the parent or adult walking around nude in front of the child with the intention of sexual enticement, to actual intercourse between a parent and a child. Recent statistics regarding incidents of child molestation are dramatic; approximately one out of every four girls and one out of every seven boys have been sexually abused.

Characteristics of the Victim and Abuser

Although child abuse tends to be more common among families from lower socioeconomic levels, it also occurs frequently among more educated parents and in higher socioeconomic levels. Although there are no specific characteristics associated with abusive parents that are not also characteristics of nonabusers, the presence of certain factors tends to increase the likelihood of a parent abusing his or her child. Some of these factors include: financial difficulties, pressures from work, marital problems, low levels of self-esteem in the parent, and the presence of abuse in the parent's own childhood history. Parents who abuse their children tend to be impulsive and defensive, have a poor self-concept, and to project their problems onto their children. They state their fear of spoiling the children and the value of physical punishment. They are likely to use more severe forms of punishment, such as hitting a child with an object, pulling the child's hair or slapping the child's face. Parents who abuse children report being less satisfied with their children, see the parenting experience as being difficult and not very enjoyable, and report that the conflict within the family is high.

Children who are victims of abuse share some common qualities that may inadvertently contribute to their own maltreatment. These children tend to be highly demanding infants who are more likely to be physically unattractive, irritable, unresponsive, and more active than children who are not abused. They are more likely to have been premature or low-birth-weight babies, or mentally retarded or physically handicapped or have some behavioral abnormalities. Children who have been sexually abused show a higher than normal need for affection, which may contribute to their availability to sexual molesters.

Consequences of Abuse

Abused infants tend to show more resistant, avoidant, and noncompliant behavior than nonabused infants. Physically abused toddlers show more aggressive behavior toward their peers, are more wary and ambivalent toward their caretakers, and even sometimes show threat or attack behavior. These toddlers have little or no concern, or empathy, when confronted with a same-age peer who is crying. In later years, abused children show self-destructive behavior, school failure, poor self-concepts, and delinquency.

Those who are victims of sexual abuse show somewhat unique behaviors and feelings. The most important signs of sexual abuse are a strong interest in sexual organs, nudity, and excessive or public masturbation. Nonsexual symptoms such as headaches, vomiting, and rashes also occur. Other nonspecific symptoms include anxieties, anger, withdrawal, aggressiveness, and sleeping disturbances.

Treatment

Numerous methods of treatment have been designed to help abusers' recovery: individual therapy, self-help groups such as Parents Anonymous and Parents United, child foster care, group therapy, and family therapy. At-risk families are sometimes targeted to receive treatment early in the life of the infant. These include programs such as parent education, parent-newborn bonding programs, and support from social service agencies. These programs have received mixed reviews. In Sweden in 1979, legislation was enacted to legally protect children within the home. Parents are forbidden by law to harm, spank or physically punish their children in any way. This antispanking law is vague and difficult to enforce. Research shows that although Swedish children may be abused just as often as American children, Swedish children are less likely to sustain severe injuries from physical abuse or to require hospitalization.

NONORGANIC FAILURE TO THRIVE (NFT)

Children who receive proper medical care and who do not show any organic problems yet fail to gain weight are sometimes diagnosed as exhibiting Nonorganic Failure to Thrive (NFT). In industrialized countries, such undernourishment results from psychological problems within the family. Mothers of these infants tend to feed their children on an erratic schedule or are arbitrary in gauging the end of a meal, tend to be depressed, and/or are undergoing significant conflict and stress in the home.

Some common features have been noted regarding the families of NFT babies. The infants tend to have had medical complications during their gestation period, were premature, and experienced other minor problems around the time of discharge from the hospital. Mothers of NFT infants show somewhat more disturbed or disrupted relationships with infants' fathers and have a poor nurturing history themselves as infants. These mothers also show less physical contact with their babies and a lower communication level. Long-term consequences of NFT include lower stature and weight in the teenage years, social immaturity, and lower scores in the areas of verbal intelligence and reading. To prevent later deficits, children who are diagnosed with NFT at an early age, along with their families, should be considered for remedial programs early in life.

*M*any *areas in the study of infancy and toddlerhood require special attention or closer examination. Sudden Infant Death Syndrome (SIDS) is the leading cause of death in infants age one month to one year. Although many factors appear to correlate with its occurrence, the exact causes are unknown. Most theories revolve around some sort of brain malfunction or other physiological abnormality. Any child at risk or having more than one of the risk factors for SIDS should be watched closely.*

With regard to cognitive development, many parents and researchers have wondered whether it is possible to speed this process during infancy and toddlerhood. Pushing infants through Piaget's substages is unlikely to be effective for two reasons: (1) biological maturation of the brain appears necessary before specific cognitive abilities can be demonstrated; and (2) cognitive development appears more dependent on the psychosocial relationship between the infant and its parents than on any other environmental factor. Basically, pushing the infant works against development, whereas a supportive parenting style encourages the child to be eager to learn on his or her own.

Parental deprivation tends to be traumatic for infants, but the overall result depends greatly on the amount of emotional stress surrounding the event. Therefore, the psychosocial relationship between parents and child again appears to have a significant impact on the development of the child.

Four areas of child abuse have been studied: physical, sexual, and emotional abuse and child neglect. Even though there are no specific predictors of who will be an abuser, a number of behavioral and historical characteristics are common to abusers. Likewise, the victims of abuse also appear to share characteristics. This leads to the supposition that the problem of child abuse may actually occur because of factors that both the victim and the abuser bring to the situation. Treatment is available for abusers and victims. A similar psychosocial problem, nonorganic failure to thrive (NFT), occurs when the nurturing process breaks down because of psychological problems in the family. Remedial family training programs help remedy this problem.

Selected Readings

Black, R., and J. Mayer. (1980). *The battered child*. Chicago: University of Chicago Press.

Brassard, M. R., and L. E. McNeil. (1987). *Psychological maltreatment of children and youth.* NY: Pergamon.

DeFrain, J., J. Taylor, and L. Ernst. (1982). *Coping with sudden infant death.* Lexington, MA: Heath.

Spitz, R. (1965). *The first year of life: A psychoanalytic study of normal and deviant development of object relations.* NY: International Universities Press.

Wallerstein, J. S., and J.B. Kelly. (1980). *Surviving the breakup: How children and parents cope with divorce.* NY: Basic Books.

White, B. L., B. Kaban, and J. Attanucci. (1979). *The origins of human competence.* Lexington, MA: Heath.

11

The Preschool Years: Physical Development

*S*ize and shape changes will slow down during this period of development, with genetics and nutrition the two most important factors in the amount of change. Because of the slower growth rate, children this age will usually be pickier eaters than when they were younger. As their caloric needs diminish, "empty calorie" foods, that is, sweets, may be a problem in maintaining a nutritious diet.

Although illness in childhood is common, bouts with major diseases are uncommon in industrialized societies because of community health and vaccination programs. However, in developing nations major diseases, malnutrition, and dehydration are common causes of childhood mortality. Accidents are the major cause of death in industrialized societies.

Maturation of the brain revolves around increased myelinization of the neurons and specialization of the brain into two functioning hemispheres. This process is demonstrated in the activity patterns of preschoolers; activity levels peak at age 3 and decline thereafter. Gross and fine motor skills also become specialized during this period as gender differences arise.

Finally, physical and brain maturation are demonstrated in the three types of physical play that can be differentiated during this stage: sensorimotor, mastery, and rough-and-tumble. These types of play also demonstrate the importance of environmental practice in refining the skills that biology awakens.

GENERAL PHYSICAL CHARACTERISTICS

Size and Shape Changes

Between the ages of two and six, the rate of growth slows to about half of what it was between the ages of birth and two. During these years, the average child (boy or girl) grows approximately 3 inches and gains about 4½ pounds per year. Boys appear to be somewhat taller and heavier throughout this stage, although the differences are marginal and the ranges of height and weight consistently overlap between genders. (There are no significant gender differences in size and shape during this time span.) At age three, girls average about 37 inches (94 centimeters) in height and 30 pounds (13 kilograms) in weight; boys average about 37 inches, but weigh approximately 32 pounds (14.6 kilograms). Individual variations from these general trends and averages are greater in weight than in height. The most significant factors influencing those variations appear to be individual genetics and nutrition.

During these four years, children lose their toddler look and their pot bellies. They will generally trim down to the slender, athletic appearance of youngsters in the elementary school years. Fat accumulated during infancy tends to be burned off, limbs lengthen, and the face becomes more angular. By the age of six, the body proportions are similar to those of an adult. The one main gender difference during this time span is that boys tend to have more muscle tissue, while girls tend to have more fat.

Eating Habits—Diet

Because a child's growth rate slows during this age range, caloric requirements also decline. Parents may worry that their child's appetite seems smaller since almost half of all boys and girls in this age group appear to not eat well. In addition, preschool children develop clearer food likes and dislikes. New foods are more likely to be turned down during this age; preschoolers are "picky" eaters.

Experts generally agree that parental pressure on a preschooler to eat more food is not a wise idea. Some researchers hypothesize that teaching children to ignore body signals that appetite has been satisfied increases a later risk of eating disorders such as anorexia, bulimia, and obesity. Peer modeling tends to be one of the most powerful ways to get preschoolers to try new foods. If other children are seen eating a new food with enjoyment, the preschooler is more likely to try this food than when urged by parents to have "just one bite." In any event, the appetite decline of this age range usually reverses itself around age eight, during the elementary school years.

Although parents fear that their preschool child will become malnourished due to picky eating habits, the majority of children in industrialized societies are well nourished. Some dietary problems do occur, however. For example, children growing up in households where the parents enforce consistent vaccination programs these easily preventable diseases can be kept at low levels.

SOCIOLOGICAL CONSIDERATIONS IN CHILDHOOD ILLNESSES

In times past, the biggest threats to a child's health were infectious diseases and malnutrition. However, in industrialized nations improvements in medical and economic conditions have greatly reduced deaths from malnutrition. In nonindustrialized nations, the most common cause of death in children under the age of five is diarrhea (resulting in dehydration). Many other children die of multiple causes, with malnutrition generally contributing to one-third of all deaths of children under the age of five. Deaths from disease are quite rare in Western countries, but measles, tetanus and whooping cough kill millions of children in the developing world each year. Polio has been virtually eliminated in the United States, but worldwide more than 200,000 children are permanently disabled each year by polio.

Childhood deaths can be greatly reduced or eliminated through inoculations against disease (such as measles, tetanus, and whooping cough), as well as through improvements in medical care. By making these available to all individuals in developing countries, child and infant mortality rates could be greatly reduced. For example, educating parents about oral rehydration therapy could greatly reduce the leading cause of death (diarrhea) in young children worldwide. This therapy involves giving children a special solution of sugar, salt, and water in the correct proportions to combat the dehydration that occurs with diarrhea. This low-cost and easily mixed solution, is standard treatment in industrialized nations for children who are suffering from diarrhea.

CHILDHOOD MORTALITY

In most industrialized nations, the major cause of death (estimates range between 30 and 50 percent) in preschoolers is injury due to accidents. There appear to be a number of factors that influence the accident potential of any situation: the amount of adult supervision (e.g., greater supervision means less chance of injury); the safety of the play space (e.g., running around parked cars in a street would be less safe than playing in a playground); the activity level of the child (i.e., as age increases the activity level decreases); gender (i.e., boys have higher accident rates than girls); and social class (i.e., accident rates increase as socioeconomic status decreases).

All 52 states have enacted laws requiring the use of seat belts for children in automobiles as they are 11 times more likely to die in an automobile accident if they are not restrained. The use of childproof caps on medicine bottles has reduced the number of accidental poisonings. Legislation has regulated the amount of space between the bars on cribs, so that children will not accidentally get their heads caught and strangle. New

a vegetarian diet may suffer from
protein such as cheese, eggs or
proteins alone are incomplete; ve
that are important for growth. L
duced young children to low-fa
risk of health problems such
however, are not recommend
specific dietary requirements t
of the nervous system and f
important in these processes
common; over 20 percent of
because of low-iron blood l
found in areas of poverty, the
ized societies puts children

Preschoolers who consu
nutritional deficiencies. S
"empty calorie" foods (i.e.,
or proteins) serve only to
additional sidelight to the
on dental health. Basically
related to the amount of
years, regardless of the qu

Health and Illness Patterns

CHILDHOOD ILLNESSES

If there is one thing
they all get sick. Gener
colds, upper respiratory
nine times a year. Pres
times per year. Of note
unusually frequent ill
have higher than aver

More than 90 per
are immunized again
rubella (German me
These vaccines are
polio and diphtheri
vaccine became ava
United States. By

Because the i
creased over time
their children vac
as red measles. H
educate parents

York City currently requires window guards on high-rise apartments, which has reduced by 50 percent the number of accidental deaths by falling. A few researchers suggest the controversial theory that some childhood "accidents" may actually be suicide attempts. Such cases may entail an overdose of medicine, leaping out a window or such impulsive behavior as running into traffic. In any event, some children may be significantly depressed and choose these behaviors to escape from their depressive, anxiety-producing living situations.

Improvements in medical science have also lead to a decrease in childhood deaths from influenza, pneumonia, cancer, birth defects, and heart disease. Although the number of children infected with AIDS (Acquired Immune Deficiency Syndrome) in this age group is small, this disease is becoming a growing concern for children. Most AIDS-infected children come from three states: Florida, New York, and New Jersey. In addition, almost 80 percent of childhood AIDS cases come from racial and cultural minority groups. Infection occurs primarily through blood transfusions due to hemophilia or through a child's AIDS-infected mother. If they survive to reach preschool age, AIDS-infected children generally show neurological and physiological impairments.

Parents of noninfected preschoolers show significant concern about the possibility of their children catching AIDS from AIDS-infected children, especially in a day care environment. Their worry seems misplaced since there are a number of sets of twins in which only one twin has been infected. Even though they have generally shared everything, including toys, bottles, clothing, and living space, the uninfected twin remains so. Most of the children diagnosed with AIDS die between the ages of three to five. Those that survive to adolescence usually have some significant physiological problems. In 1992 an estimated 10,000 children had AIDS.

BRAIN MATURATION

The brain of a five-year-old has attained approximately 90 percent of its adult weight. Myelinization of nerve fibers is complete in the spinal cord and has been since age two; but neurons in the brain will not be completely myelinated until near the end of adolescence. As discussed in chapter 7, myelinization covers the nerves with a fatty sheath or coating that allows for faster and more controlled transmission of nerve impulses. This process contributes significantly to improvement in a preschooler's abilities. For example, visual motor functioning and control of eye movements increase as myelinization increases so that by age six the majority of children have adequate focusing and scanning skills (exactly the ones that will be needed when the children enter school). Up to age five or six, many children are slightly farsighted, yet this deficit usually disappears as myelinization is completed.

Brain maturation includes the organization of the brain into right and left hemispheres. Each hemisphere has developed specific functions and duties relative to the overall maturation of the brain. By the end of the preschool years, the left hemisphere is responsible for such characteristics as speech, writing, calculation, comprehension of time, logical analysis, and complex movement; the right hemisphere handles perception, imagery, pattern recognition (e.g., melodies, faces, and emotion), emotional expression, and creativity. Plasticity of the brain, that is, flexibility of parts of the brain to take over functions from other damaged parts, has slowed. This ability will be virtually nonexistent by the end of elementary school. Hemispheric specialization is demonstrated in the emergence of hand preference. By age five, over 90 percent of children show a right- or left-hand preference. Psychologists agree that a child can be forced to use the nonpreferred hand, that is, to make it dominant; however, this is generally frustrating for both the parent and child and is likely to be harmful emotionally as well as to cause some decline in perceptual and motor skills. It is interesting to note that whichever hand is the one of preference, the other hand will usually have a more acute sense of touch.

Activity Levels

Activity levels (i.e., the amount and frequency of body movements) in preschool children show a definite age-related pattern that peaks at about age three and then decreases throughout the rest of childhood. This pattern is believed to be related to maturation of the brain itself and the myelinization process, to the production of certain hormones in the brain, and to the brain's need for mental and physical stimulation. Regardless of the cause, several trends in activity levels have been noted: (1) boys tend to be more active than girls; (2) activity levels among children are at least partially genetically influenced (i.e., monozygotic twins are almost identical in the amount of activity they exhibit and dizygotic twins are no more similar than any other pair of brothers and sisters); (3) context of the activity (the environment in which it occurs) can intensify or decrease the child's rate of activity (e.g., having to sit waiting in a doctor's office decreases the rate of activity). Overall, there is a wide variation in normal activity levels for preschool children, indicating the importance of understanding that individual differences will probably be the greatest influence on activity levels in school and family settings.

Mastering Motor Skills

GROSS VERSUS FINE MOTOR SKILLS

Gross motor (large muscle) skills are those body movements that generally involve movement of the body through space, for example, running, jumping, throwing, climbing, and so on. With both maturation and practice, these skills improve dramatically during the preschool years. For example, two-year-olds are quite clumsy, easily falling down and appearing somewhat ungraceful. By age five, children in industrialized nations appear much more coordinated, mastering many fundamental motor skills: climbing a ladder, riding a tricycle, kicking a ball, hopping, jumping, and balancing. The principle of motor primacy (mentioned in chapter 7) is also important here. Specifically, biology and genetics serve to bring the basic abilities to the surface at the appropriate maturational time, and then practice serves to help the child perform these activities smoothly and adeptly. For example, an 18-month-old toddler has only recently acquired the skill of "running": it looks essentially like fast walking. However, a three-year-old shows a more adultlike pattern of body movement: springing off with the feet, leaving the ground, and landing on the balls of the feet rather than flat-footed.

GENDER DIFFERENCES

Gender differences exist in gross motor skills. Boys tend to be stronger than girls and to have more muscle coordination in motor skills, making them better at throwing a ball, going down ladders, and jumping. On the other hand, girls outdo boys at tasks involving limb coordination. Girls are generally better than boys at hopping, catching a ball, balancing on one foot, jumping jacks, and foot tapping. It is not clear whether these differences reflect sex differences or societal attitudes that encourage sex-typed activities.

Girls tend to excel in small muscle (fine motor) coordination. Fine motor skills tend to develop more slowly than gross motor skills. This has been true to a great extent because of the proximodistal principle. That is, fine muscle skills of the fingers and toes have usually lagged behind the large muscle skills of the arms and legs, respectively. The activities in question include such things as cutting food with a knife and fork, tying shoelaces, and pouring juice from a pitcher into a glass without spilling it. Such manual dexterity and manipulation skills develop over the entire preschool period.

Because fine motor skills use hands and fingers to manipulate objects, Marie Montessori developed a series of small motor tasks and materials that encourage the development of eye-hand-brain coordination. Her tasks and approach to teaching preschool children developed into the Montessori school curriculum. Such fine motor skill tasks have been shown to prepare children well for elementary school curricula and the process of formal learning.

DEVELOPMENT OF CHILDREN'S ARTISTIC ABILITIES

One application of fine motor development is in the area of art and drawing. Children have a natural enjoyment in artistic expression, such as drawing and painting, which appears to follow an inborn pattern of neurological growth and refinement that significantly influences the art children produce. At one year, when fine motor skills are rudimentary and poorly controlled, a crayon would be enveloped in the palm and used with full arm movements. At two years, fingers can extend along the shaft of the crayon, and the movements are more controlled. At age three, a child starts to imitate adults by resting a crayon on the hand and having the thumb oppose the index finger. Finally, at age four, when motor control is more advanced, the crayon can be firmly gripped and moved with the fingers only, much as an adult can do.

Scribbling, Shape, and Design Stages. Drawings also progress at a sequential rate, which is divided into four stages. The first is scribbling. Rhoda Kellogg found that scribbles could be classified into twenty basic categories such as zigzags and vertical lines. Children are skilled at scribbling by age two. Motor coordination is not yet finely tuned, hence children are very involved just with the placement of the scribbles on the paper. Early in the scribbling stage, crayon marks may go off the paper; but by the end of this stage the child can stay within the boundaries of the paper, showing more voluntary control. At age three, the shape stage appears, and the child is able to draw such basic forms as ovals, crosses, and circles.

By age four, children usually move into the design stage, where basic shapes are combined into complex patterns. This is an abstract process where the shape combinations generally do not represent anything that the child sees. The child's purpose is to produce aesthetic combinations rather than to draw real-life objects.

Pictorial Stage. A short time after the design stage begins, the pictorial stage also begins (between ages four to five). Here, the "tadpole person" is drawn, that is, a bodiless person with a large head and sticks for legs. This stage culminates the process that has been progressing with better eye-hand coordination: moving from abstract form (scribbles and shapes) to simple design (placing shapes together) to representational focus (recreating a more explicit picture of what is in the world). Around age five to six the preschooler begins to draw a complete person with a body, head, and appendages. It is at this point that formal learning generally begins. In school, children are usually encouraged to move away from a focus on form and design to "staying within the lines" and representing the world more exactly. It is interesting to note that much of what our culture considers "good" art is a return to the abstract and design stage of art development. In essence, the tendency to emphasize pictorial representation may actually impede a child's growing interest in design and form.

Physical Play

Developmentalists refer to the work of childhood as play. Through play, children develop and practice their physical, cognitive, and psychosocial skills. Play behaviors, however, are not all of the same type. Generally, they are subdivided into three distinct types, each of which stimulates the development of motor, cognitive, and social skills.

SENSORIMOTOR PLAY

This is any play that explores, or is simply done for, the enjoyment of the sensory or motor experience. It is the type of play often seen in infants (e.g., shaking a rattle or kicking the side of a crib). As the child's motor abilities become more complex, the types of sensorimotor play behaviors also become more complex. Preschoolers, for example, stimulate their senses by tasting, feeling, and smelling odd flavors, food combinations or textures. Chewing and cracking ice with their teeth as well as sticking their hands outside a moving car window are also examples of this type of play. Sensorimotor play shows pleasure in sensory and motor experiences, and assists neurological development.

MASTERY PLAY

Most physical play is of this type as it helps children master new skills and sharpen old ones. These skills vary from large gross motor skills, such as jumping over objects or walking backwards, to fine motor skills, such as tying shoes or buttering a slice of bread. As they get older, children engage in mastery play that becomes more cognitive, such as word games. Nonetheless, preschoolers take joy in practicing and developing the physical skills that are perfected through such play. Parents influence which of these skills children become adept at simply by example and encouragement, such as playing catch with the child.

ROUGH-AND-TUMBLE PLAY

This type of physical play helps develop social awareness as well as physical capabilities, however, at first glance it may look like aggression. Young animals participate in such play by pouncing on one another, tumbling, and mimicking aggression. Preschoolers can frequently be found in a heap laying all over each other, wrestling and punching amid laughs of glee. What distinguishes this "wrestling" behavior from aggression is the presence of a "play face" (i.e., smiling and laughing). The children involved seem happy and playful and emerge generally unhurt. Aggressive behavior would be accompanied by frowns or scowls. Social roles between children are learned and strengthened in addition to further development of gross and fine motor skills.

GENDER DIFFERENCES IN PHYSICAL PLAY

Gender differences in children's play patterns appear to exist. Even though the rate and sequence of physical development between the sexes is almost identical during the preschool years, society appears to encourage gender differences in play behaviors. Thus, boys and girls in early childhood become skilled at different activities. Boys spend more time outside participating in gross motor activities, such as playing ball, climbing, and running. More of their activities involve playful aggression and competition (i.e., rough-and-tumble play). In contrast, girls are generally encouraged to play more indoors, participating in activities that utilize fine motor coordination, lower activity levels, and apparent cooperation. For example, girls spend more time in games that require taking turns. Jumping rope is primarily a girls' outdoor activity in which the rope turners must cooperate, synchronizing their rope turning. These gender differences appear to be mostly the result of social rather than biological factors. In addition, children are often encouraged to play with gender-appropriate toys. One is likely to find girls playing with dolls (e.g., Barbie and Ken) while boys might play with action figures (e.g., Ninja Turtles).

Between the ages of two and six, children grow an average of 3 inches and gain an average of 4½ pounds per year. In addition, body shape during this age range will generally transform the child from pudgy to slender. Whereas biology determines this slower growth rate that is seen, parental and nutritional factors influence food choice and nutritional quality of a child's diet. Since the caloric needs diminish over this stage, "empty calorie" foods (such as sweets) need to be secondary in a diet that meets basic nutritional requirements.

The incidence rate of minor illnesses (colds, ear infections, and so on) in preschoolers is less than in infants. A health concern during this time is the immunization of children against the major childhood diseases: whooping cough, polio, diphtheria, red and German measles. Even though these diseases are on the decline in industrialized societies, they are a significant health problem in the rest of the world. Dehydration and malnutrition, whether as a result of disease or poor diet, are leading causes of preschooler mortality in developing nations. These are not significant problems in developed countries, where the leading cause of childhood deaths is accidents. AIDS is becoming a significant cause of childhood mortality. Infection occurs primarily through blood transfusions postnatally or through a child's AIDS-infected mother prenatally. Most children who contract AIDS early in life die during the preschool years.

Brain maturation during this time is demonstrated by increased myelinization and hemispheric specialization. At the end of this stage, the child's brain is 90 percent the weight of an adult brain and has all of the functions that an adult brain has with respect to specialization, as is shown by consistent hand preference by age five. In addition, by age six increases in myelinization have brought about the visual focusing and scanning skills that will be necessary for school. The fall in activity levels over time is also a result of brain myelinization.

Motor skill development shows biological and environmental influences together. Specifically, biology (proximodistal principle) brings new skills to the surface or makes them possible, and practice with them improves proficiency. This can be seen in the development of children's art (fine motor skills) and running or riding a bicycle (gross motor skills). Some gender differences appear to exist with regard to the development of gross versus fine motor skills; however, these differences may reflect socialization pressures from parents and society rather than basic biological differences.

Finally, physical play behaviors are the work of preschool children. These behaviors take three forms: sensorimotor (those that result in pure sensory or motor experiences); mastery (those that are used to learn new skills); and rough-and-tumble (those that help children learn different social roles). These last play behaviors can be distinguished from aggression by the presence of a smiling "play face."

Selected Readings

Aslin, R. N. (1987). Visual and auditory development in infancy. In J. D. Osofsky (ed.). *Handbook of infant development.* 2d ed. NY: Wiley.

Bailey, D. A. (1977). *Readings in child development and relationships.* NY: Macmillan.

Cohen, D. (1987). *The development of play.* NY: New York University Press.

Gardner, H. (1980). *Artful scribbles: The significance of children's drawings.* NY: Basic Books.

Laszio, J. I. ((1990). *Development psychology: Cognitive, perceptual-motor, and neuropsychological perspectives.* Amsterdam: North Holland.

Rallison, M. L. (1988). *Growth disorders in infants, children, and adolescents.* NY: Wiley.

Sinclair, D. (1978). *Human growth after birth.* 3d ed. London: Oxford University Press.

Singer, D. G., and J. L. Singer. (1977). *Partners in play: A step-by step guide to imaginative play in children.* NY: Harper & Row.

Taitz, L. S., and B. I. Wardley. (1989). *Handbook of child nutrition.* NY: Oxford.

12

The Preschool Years: Cognitive Development

*P*hysical development in the preschool years also ushers in a major shift in the thinking (cognitive) skills in a child: the ability to represent his or her thoughts or actions symbolically. However, the child is still tied to the "real" world, meaning that he or she is still a long way from thinking abstractly.

The use and meaning of a child's symbols can be viewed through Piaget's examination of the thinking problems of this age range: egocentrism, animism, centration, illogical reasoning, and so on. All of these problems involve a child's blossoming use and understanding of symbols both in thinking and language.

This chapter will explore Piaget's theory of cognitive development as well as the IQ and information-processing theories. In addition to the above problems of preschool thinkers, we will explore the parental and family characteristics that foster and help mold a child's thinking through these years.

ROLE OF SYMBOLIC THOUGHT

The major change in the cognitive ability of the preschooler is in the ability to use symbolic thought. Unlike the infant, the preschool child is able to use an object or name or event to symbolize another. The use of language fully reflects this newfound ability, since all language is symbolic in form; that is, a word or group of sounds represents an object, person, action or event.

Passage from the sensorimotor to the preoperational stage occurs because of the effects of the last sensorimotor substage (substage six), which may be a transition stage from sensorimotor to preoperational cognitive thinking. In substage six, the infant imitates with voluntary control and uses deferred representation; he or she can create a visual image of an act or event and mimic it later when the event is not actually occurring. The infant is thinking symbolically.

You can see the development of symbolic thought and symbolic thinking processes by reviewing the development of pretend play behaviors. The first stage of pretend play, sensorimotor play takes place during the infant's first year of life. At this stage an infant develops different schemas that help it understand what objects are as well as what they can and can't do. Essentially, the child does not pretend yet, but this period corresponds with the development of the object concept (see chapter 8). The first sign of pretending (stage 2) occurs when a child displays some self-oriented action (e.g., washing his or her hands) but uses a toy to complete the action rather than the appropriate item (e.g., a toy bar of soap). In stage 3, between the ages of 15 and 21 months, the child uses another person or toy to receive the action of the pretending. Even though objects may be used for their exact purposes, such as a teacup being used for tea, the person receiving this play may be a doll, dog or stuffed animal.

In stage 4, between the ages of two and three, objects are used for other than their real purposes. For example, a cup of water can now be used to mimic sand at the beach. Schoolteachers see this stage of pretend play as more indicative of social competence: children who use it are generally more popular and less egocentric. In stage 5, about age four or five, children start developing sociodramatic play. Here they take on parts in social roles, such as playing mommy and daddy. This stage of pretending encourages them to think less about themselves and more about the perspectives of other people.

In stage 6, around age six, pretend play becomes very dramatic, including extensive and elaborate roles. These roles mimic what children see in everyday life. The play will be planned ahead of time with people assigned to different roles, which may change within the course of the play. This stage begins late in the preoperational range and extends into the elementary school years. However, pretend play tends to wane over time, although it never quite disappears. What takes its place is a tendency to play with specific rules and elaborate games.

PIAGET AND PREOPERATIONAL THOUGHT

As we saw in chapter 8, Piaget summarized infants between birth and age two (sensorimotor stage) as being incapable of seeing beyond themselves cognitively. The information they gather from the environment and the schemas they develop are intimately related to their own sensory and motor experiences in and around the environment.

A child in the preoperational stage (ages two to six) takes the schemas learned in the sensorimotor stage and applies them outside his or her own frame of reference. This means that children attempt to see the world as something greater than themselves. Piaget noticed an obstacle to this understanding, however, in that children come into this stage thinking they are the center of the universe. Therefore, this "center of the universe" concept needs to be unlearned before children move into the next stage of development, where they begin to understand that each person has his or her own particular perspective.

In describing preoperational thought, Piaget defined a number of concepts that begin at the end of the sensorimotor stage. These are initially restrictive but over the course of preoperational development become broader and acquire many of the characteristics found in the concrete operational stage of elementary school. The following is a sampling of the characteristics of preoperational thought as Piaget defined them.

REVERSIBILITY

Preoperational children cannot reverse their thought processes. If a preoperational boy says he has a sister and is then asked if his sister also has a brother, he will have difficulty reversing his role and seeing himself as someone else's brother. Therefore, he is more likely to say that his sister does not have a brother. This same reversibility problem is often seen when children begin to learn mathematics; a child lacking reversibility views 3 + 4 as being different from 4 + 3.

CENTRATION

Preoperational children appear unable to see beyond a single dimension of an object or person. For example, a child may easily understand that Mommy is a parent but not understand that mommy is also a daughter, a sister, or an aunt. Children at this stage center or concentrate on one dimension to the exclusion of others. The one centered on may very well be the more obvious or familiar one to the child. A broad view of any one person or situation is difficult for the preoperational child.

CONSERVATION

Preoperational children rely heavily on their visual perceptions, making it difficult for them to distinguish between appearance and reality. They do not understand that qualities of an object or a person remain the same, regardless of changes in appearance. This can be seen with respect to changes in matter, number, and identity.

Matter. Preoperational children do not distinguish between substantial and superficial transformations of objects. For example, a single piece of 8½-by-11-inch paper contains the same amount of paper unfolded as it does folded, regardless of the number of folds. The preoperational child would believe the unfolded piece to have more paper.

Number. Children at this stage usually presume that changes in the appearance of objects also change the number of objects. For example, two plates of five identically shaped cookies will be seen as having different numbers of cookies, depending on the placement of the cookies on each plate. Cookies positioned entirely in the center of the plate will be interpreted as fewer than cookies placed entirely around the edge of the plate.

Identity. Preoperational children interpret changes in the outward appearance of people to be changes in the people themselves. For example, a father who has let his hair grow long may be seen by his child as becoming "female," if having long hair is included in the child's definition of femaleness.

EGOCENTRISM

Preoperational children see the world from their own perspective. This viewpoint is not selfish but demonstrates a lack of maturity in their thinking. A preoperational child who prefers chocolate ice cream assumes that everyone prefers chocolate ice cream. As may be apparent, this process is a part of each of the other thinking problems the preoperational child has.

REALITY = FANTASY

Preoperational children also have trouble distinguishing fantasy from reality. They have not yet mastered the concept of conservation or logical thinking and therefore lack the ability to question the reality of figures such as Santa Claus, the Tooth Fairy, and the Easter Bunny. For example, a child can pretend to be Santa Claus while knowing he or she is not, yet the same child lacks the logical understanding to question whether Santa Claus could deliver toys to everyone in one night.

ANIMISM

Animism is the belief that objects are conscious or alive. A child might believe that burned cookies are the result of the oven's anger at the person baking and that a car might get a flat tire in order to "avoid" going to the garage for repairs.

TRANSDUCTIVE REASONING

A preoperational child's reasoning is not logical but rather transductive: it uses no abstract logical thinking. Basically, the child assumes that a correlation means cause and effect. For example, a preoperational child who touches a hot stove would assume it was hot because he or she touched it, not because it was on.

CLASSIFICATION

Classification is the ability to places objects, people, and thoughts into one or more schemas. Piaget thought that a preoperational child could not take a group of toys and put them into any logical classes, such as wind-up toys versus pull toys, or red toys versus blue toys. Nor could he or she place a dog into a mammal schema, an animal schema or a pet schema. In addition, the preoperational child could not place the toys in seriation (size order) from smallest to largest.

Piaget Updated

Piaget is by far the most influential theorist in cognitive development. His stages offer evidence of a particular order in cognitive development, but according to new test data he may have miscalculated the age at which a child develops a particular cognitive process. This apparent inaccuracy can be seen in two areas: conservation and egocentrism (or understanding another's perspective).

CONSERVATION

According to Piaget, this concept does not appear in all three areas of matter, number, and identity until about age eight. New research suggests, however, that understanding conservation as a general principle may start as early as age three and not be complete until at least age ten. For example, three-year-olds have demonstrated conservation of number so long as the number of objects is no more than three. Note that in these studies the objects were familiar to the children (checkers), misarrangement of the objects was done by a familiar rather than a strange individual (a "naughty" teddy bear vs. an adult experimenter), and each child was given very simple, easy-to-understand instructions. In addition, three-year-olds have demonstrated counting ability when confronted with conservation of number problems using toys (again familiar objects). Lastly, conservation of matter has been seen with four-year-olds who were the children of potters. Essentially, these four-year-olds were able to continually observe the transformation of a ball of clay into a plate or pitcher, that is, changes in the shape of matter without changes in the amount.

EGOCENTRISM (PERSPECTIVE TAKING)

Piaget said that understanding another's perspective would not occur until the end of the preoperational period (about age six). However, in an experiment using a picture pasted to the bottom of the inside of a hollow cube so that the only way to see the picture was to look into the cube, two-year-olds would turn the opening toward an observer when asked to show the picture.

Evidence of perspective taking in preoperational children also comes from what psychologists call "theory of mind" research. This means that each of us has a personal understanding of our own mental processes (emotions, thoughts, perceptions, actions, and so on) and makes guesses about the mental processes of others. This process appears to exist in children's attempts to mislead one another. The knowledge that one is creating false beliefs in another person would indicate an understanding of a difference in perspective: the "liar" would understand what the listener might believe and might not believe. This appears to be the case for children between two-and-a-half and five-years-old.

UPDATE ON PIAGET

Piaget provided a way to organize the thinking processes and abilities of the preschool child. About that there is little argument; the kinds of thinking problems Piaget recognized and defined are indeed present. Likewise, a three-year-old does not in any way have the ability that an eight-year-old has (see chapter 16). However, Piaget errs in seeing cognitive development in absolute terms.

When experiments have been set up to undermine Piaget's analysis, researchers have found rudiments of some more mature cognitive functions, especially in the areas of conservation and egocentrism. Specifically, making the task very simple, encouraging active participation on the child's part, using situations or materials that children are familiar with, making the experiment seem more like a game, and using language familiar to the child all increase the likelihood of finding aspects of advanced skills at younger ages. Therefore, younger children may actually grasp aspects of many of the concepts necessary for adult functioning and lack only sufficient experience, maturation, and understanding. Put into practice, this new evidence could have profound effects on the developmental rate of cognitive thought processes. Essentially, an environment that provides a child with familiar and simple learning tools will encourage that child to develop faster cognitively.

Alternative Approaches to Cognitive Development

(See chapter 8 for a general introduction to the theoretical areas discussed below.)

PSYCHOMETRIC

Whereas IQ tests are essentially unreliable for infants and toddlers, the same is not necessarily true for the preschool child. A few points are helpful here. First, IQ testing becomes easier as children age, partly because of their increased use and understanding of language and partly because the tests may measure cognitive functions that are more stable as children age. Second, the tests are designed for older children and adults, making their scores and interpretations more reliable with older subjects. Third, since IQ tests measure a kind of cognitive "power," scores for older children should be better predictors of later intelligence than scores of younger children.

With these points in mind, researchers have found some reliable results when testing IQ in children. The IQ scores do indeed become more stable over time, and they do indeed predict later performance better when older rather than younger children are tested. Fluctuations within individual scores may be as much as twenty to thirty points from one testing time to another; the younger the children being tested, the greater the fluctuations. In addition, the shorter the time between testing, the more similar the scores.

Whereas reliability in predicting later performance is virtually nonexistent for children below age two, scores at age three can better predict scores at age five. By age eight, the IQ scores are even more stable and therefore even better predictors of IQ at age ten. Large changes become less frequent over time, improving predictability. In the final analysis, prediction is more accurate through the preschool years, but it is far from precise. The improvement is probably directly related to brain maturation and increased myelinization.

Two further notes: First, as discussed in chapters 8 and 9, the home environment influences intelligence. A stable home appears to cause more stable cognitive development, especially if the child is securely attached to the parents. Those home environments that score high on the HOME survey with regard to attention to play and the availability of different stimuli encourage higher IQs.

Second, the number of children in the home appears to influence IQs. This effect is referred to as the confluence model. Essentially, if there is more than one child in the home, the IQ level of each child after the first appears to progressively decline. Rather than there being some biological or genetic "weakness" that shows up with increased numbers of children, the decline is more likely due to a decrease in environmental stimulation. Parents can spend an enormous amount of time with an only child, but the amount of time per child decreases with each new child, thereby reducing the stimulation needed to foster the same level of cognitive development in each child.

INFORMATION PROCESSING

Since this aspect of cognitive development depends on how information is processed and on the workings of memory, the preschooler is a better information processor than the infant or toddler. This would be expected with maturation. Where an infant's attention can be "captured" by some stimulus in the environment or the infant can be easily distracted, the preschooler has a better command over those faculties. The preschooler is better able to decide what will grab his or her attention, to focus the attention or leave it unfocused, and to divide that attention among many activities going on at the same time (watching the television, listening to Mom talk about work, and watching the dog).

An infant's memory is limited in size and duration. The preschooler's memory has expanded in both of those areas. Recognition memory (realizing that one has seen something before) is very good in four-year-olds whereas recall memory (retrieving as many recollections as possible about a situation) is less developed. Recall memory improves over the preschool and elementary school years as children learn more about how to memorize and retrieve information, that is, how to make memory work.

Preschoolers can also distinguish between information that is central to a message and that which is peripheral. After watching segments of "Sesame Street," for example, four-, five-, and six-year-olds can name the central theme of the segment reliably, disregarding the unnecessary material. However, they have a much harder time being selective about central themes if the period of time they are asked to summarize is long. Asking a preschooler to tell you what happened during the school day may result in no answer at all; asking the same child what interested him during "show and tell" can result in an exquisitely detailed response.

In summary, while preschoolers have some problems interpreting their perceptions, their capacities and processing abilities improve over time. In effect, the deficiencies Piaget pointed out may simply reflect immature processing and retrieval capabilities, which might also be reflected in the low psychometric reliability scores.

LANGUAGE DEVELOPMENT

Language/ Thought Relationship

Children's capacity for language explodes during the preschool years. The question remains, however, whether language precedes thought or vice versa. That is, do preschoolers increase their vocabulary as a means of describing concepts that already exist for them, or do new words generate new concepts? Probably both. For example, infants and toddlers probably understand the concept of "love" by virtue of the care they receive from their parents long before the word enters their vocabulary.

Vocabulary and Grammar Development

VOCABULARY SIZE AND USAGE

Children's vocabulary increases dramatically through this age range, as can be seen in Table 12.1, which shows the average vocabulary for children between the ages of eighteen months and six-and-a-half years. As vocabulary increases, so does the rate of speech, the length of sentences, and the information content. One also finds an increased use of words denoting time ("when"), as well as of those dealing with questions and explanations ("because").

Age (years)	Average size of vocabulary (number of words)
1	0
1½	100
2	250
2½	500
3	900
3½	1,200
4	1,500
4½	1,800
5	2,200
5½	2,300
6	2,500
6½	2,600

Table 12.1 Typical acquisition rate of vocabulary in children. Children's average vocabulary size increases rapidly between the ages of 1½ and 6½ years.

GRAMMAR

Grammar deals with how words are put together to convey meaning. Initially, much of the language used by preschoolers represents an egocentric viewpoint; language may not be precise because preschoolers expect the listener to understand. A preschooler may say, "I want it for breakfast," assuming that the parent knows what "it" is. Until the child begins to see that others may not share his or her perspective, the clarity of language will improve only slowly. Likewise, using past tense, adult logic, and putting things in order by time are difficult for preschoolers. Two grammar problems are indicative of this age.

Overextension. This usually occurs with nouns and involves difficulty with classification. For example, calling all vehicles with wheels that drive on highways "cars" is overextending the class. This problem disappears with time but can be seen whenever the child is exposed to new items that are similar to each other. From a cognitive viewpoint, overextension may be an attempt to assimilate new information. When that fails, the child must accommodate that information and change his or her schemas.

Overregularization. This problem is usually found with verbs, especially those that are conjugated irregularly. For example, "Yesterday I wanted . . ." is the past tense of "today I want." It is accomplished by the addition of "ed." The preschooler will apply the "ed" rule across the board as in "today I go," "yesterday I goed." This problem results from an incomplete understanding of the rules for the past tense, which will likely not be well learned until the child is nearly in elementary school.

PRAGMATICS

One aspect of language that represents a lack of egocentrism at this age relates to the concept of pragmatics. That is, preschoolers are able to comprehend that children younger than they are understand differently from older children or adults. The four-year-old will talk very simply to a two-year-old baby brother or sister and will use larger words and longer sentences when talking with parents. This ability can help the four-year-old translate the speech of a two-year-old for an adult who does not understand.

Factors Influencing Language Development

Several factors are important to language development. Generally speaking, a female, middle-class, first-born or only child will have a faster rate of language development, a larger vocabulary, and a better command of grammar rules than other children.

Apart from those personal factors, the major influence on language appears to be the family, specifically the emphasis that the parents or caregivers place on language development. (This same statement is also true of cognitive development in general.) That is, language development proceeds very well when the amount and quality of adult's conversation with the child are high. Reading stories and books, telling stories, conversing with the child in simple language, asking questions that require more than simple yes or no answers, repeating back what the child says to be sure that you understand, and making conversation time a special time are all ways to improve the language content and language organization of the preschool child.

*C*ognitive development in the preschool child is marked by the child's use of symbols, primarily in language. The development of symbol use is apparent in the changes in the child's pretend play, which may range from mimicking the real use of an object (using a cup and saucer for tea) to expanding the symbol meanings beyond the real use of the object (using the cup and saucer as a bathtub for fairies).

Piaget defined a number of thinking problems that are hallmarks of the preoperational child. These include: an inability to see more than one aspect of an object (centration), difficulty in understanding another's perspective (egocentrism), seeing personality in inanimate objects (animism), and believing that fantasy is the same thing as reality, among others. However, preschooler's lack of understanding of these concepts does not mean that rudiments of those concepts are not present. For example, the ability of a preschooler to deceive another child implies an understanding of the other child's beliefs and perspective.

Psychometric and information-processing approaches to the study of cognitive growth during this period are more informative than they were during the sensorimotor stage. This can be seen with IQ scores, which, as the child matures become better predictors of later intelligence scores. Likewise, better control over attention and memory capacities demonstrates that with maturation and environmental practice comes better cognitive functioning.

Lastly, language development moves ahead quickly through the preschool years, and the child makes great strides in vocabulary and in understanding the rules of grammar. Two problems develop here: overextension (literally an overuse of assimilation) and overregularization (attempts to apply the rules of grammar to verb tenses). All in all, language improvement seems to be fostered greatly by a supportive family and a home environment where communication with rather than to the child is stressed.

Selected Readings

Carey, S. (1978). *Linguistic theory and psychological reality.* Cambridge, MA: MIT Press.

Chomsky, N. (1968). *Language and mind.* NY: Harcourt, Brace, World.

Cox, M. (1986). *The child's point of view: The development of cognition and language.* NY: St. Martin's Press.

Flavell, J. H. (1985). *Cognitive development.* 2d ed. Englewood Cliffs, NJ: Prentice-Hall.

Mussen, P. H. (1983). *Socialization, personality and social development.* Vol. 4. *Handbook of child psychology.* NY: Wiley.

Piaget, J. (1959). *The language and thought of the child.* 3d ed. Trans. M. and R. Gabain. London: Routledge and Kegan Paul.

13

The Preschool Years: Psychosocial Development

Between the ages of two and five, children's social interactions dramatically increase. This chapter covers the importance of a preschooler's social world and what influences it; Of particular interest are the theories about the development of self-concept, cognition and learning. The roles of peers, play, and friendship in the development of self-concept are also discussed.

A continuing influence in the social lives of children is the family. Parenting styles are examined along with the influence of siblings. Topics covered include: the use of punishment, three general parenting styles, and the most effective ways to raise children.

Finally, prosocial behavior and sex roles are addressed. This chapter looks at how children develop altruism and what form it takes in early childhood. Theoretical explanations of how sex-role behavior develops at this age are examined, especially through the perspectives of Freud, learning theory, and cognitive theoretical models.

DEVELOPMENT OF THE SELF-CONCEPT

A person's self-concept is like a self-portrait. It is how one sees oneself either in general or in specific situations, and it is a picture one creates based on one's experiences in different situations. That is, a student might see herself as a good student in one class where she performs well and as a struggling student in another where she does not perform well. Likewise, a two-month-old has a self-concept that intimately involves his or her dependence on parents in order to move around, eat, bathe, and so on, whereas a two-year-old sees himself as more mobile and independent. Thus self-concept does not necessarily amount to self-awareness but rather to a view of the world with oneself in it.

One can imagine the self-concept as being similar to a mental photo album for which the "self" takes all the pictures and is the central character in each picture. In that sense, we all come equipped with an inborn "instamatic camera" that takes pictures of every situation we find ourselves in and develops them immediately. Significantly, each picture also adequately reflects our feelings about the situation. That is, when we look at these pictures of ourselves, they evoke feelings about ourselves as well.

This implies that the self-concept is not static and unchanging. On the contrary, as our experiences change, so can our self-concept. If the struggling student mentioned above sets aside more time for study and preparation, then the grades will improve and the self-concept will improve also. The self-concept is dynamic with the environment: they influence each other.

In general, preschool children have exuberant self-concepts. They believe they can do virtually anything. If left alone, they interpret their own mistakes as having little influence over later attempts to solve a problem, largely because mistakes do not represent to them an inadequacy on their part. This probably results from the lack of cause/effect reasoning indicative of this age range (see chapter 12). Their exuberance shows in their unbridled happiness and resolve when they enter new situations.

Theoretical Explanations for the Self-Concept

ERIK ERIKSON (PSYCHOANALYTIC THEORY)

According to Erikson, the crisis during the preschool years involves the conflict between the child's initiative in starting and completing her or his own activities regardless of the outcome versus feeling guilt for not completing a task successfully or for doing it the wrong way. Erikson, then, sees this portion of the lifespan as the time when children begin to take on adult (independent, responsible) components to their personalities or form strong child (dependent, irresponsible) components. The child begins developing an awareness of society, a clear sense of self, and takes initiative in accomplishing things. This stems from but is different from the toddler's desire to assert autonomy. Learning about autonomy meant learning about what the new physical, cognitive, and psychosocial abilities could accomplish. Now the child can put these abilities to work while playing and creating.

Should the purposeful attempts at initiating tasks or exploring lead to failure, then the important social component of Erikson's view becomes apparent. That is, because of children's egocentric viewpoint on life, harsh or continual criticism will be viewed as relating to themselves personally rather than just to their behavior; the result is guilt. In and of itself, guilt is not all bad because it can serve as a motivator or inhibitor for some behaviors. For example, most people buy items from stores rather than shoplift them because the latter is wrong behavior. But then if the child equates feelings of guilt with his or her self-concept, then the child may see him- or herself as not merely *doing* wrong but as *being* wrong or bad. The ability to feel guilt is closely tied to the development of a self-concept.

LEARNING AND COGNITIVE THEORIES

The learning theory approach explains preschoolers' self-concepts as resulting from an awareness of themselves and their behavior and of how they are perceived by others. Praise (attention and acceptance) and blame (rejection) now become powerful reinforcements and punishments. Thus preschoolers' self concepts are formed according to normal rules of operant and classical conditioning. Likewise, they can imitate behaviors of adults and their peers using the reinforcement/punishment consequences of those behaviors to mold a self-concept. Preschoolers can also begin to take pride in their own self-control, thus reinforcing their own self-esteem as they decide that they are "good boys" or "good girls."

Cognitive theorists propose that preschoolers acquire a rudimentary psychological understanding of themselves, or a self-schema. They begin to distinguish between their own perceptions and motives and those of others. This self-schema is composed of a basic self-knowledge, which becomes the basis of the self-concept. Because of the limitations in cognitive functioning at this age, a preschooler's understanding of psychological processes is general and simplistic. For example, a five-year-old has difficulty grasping that a person can be good at doing some things and bad at doing others (a characteristic of centration).

Self-Concept and Social Interactions

As preschoolers understand themselves better, their understanding of others both individually and in social interactions also improves. Research has shown that those preschoolers who have a more positive sense of themselves are better able to cooperate in social interactions. Other studies have shown that children who are more socialized score higher in measures of self-concept. These children tend to be less dependent on teacher support in preschools and more skilled at making friendships in the playground. Again, the interaction between self-concept and experience appears to be a dynamic one.

SOCIAL PLAY

In infancy and toddlerhood, many of the child's play behaviors are solitary: the child's sensorimotor experiences predominate over social interchange because the infant is learning about the world around it. However, with increased mobility and an apparent desire to learn more about the people in the world, the preschooler's play behaviors take on more of a quality of social interchange. Playing with someone or imagining playing with someone comprise much of a preschooler's social interaction.

Categories of Social Play

Over fifty years ago, a method of detailed categorization was developed to summarize the ways children play. These categories, based on observations made during free play in a nursery school, are unoccupied play, solitary play, onlooker play, parallel play, associative play, and cooperative play.

UNOCCUPIED PLAY

The child is not engaged in any obvious play. He or she may show random movements or may merely stand in one spot. Babies, for example, may play with their hands or bang a toy. This type of behavior is most common in children who appear to lack motivation to play socially and are simply watching whatever interests them at that moment.

SOLITARY PLAY

The child plays alone and seems unconcerned with the activities of others. This child's games become more complex during the second or third year of life. This play may incorporate imaginary people; hence there may be inherent social qualities to it. Nonetheless, the child makes no effort to join or interact with other children.

ONLOOKER PLAY

Here the preschooler is aware of other children nearby. He or she watches them play and may even comment or ask questions.

PARALLEL PLAY

Although the child plays alone, he or she watches other children, mimicking their behavior or playing with similar toys. The child makes no attempt to control the action of the play or to modify actions of other children. The social quality consists of being alongside the other play activities rather than in the middle of them.

ASSOCIATIVE PLAY

Children play with each other but seem to be more interested in associating together than in the games themselves. Play materials are borrowed or loaned. The play activity is similar for all children, but it is not organized as a group activity.

COOPERATIVE PLAY

Children play together in some organized way for a particular purpose. This could be a competitive game or a cooperative venture, such as a dramatic play, that requires a division of labor. The group or social organization takes on an importance of its own.

Importance of Social Play

Older children spend more time in associative or cooperative play than younger children, who are more likely to engage in parallel or solitary play. Although the more social forms of play are characteristic of older, more mature children, solitary play in an older child shows the ability to concentrate on a task. Also, younger preschoolers who have had experience with older children frequently engage in more mature types of play, such as chasing each other or cooperating in simple games. Moreover, the higher forms of social play are critical in the developmental life of the preschooler. Children grow in the skills they need to be competent in the social world through the social interactions found in higher levels of play.

One should not use these play behaviors in a diagnostic sense to pick out some problem a child might be having. On the contrary, environmental situations can greatly influence play behaviors. A highly social and gregarious child in one situation might use solitary or onlooker play in a new environment until the "rules" of the new situation are understood. It is more appropriate to see play behaviors as tools for learning social interaction skills and for trying out different social roles.

Primate studies give evidence of the importance of social play in the development of children. In a number of studies conducted by Harry Harlow, rhesus monkeys were raised isolated from their playmates. The isolation-reared monkeys were withdrawn socially and highly aggressive. They had few social skills and during adolescence had a lower survival rate because of attacks they initiated on larger male monkeys or nursing females. If these undersocialized monkeys made it to adulthood, they appeared relatively normal, although they tended to be overly aggressive and were unable to show or accept affection. Although primate studies must be applied to human situations with caution, this research suggests that it may be adaptive in the long run for young children to be encouraged to interact with peers in order to develop social skills.

Dramatic Play

Dramatic or pretend play begins when the child is able to use symbols, usually around the age of two. This type of play peaks at ages five to six years and gradually declines as children's interests shift more to games. The first sign of this play usually is the toddler feeding a doll or stuffed animal. This style of play expands over time to include other children as well. Mutual fantasy play becomes common and more complicated at ages four to six, when children begin to interact in dramatic play. Several standard plots emerge as such play develops: parent/child interactions; one player becomes hurt or dies and the other administers a healing potion; one child rescues another from some threatening situation.

Dramatic play allows preschoolers to develop their world in a number of ways. They can exercise and develop their creativity. They explore rules. They coordinate complex rules. They cooperate and share in directing. Dramatic play also allows children to express fears and fantasies and then attempt to master them.

Development of Friendships

The preschooler begins to make rudimentary friendships as children play repeatedly with the same children either in the neighborhood or at preschool. Many of these relationships are transitory because commitment is beyond the cognitive capabilities of the preschooler. A few persist if the children keep attending schools together or remain neighbors. Young children describe friends as those who participate in shared activities, who are physically present, and with whom they can share things. Most of these friendships are fleeting and depend upon the shared physical presence of the children. Also, as children get older, they tend to play more and more with same-sex children. It is unclear how much influence gender-role stereotypes have on these associations.

PARENTING

As children enter the preschool years with increased mobility, communication, and social skills, they strive to develop a sense of independence from the parents. For their part, parents generally want to raise "good," self-reliant children. However, despite this shared goal, parents and children often do not share an understanding of what children should learn and how they should learn it. Because of the inherent conflict between parents and children, parents need to approach parenting with care. For example, despite the temptation to be hostile toward an unruly child, staying calm and showing affection may actually be more helpful.

Parenting Styles

The pioneering research in this area was conducted by Diana Baumrind, who outlined three basic parenting styles by observing more than 100 nursery school children and interviewing their parents. Much of what follows can be viewed from the perspective of children's rights versus their responsibilities.

AUTHORITARIAN

These parents believe in "old-fashioned strictness." Children are expected to follow unquestioningly the rules of the family and the household. Any resistance is met with punishment and force. The parents rule this household with little or no input from the children. The parent/child relationship is tenuous, with little affection, nurturing or communication. The children are given little freedom. Hence children have few if any rights but are required to fulfill responsibilities they probably do not understand. For example, in an authoritarian home an eight-year-old may be required to babysit for a three-year-old for an hour while a parent goes to the store. Taking care of a three-year-old is hard enough for an adult; an eight-year-old may not have the patience or experience to handle every situation that may develop.

PERMISSIVE

These parents tend to demand very little of their children, giving them much freedom and little discipline. These parents tend to be highly affectionate, communicative, and accepting of their children. Permissive parents see their role as to support their children rather than to shape their lives. Since these parents set few if any limits and enforce them only sporadically, their children have many rights and few responsibilities.

AUTHORITATIVE

These parents firmly enforce family rules; however, they explain their reasons to children and maintain flexibility. Input from children is also actively encouraged as they are an integral part of the family. Children are allowed to object to the rules. These parents, however, take final responsibility for making the decisions. Both rights and responsibilities match the ability of the children to understand and fulfill them. The parents expect their children to be independent and to grow in maturity. Parent/child interactions are open and nurturing.

Baumrind's studies concluded that children of authoritative parents fared best in the long run; they tended to be the most contented, self-reliant, cooperative, self-controlled, and achievement-oriented of all the children studied. Children whose parents were overly strict (authoritarian) tended to be unhappy. Children of permissive parents, however, were the unhappiest and the least self-controlled of the three groups. Thus both authoritarian and permissive parenting styles produced children who were less motivated and more distrustful, self-centered, and unhappy. Baumrind concluded that the key factors in raising happy children are making demands and being responsive. Either without the other produced unhappy children. Parents who demand and expect much of their children while maintaining open communications and flexibility, and providing encouragement and warmth produce independent, competent children.

Punishment and Reward

A survey taken in 1983 found that only 3 percent of children in the United States grow up without ever having experienced physical punishment from their parents. This punishment varies from taking away a pleasurable activity (restriction) to severe physical punishment that results in permanent physical damage or death (see the section on child abuse in chapter 10). Almost every research study that has investigated the use of harsh physical punishment has found long-term negative effects. Properly used punishment that results in long-term positive behavioral changes without negative side effects includes: the lowest level of emotion possible (no loud, angry yelling); mildest level of punishment (no physical punishment); and intervention as early as possible in the behavioral sequence (no saying: "Wait until your father gets home").

Superficially, it does seem that using harsh punishment has the immediate effect of making a child immediately obedient, which may serve to make parents proud that they don't "spare the rod" and thus spoil the child. However, in the long run, severe punishment is less successful and even damaging compared with using the mildest forms of punishment, such as taking away privileges. Numerous studies have shown that children who receive harsh punishment tend to grow up to be juvenile delinquents. These children are apt to be more mistrustful of adults and authority figures, to be sullen, to experience more school and behavior problems, and to be more aggressive.

Harsh punishment has other long-term effects. A parent who disciplines with physical punishment models for a child that physical aggression is an acceptable, mature outlet. Spanking a child out of anger tends to communicate rejection, anger, and dislike of the child. In addition, pairing physical pain with the presence of a parent tends to make the parent's presence less desirable for the child. Children tend to avoid parents who use harsh physical punishment because of the associated anxiety and discomfort.

Verbal punishment in the form of criticism tends to result in children who are withdrawn and anxious. This can occur because of the esteem with which children regard their parents. When criticism comes from "on high," children take it personally. Children who are often criticized generally do not act out physically but rather internalize the criticism and become more dependent.

There are some overall guidelines for discipline that most experts agree on. Overall, positive reinforcement works more effectively than punishment. Children behave better when they are praised for correct behavior rather than when they are punished for bad behavior. Parents should keep in mind that children's thinking is less mature than adults' and should make sure the child clearly understands the rules. Expectations for a child's behavior should be kept well within developmental limits. Parents should model good behavior, which is a very effective method of behavioral control. Parents should also make sure they listen to their children and have an ongoing re-evaluation of the family rules. Consistency and support are two other principles of good parenting.

INFLUENCE OF SIBLINGS ON INDIVIDUAL GROWTH

A sibling's influence on a young child is complex. Recent research shows that the commonly accepted existence of sibling rivalry has come into question. The interactions and effects of siblings are multifaceted and tend to set the stage for later interpersonal relationships.

When a preschool child first meets a new infant sibling, some conflict and behavioral changes are bound to result. The first-born child is likely to imitate the behaviors of the infant in order to maintain or reattain the attention of the parents. Although some conflict frequently occurs, the mother's behavior toward the new infant is an important factor in the eventual response of the older sibling. If the mother encourages the older child to help care for the new baby and refers to the infant as a person rather than "the baby," then the older sibling tends to be more interested and affectionate toward the new child.

Other research has shown that siblings have a powerful yet complex influence on one another. Even siblings who get along well with one another tend to have episodes of conflict. This is likely the result of spending so much time together. Opposite-gender siblings tend to have stormier relationships than same-gender ones. In observing young (under age six) siblings, researchers have found that brothers and sisters get along better when the mother is absent than when she is with them. This suggests that much of the conflict between siblings is a bid for the parent's attention. In this preschool age group, older siblings can serve as effective teachers for their younger brothers and sisters. Older girls especially tend to be more patient and accepting of their younger siblings when they function as teachers.

Sibling relationships in nonindustrialized countries tend to be different yet equally important. Older siblings in non-Western nations take more of a role in raising their younger siblings, even when they themselves are still very young. Only children have frequently been described as self-centered, dependent on others, temperamental, and generally unlikable. Research, however, has shown that only children do not suffer any developmental disadvantages; rather they tend to resemble first-born children. Only and oldest children tend to be more intelligent and more achievement-oriented. A massive cultural study of only children is being undertaken in China, where 98 percent of all urban children between the ages of three and six have no siblings. This is the result of a vigorous government program to halt the rapid population growth. The typical Chinese four-year-old lives with four grandparents, two parents, and no siblings. The adults in the family tend to try to satisfy all the child's demands and give the child very little discipline. Although the research is incomplete, preliminary studies show that only children are not as well liked, are less persistent and less coopera- tive, and show fewer leadership qualities than children with siblings.

DEVELOPMENT OF PROSOCIAL BEHAVIOR

Prosocial behaviors, or altruism, are those actions that are intended to help or benefit another individual without expectation of reward. Such behaviors include helping someone in need, empathizing with someone, and sharing. Although older children tend to be more altruistic than younger children, prosocial behavior begins very early in development. By the age of two, it is not unusual for a toddler to offer hugs or toys to a suffering playmate. Although prosocial behaviors occur in the preschool years, they are outnumbered by selfish and aggressive behaviors. Children of this age are more likely to help adults than their peers. Preschoolers are capable of showing helping behaviors at this age; they very often just don't.

Studies examining factors influencing altruism have found that socio-economic status and sex make no difference in the number of helping behaviors preschoolers exhibit. Factors that do have an effect on altruism include chronological age and stage of mental reasoning. The older the child and the more advanced he or she is in mental reasoning, the more likely it is that the child will exhibit altruistic behaviors. Also, the parents of these children tend to sit down with them and discuss the implications of their actions. Such parents model helping behaviors for their children. Prosocial parents expect their children to uphold high moral standards and encourage their children to help others. In addition, prosocial parents encourage their children to watch prosocial television programs (e.g., "Sesame Street") and discourage them from watching programs with aggressive content. Proso-cial children are encouraged to engage in altruistic behaviors by prosocial parents who act altruistically themselves.

SEX ROLES AND STEREOTYPES

General Characteristics

During the preschool years a child begins to understand gender and sex roles. Most two-year-olds have some idea of the differences between sexes and some understanding of their own sexual identity. By age three, children are able to consistently and correctly apply gender labels to other people and to enact sex-typed roles. Around age four, preschoolers have definite opinions about which activities and toys are appropriate for which sexes and have little trouble expressing this to their peers.

Research has shown that, although many differences exist between children, few of these are due to differences between the sexes, and even these differences are small. Boys tend to be somewhat more aggressive in early childhood. Girls appear to be more responsive to babies and younger children. Boys play more boisterously, fight more, and tend to try to dominate other children. Girls tend to be more cooperative with their parents and boys to be more challenging. These overall differences are minimal, making boys and girls generally more alike than different.

Two other terms are frequently used to help clarify the origins of the gender differences between children. *Sex roles* are those attitudes and behaviors that the culture dictates are necessary and appropriate for each sex. In Western culture, men have been viewed traditionally as strong, active, competitive, and dominant. Women's roles include nurturing, mothering, compliance, and relative physical weakness compared with men. Although such sex-role stereotypes are crumbling, they are still being communicated to young children. Through the process of *sex-typing*, preschool girls learn they are supposed to play with dolls and that boys are supposed to play with trucks. Sex-typing enhances and adds to real sex differences and results in gender-identity in the five-year-old.

Origin of Sex Differences

BIOLOGY

Biology has a strong influence on and sets the stage for any environmental expression of gender- or sex-role behaviors. Hormonal influences early in gestation determine the formation of the sexual organs but also can affect the behavior of adult animals. Studies have shown testosterone to cause increased aggression in adult animals and prolactin to cause maternal behavior in virgin or male animals. Male brain hemispheres appear to be more specialized than female brains, which are more flexible in their functions.

ENVIRONMENTAL INFLUENCES

Environment appears to be the strongest influence on gender expression. The roles of males and females vary from culture to culture. Different societies are dominated by different sexes, and what might seem strange as female behavior in one culture is the norm in another. Parents tend to treat their children differently depending on their sex. In Western cultures, parents focus more on and expect more from their male children. Females tend to be more protected and have more latitude to experiment with cross-sex behaviors: it is culturally easier for a woman to become an engineer than for a man to stay at home with the children. Television and other media promote these cultural sex-role differences. Women should be beautiful and men should be tough, television commercials say. Research has found that children who watch a lot of television develop more traditional sex-role stereotypes than children who watch less. Children absorb the sex-role characterizations presented in the environment and base their own sexual and interpersonal activities on them.

Theories to Explain Sex Roles and Stereotypes

PSYCHOANALYTIC (SIGMUND FREUD)

According to Freud, between the ages of three and seven a little boy enters the phallic stage. During this time he begins to notice the importance of his penis, to masturbate, and to have sexual feelings about his mother. Because of the jealousy these feelings arouse, the little boy fantasizes about killing his father due to jealousy, and then feels guilty for such thoughts. The little boy also fears that his father will castrate him if he ever learns about such taboo thoughts. This phenomenon is know as the Oedipus Complex. The little boy learns to cope with his guilt and fear through the defense mechanism of identification. The boy strives to become like his father (identification) by adopting his masculinity, moral values, and other attributes. In this way the forbidden impulses of a little boy's id are controlled by the growth of his superego.

Freud postulated that the phallic stage also occurs in little girls, but with a slightly different twist. The little girl becomes envious of males because they have a penis and she does not (penis envy). The girl blames her mother for the lack of this important body part. She also feels a sexual attraction for her father because he has a penis and wants to kill her mother to win her father (i.e., Electra Complex). Freud thought girls are less likely to resolve the complex because they have no fear of being castrated; thus the little girl is less likely to fully accept her gender role by identifying with her mother.

LEARNING AND MODELING

Learning theorists, on the other hand, propose that all sexual behavior is learned and that the environment is responsible for shaping gender-stereotyped behaviors. Not all the research supports such a proposition. Some research findings conclude that fathers tend to play rougher with boys than with girls and that they are more insistent than mothers in feminine and masculine sex-role expectations. Teachers, parents, and peers are more likely to reward sex-appropriate behavior in preschool age groups, and boys are more likely to be criticized for playing with sex-inappropriate toys. Parents tend to demand independence from their boys and come to the aid of their girls more quickly. Parents also tend to allow their boys more freedom than their girls. Female preschoolers are more flexible in their gender-behavior than boys. It is more acceptable for girls to play with trucks and climb trees than for boys to play with dolls and apply makeup.

Social-learning theorists use the concepts of modeling and imitation to explain gender-role acquisition. Little girls tend to act like their mothers and other female role models. Little boys imitate Dad and older brothers. Sex-role stereotypes are reinforced by the fact that only women can have children and breast-feed. Thus when a woman becomes pregnant and has a child it is more likely that she will stay home and take care of the child in a stereotypically female role. If she does work outside the home, it is likely that a woman will still have primary responsibility for child care. Although a woman may verbally espouse role equality, practicality and biology may necessitate a more traditional female role that she will, in turn, model to her children.

COGNITIVE THEORY

Cognitive developmental and gender schema theories emphasize the influence of internal rather than external forces on gender role. According to cognitive developmental theory, preschoolers believe that sex differences depend on a person's appearance and dress rather than biology. Thus a preschooler believes that if boys wore dresses they could be mommies, too. Around age four or five, children begin to attain a sense of gender constancy; that is, each person is permanently male or permanently female. At this point the child begins to actively search the environment for information about how boys and girls behave.

Research shows that even prior to age four, children exhibit sex-typed behaviors and many have an elaborate understanding of sex roles long before their awareness of gender constancy has developed.

Another cognitive theory holds that gender constancy is unnecessary in developing sex-role typing. All that is necessary is a rudimentary understanding of the category or schema of male and female. This schema, or organized body of knowledge, helps children interpret environmental information and influences their subsequent reactions. Once the child forms this gender structure, he or she can select what is appropriate for his or her sex and incorporate it. For example, part of the gender schema for males is strength which is not included in the female schema. Nurturing generally is not part of the male schema, while it is a central part of the female schema. Such a concept helps explain how children will maintain their gender-role stereotypes in spite of receiving some contrary information. These schemata will cause children to distort contrary information in order to fit the schema. Thus preschoolers will view a photograph of a white-coated male and female and label the male as a doctor and the female as a nurse in spite of contrary information.

Self-concept (the individual's self-portrait) formation is an important aspect of the preschooler's development. Erikson describes the crisis at this stage as one of initiative vs. guilt. A child begins to take initiative in accomplishing things while also experiencing guilt caused by failure or criticism. Learning theorists see self-concept as developing from societal punishments and reinforcements. Cognitive theory holds that a child develops a psychological understanding of himself or herself through self-perceptions and a rudimentary self-knowledge.

Play helps young children learn about their social world. Through play they develop friendships and relationships, learn social rules, and develop creativity. Six types of play are recognized in this age group: unoccupied, solitary, onlooker, parallel, associative, and cooperative. Primate studies support the conclusion that play is important to children's development. Primates who were socially isolated were more aggressive and were unable to give or receive affection.

Parenting styles, punishment, and siblings have a great influence on the social development of children in this age group. Three general parenting styles have been postulated: authoritarian, authoritative, and permissive. Studies have shown that children of authoritative parents tend to be more contented, self-reliant, and achievement-oriented than children of parents with other styles of parenting. The studies of parental punishment show that spanking tends to result in aggressive children and the best form of discipline is to intervene in the misbehavior as quickly as possible and to use a very mild form of punishment, such as taking away a privilege. The influence of siblings on social behavior is complex and poorly investigated.

Prosocial behavior in children is encouraged by exposure to parents acting in prosocial ways and by viewing prosocial television such as "Sesame Street." Prosocial behavior also tends to increase with the age and stage of mental reasoning.

Finally, it is during the preschool years that children begin to gain an understanding of gender and sex roles. Freud proposed that boys and girls go through a phallic stage during which they give up their sexual attraction for the opposite-sex parent and identify with the same-sex parent. Cognitive theorists describe how children gain an understanding of gender; gender constancy occurs around age five. Learning theorists propose that children receive reinforcement for acting in accordance with the cultural sex roles. Overall, sex role development is influenced by both biology and environment.

Selected Readings

Abranovitch, P. R. R., and C. Corter. (1982). *Sibling relationships*. Hillsdale, NJ: Erlbaum.

Baumrind, D. (1967). Child-care practices anteceding three patterns of preschool behavior. *Genetic psychology monographs (75)*.

Bem, S. L. (1981). Gender schema theory: A cognitive account of sex typing. *Psychological Review (88)*.

Erikson, E. H. (1963). *Childhood and society*. NY: Norton.

Garvey, C. (1977). *Play*. Cambridge, MA.: Harvard University Press.

Mussen, P. H. (1983). *Handbook of child psychology. Vol. 4, Socialization, personality and social development*. New York: Wiley.

Overton, W. F. (1982). *The relationship between social and cognitive development*. Hillsdale, NJ: Erlbaum.

Parten, M. B. (1932). Social participation among preschool children. *Journal of abnormal and social psychology (27)*.

14

The Preschool Years: Special Issues

The preschool years are a period of transition from infancy to elementary school age. During this time children undergo a variety of changes affecting all three domains (physical, cognitive, and psychosocial). This chapter discusses sleep-related behaviors as they pertain to the preschooler's changing abilities to cope with emotional stresses, the influence of toys on children's motor development and cognitive functioning is also discussed.

This chapter addresses sex-role and gender issues. Since many sex-role behaviors and gender characteristics are learned in the preschool years, many researchers now suggest teaching and modeling a combination of both types of gender behaviors for children (i.e., androgyny). One major influence on gender identity learning as well as on other physical, cognitive, and social functioning is television. The pros and cons of extended television viewing are reviewed.

Finally, the value of preschool intervention or education at this age is covered, with a close look at the Head Start program.

SLEEP BEHAVIORS

Children in this age group display unique sleep rituals and patterns. The older the child within this age group, the longer the bedtime ritual. Normal behavior includes demanding that the light be left on, asking for a drink of water and one last "tuck in," and inquiring about noises in and outside the house. Preschoolers also tend to take a longer time falling asleep, frequently playing by themselves or with a sibling in their room. "Transitional" objects, such as a favorite blanket, stuffed animal or a soft toy, frequently help children fall asleep. Dependence or clinging to such an object may cause parents some concern, but research shows that children who have favorite objects during this age tend to be outgoing and well-adjusted as teenagers and adults.

Some other sleep-related behaviors signify significant and persistent problems as well as underlying emotional issues. "Night terrors" occur without awakening the child while he or she is in a very deep sleep. These children show autonomic arousal (sweating and rapid heart rate). They scream, appear fearful, and are unable to be awakened. When asked about the incidents in the morning, the children don't remember them. Although this can be a frightening experience for parents, night terrors usually go away by themselves with no residual affects. The causes may vary from underlying emotional problems to a physiological condition.

Other sleep problems include struggles (e.g., tantrums) at bedtime, nightmares, sleep walking and talking, as well as bedtime fears (e.g., of bogeymen in the closet). During this age, many children have problems going to sleep, frequently arousing their parents during the night. The majority of children with these problems are experiencing some significant family stressors and may attempt to share their parents' bed. While many children have nightmares, having them frequently indicates a significant amount of stress. Sleep walking and talking occur occasionally, but few children do them frequently or pose any danger to themselves. Finally, nighttime fears (fear of the dark or of monsters) are also experienced by many children but are no cause for alarm unless they are prolonged and debilitating.

TOYS GEARED TO MOTOR DEVELOPMENT OF THE CHILD

During the preschool years, a child's small and large muscles develop and grow. Activities are more demanding, and overall muscle growth and coordination related to these activities develop the child's self-confidence. When children are between two and three years old large muscles develop rapidly, and toys should be chosen to encourage such development. Two- and three year olds can play with wheeled toys, usually ones they can push, because the child can see the toy while it is in use. The second and third year of life is also an appropriate time for art materials and activities such as painting, working with clay, and drawing with crayons and pencils. Children's work is crude during this period as they begin experimenting with large movements using crayons. During the third year, construction toys (such as blocks or small boxes) become interesting because of the many ways children can be creative with them. Around age four the small muscles begin to develop, and toys should be chosen to encourage related new skills. Four-year-olds can string beads and perform more complex, small muscle tasks. Large muscles are also still developing, so children may start riding bicycles and playing team sports like tee-ball and softball.

While they are helping their children develop muscle groups and motor coordination, parents should remember that children do not develop at the same rate even if they are the same age and that if a child is successful in one area of motor skill development, this does not ensure success in another area. Patience and encouragement, no matter what a child's accomplishments, help children develop their self-esteem and self-concept.

ANDROGYNY VS. NORMAL SEX-ROLE DEVELOPMENT

Sometime between the ages of one and a half to three years, children develop a simple gender identity. During this time they learn to label males and females, or girls and boys. Sometime later they learn that gender does not change over time, and by age six children generally understand that gender is constant, regardless of changes in clothing or activities. By age two the preschool child tends to select toys and activities that fit his or her sex stereotype. Gender identity begins in early childhood, persisting and strengthening throughout the rest of childhood and adolescence.

The concept of androgyny was introduced in the early 1970s as an alternative to sex-role stereotyping. A child is androgynous if he or she combines female and male psychological qualities. This concept was introduced by Sandra Bem. She maintained that the most psychologically healthy person is one whose personality traits include balanced combinations of the most positive characteristics that are typically associated with each sex. She felt that sex-role stereotyping restricts people in their functioning, even in simple everyday behaviors. The androgynous person is one who is assertive, sensitive, nurturing, dominant, affectionate, and self-sufficient (a combination of traditional male and female qualities).

It is has been shown that androgynous individuals deal more effectively with their surroundings. They score higher in measures of self-esteem and behavioral flexibility. They score lower in some issues of anxiety. Parents scoring high in androgynous traits tend to spend more time with their children. Although there is a significant body of research to support the idea that androgyny is a more positive orientation in raising children, it has been criticized.

Several researchers contend, however, that the presence of masculine traits, such as assertiveness, dominance, and independence, is responsible for the superior performance of androgynous women in traditionally male-oriented occupations. Other studies of parents who followed the traditional male and female roles found that they tended to be more child-centered in their childrearing practices. Another researcher contends that traditional parental roles may help families cope with the complex tasks of parenting more efficiently. Sandra Bem admits gender-difference concepts can help children organize their perceptions of adults and the adult world.

Overall, it would be worthwhile for parents to notice the sexual stereotypes they promote. Common statements such as "boys don't cry" and "girls don't fight" discourage children from using a variety of behaviors when appropriate. Because our roles tend to be sexually stereotyped within our society, it may be particularly important to encourage girls to be more assertive and independent and boys to experience and practice nurturing and sensitivity. Such encouragement should be provided in an environment in which children of both sexes can choose from the greatest possible range of behaviors and roles.

INFLUENCE OF TELEVISION

Television is a major influence on the physical, cognitive, and psychosocial development of today's preschoolers. Prolonged television viewing obviously reduces the amount of time a child spends in physical activity. Given that the usually high level of activity at this age range removes the baby fat of infancy and toddlerhood, reducing the activity level would be expected to slow the child's fat loss. Generally speaking, a child's weight increases about 2 percent for every hour of television regularly watched. This occurs primarily because the reduced activity is not coupled with reduced caloric consumption. Children snack on foods that are usually high in fat content, such as potato chips. Thus the side effects of regular television viewing include not only reduced activity levels but also nutritional and weight problems.

Educational Television

One contemporary influence on preschoolers is educational television. The most well known educational program for this age group is "Sesame Street." Researchers have found varying influences of educational programs such as "Sesame Street," whose goal is to improve special cognitive skills, such as the ability to solve problems, to recognize and use letters and numbers; and to understand one's physical and social environment. Overall, children tend to show some improvement in these skills after watching educational television programs. Three-year-olds tend to improve more dramatically than five-year-olds, and low socioeconomic children show gains similar to those of more advantaged children who watch such programs as often. Children who are introduced to a learning regimen such as "Sesame Street" tend to have an improved attitude toward school compared with children who watch this kind of programing less. Finally, one study has shown that where one would expect television to encourage development of the imagination, children who watch a large amount of television tend to engage in less imaginative play. A possible explanation for this is that these children become used to passively accepting the images and ideas presented on television rather than generating their own.

Disadvantages of Television Viewing

Television also has an effect on the social behavior of young children. "Sesame Street" has been criticized for sexual stereotyping when it portrays women as passive. "Mr. Roger's Neighborhood" and "Here's Humphrey" (a similar Australian television program) have been shown to increase social behaviors in preschool children. Overall, the viewing of violent television programs has been consistently associated with aggression in children. Other research has found that children who view an increased amount of television that includes action, violence, and dramas tend to see the world as a frightening, threatening place. In this case, television may function to make children less trusting of others in the world. This finding has been supported by the documentation of the effect of television viewing on a small town in Canada in the early 1970s. Prior to 1973, this Canadian town had no television. After two years of television viewing, children showed poorer reading skills, lower scores on tests of creative thinking, more aggressive behavior, and more rigid sex stereotyping. Although one can't conclude that television violence causes aggressive behavior in children, viewing such violence on television has been strongly linked to increased violence in at least some groups of children.

Prosocial and Other Positive Effects

On the other hand, a number of studies have also shown that prosocial television viewing is associated with prosocial behavior in young children. "Sesame Street" has been instrumental in promoting positive social interchanges between children and adults of different ethnic backgrounds on TV.

Because preschool children spend a significant amount of time in front of the television set (up to five hours a day), many researchers have suggested similar approaches to ensure that this important influence on children affects them positively rather than negatively. Aside from sending letters to networks and sponsors, experts in this area suggest a number of things that parents can do to minimize the negative impact and maximize the positive impact of television: (1) watch television with the children and discuss the programs; (2) plan the programs children can watch rather than allowing random viewing; (3) make sure television is not used as a babysitter or as a substitute for other activities; (4) make sure the children have a balance among reading, television, and other activities; (5) discuss sexual stereotypes, role models, and prosocial behaviors with children when these occur on television; and (6) call attention to negative and violent behavior, discussing how parents feel about them.

VALUE OF PRESCHOOL EDUCATION

Over the last two decades, the number of children in preschool has dramatically increased. In the early 1970s, approximately 15 percent of three- and four-year-old children were attending nursery school. By the late 1980s almost half of all four-year-olds in the United States attended some sort of nursery school program.

The types of exposure to early learning varies widely. Traditional nursery schools place an emphasis on improving emotional and psychosocial development. The programs in this type of school tend to be flexible, varying from music to academic subjects, such as learning to read letters, to exercises in self-discovery. Montessori schools have also grown popular in the last two decades. This type of preschool program lays the groundwork for reading and writing by emphasizing the importance of the senses. Other types of programs are based on theories such as Piaget's, which stress play as an important part of the learning process.

Head Start

In 1965 the federal government began a compensatory preschool program called Project Head Start. This program was designed to provide health care, intellectual enrichment, and a supportive learning environment to the children in families of low socioeconomic status. Its aim was to improve their intellectual and social competence. The parents of these children were unemployed, absent or employed in low-paying jobs. Children from these backgrounds tended to do poorly in school, to be at higher risk of being held back, and eventually to drop out of school. IQs ranged from 15 to 20 points below that of the average middle-class child. During the first summer of Head Start in 1965, over 500,000 children were enrolled. This program has been scrutinized by legislators, educators, and researchers hoping to find beneficial effects of such early enrichment programs.

During the early years of Head Start, participants showed consistent gains in IQ, school readiness skills (understanding letters and numbers), and vocabulary. Children with the lowest initial starting skills tended to benefit most from the program. The IQs of preschool children shot up over 10 points within the first year. However, these initial dramatically positive results were somewhat tempered by a gradual decline in IQ and performance if the children entered regular school and did not receive the enrichment program anymore.

Although the research methodology for the Head Start study has been somewhat defective (lack of appropriate control groups and the grouping together of nonsimilar programs), it seems clear that Head Start children perform better in school and have fewer scholastic problems compared with similar children who did not attend a Head Start program. Disadvantaged children exposed to Head Start do not perform as well as average middle-class children, but they tend to do better overall when compared with their socioeconomic peer groups who did not attend Head Start programs.

The initial effects appear to last even into high school. Those children who had participated in Head Start preschool programs tended to complete high school more frequently and were more likely to have jobs after high school when compared with similarly disadvantaged peers. Although the female students who had received Head Start training became pregnant as frequently as non-Head Start female students, the Head Start students tended to return more often to school after having their babies.

Some long-term studies of broader scope have shown positive effects of compensatory preschool education programs such as Head Start. At age nineteen individuals who received a compensatory preschool education were much more likely to have graduated from high school, to have a job, and to be enrolled in college or vocational training. They were less likely to have been arrested and to have been classified as slow learners in high school. Head Start also gave the parents of disadvantaged youngsters an opportunity to become involved in the process. This appeared to be quite beneficial for each child: the more actively involved the parents were, the better each child performed on achievement tests.

The sleeping behaviors of preschool age children usually include a variety of rituals, many of which may inconvenience the parents of the older preschooler because of the extra time the child needs to drop off to sleep. Some sleep behaviors can indicate emotional problems, especially if the child is exposed to increased environmental stress and has difficulty coping.

Toys are important to children during these years, so care should be taken to ensure that they are appropriate. Basically, toys that encourage motor skill development as well as imaginative and creative play are probably best.

Children in this age range develop strong concepts of gender identity (i.e., what "male" and "female" mean). However, teaching children a mixture of qualities from both genders has strong support because it may allow the individual to be more flexible as an adult.

Television and formal early education strongly influence children at this age. Regular, unsupervised television viewing seems to have detrimental physical, cognitive, and psychosocial influences on the development of children: children have more weight and nutritional problems while being less active; they tend to be less creative and imaginative; and their social interactions diminish. Formal education experiences, on the other hand, appear to help children's development, especially programs for environmentally disadvantaged children, such as Head Start.

Selected Readings

Achenbach, T. M. (1982). *Developmental psychopathology.* NY: Wiley.

Bem, S. L. (1985). *Nebraska symposium on motivation 1984: Psychology and gender.* Lincoln: University of Nebraska.

Crow, L. D., W. I. Murray, and H. H. Smythe. (1966). *Educating the culturally disadvantaged child.* NY: McKay.

Evans, E. D. (1975). *Contemporary influences in early childhood education.* 2d ed. NY: Holt.

Lee, V. E., J. Brooks-Gunn, and E. Schnur. (1988). Does Headstart work? *Developmental psychology, 22.*

Liebert, R. M., J. M. Neale, and E. S. Davidson. (1973). *The early window: Effects of television on children and youth.* NY: Pergamon Press.

Murray, J. P. (1980). *Television and youth: 25 years of research and controversy.* Stanford, CA: Boys Town Center for the Study of Youth Development.

15

The Elementary
School Years:
Physical Development

Physical development during the elementary school years is less erratic and less turbulent than that of early childhood or puberty (adolescence). Essentially, growth during these years can be considered slow and steady. Physical skills improve over time and are strongly influenced by cultural values. Sex differences in physical abilities and physique are small. Children spend time practicing skills that will be perfected in adulthood. Nutrition is an important issue in both physical development and self-esteem.

SIZE AND SHAPE

During middle childhood, children's growth slows to a gain of about 5 pounds (2¼ kilograms) and 2½ inches (6 centimeters) per year. School-age children are much taller and thinner than preschoolers. Girls have more fatty tissue than boys, and black children tend to be slightly larger than white children. Both sexes are of about equal weight at about 8½ years of age. At age 9 or 10, girls start to gain weight and remain heavier than boys, on the average, until age 14. At age 10 the average boy weighs 69 pounds (31 kilograms) and the average girl weighs 72 pounds (33 kilograms). There are significant deviations from these average figures.

Variations in Physique

The sizes and shapes of individual children vary widely during the school-age years. Nonwhite boys and girls tend to be somewhat larger than white children of the same age and sex. Children from more wealthy homes tend to be taller, heavier, and more mature than children coming from less wealthy backgrounds. This variation is due to nutritional differences. Low nutrition or malnutrition hinders growth and does not allow the child to become as tall and heavy as his or her genes would allow. Overweight children mature the fastest of all, with obese girls experiencing menarche (first menstruation) earlier than their average-weight classmates. Ethnicity (representing a different genetic pool) also has a significant effect on the ultimate size of children. Worldwide, the shortest children come from Southeast Asia and South America and the tallest from the United States, eastern Australia, and north central Europe. In summary, genetics or nutrition or the interaction between them is responsible for variations in size within this age group.

Children's Age and Eruption of Teeth

Children are endowed with twenty baby teeth, also known as deciduous teeth. At about age 6, the child's first molars erupt. Second molars follow at about age 13, and the third molars (wisdom teeth) usually erupt in the early twenties. Children generally start shedding their deciduous teeth around age 6 at the rate of about four per year for the next five years. The last of the baby teeth (the canines, or "eye-teeth") fall out at around age 12. The gaps left in the mouth from the loss of these baby teeth can cause some difficulties in pronunciation along with cosmetic problems.

At age 5, children have an average of four decayed or filled surfaces in their deciduous teeth. Boys, in general, have fewer cavities than girls, and white children tend to have more cavities than nonwhite children, probably because of dietary differences such as the increased eating of candy. Many parents tend to ignore dental care for their children's baby teeth because they will "fall out anyway"; however, the premature loss of deciduous teeth can lead to later dental problems. Good nutrition is very important during these years in order to ensure the healthy formation of both the teeth and mouth. With the emphasis in recent years on better nutrition, careful tooth brushing, good dental care, and the use of fluoride supplements, children have fewer cavities. Thirty-seven percent of all children age 5 to 17 have no tooth decay at all.

This is the age range when children develop a fear of the dentist. During the preschool years, children tend to have no problems about visiting the dentist; the reluctance in the elementary school years probably has little to do with personal experience. More likely, this fear comes from modeling and social referencing of adult behaviors with regard to dental visits. That is, over time children copy the fears they have seen adults manifest.

MOTOR SKILLS

During the elementary school years, children become more skilled at controlling their bodies and can perform many adult motor skills. The skills honed during this age range include jumping, catching, cycling, climbing, becoming better coordinated, balancing, and hopping. Generally, children's skills are modified and refined through a combination of heredity and environment. That is, maturation is still responsible for the presence of new skills (remember the principle of motor primacy), and practice is now responsible for the successful coordination and improvement of those skills.

Gender Differences

Although it is generally assumed that boys' athletic abilities and strength are superior to girl's, recent studies show that much of the difference between sexes regarding motor ability is due to different rates of participation in sports as well as different cultural and family expectations. Researchers studying elementary school girls and boys taking part in similar activities have found that they exhibit similar physical abilities and skills. With age, both sexes improve in activities such as sit-ups, fast running, broad jumps, and walking. Prior to puberty, there is no reason to separate boys and girls for physical activities. However, after puberty, the boys develop heavier and larger frames, which make them more powerful in collision sports such as football. A few early studies have shown that boys tend to run faster and throw farther than girls. Two minor differences between the sexes before puberty appear to be that boys have greater forearm strength and girls greater overall flexibility. This may give girls the edge in sports such as gymnastics, and boys may be superior in sports that utilize forearm strength, such as baseball.

Another important factor in physical activities is reaction time, which is significantly influenced by brain maturation. Reaction time is the length of time it takes an individual to respond to a stimulus. Older children have a significant advantage over younger children in sports in which reaction time is the crucial ingredient. However, older children are at a disadvantage compared with adults, who have the shortest reaction times. Motor ability and coordination also improve with age, as does running speed, jumping ability, throwing accuracy, throwing distance, and balance. Girls tend to learn to skip sooner than boys, but boys can jump farther and higher than girls.

Interestingly, a recent study has found that girls' greater amount of fat tissue may account for a significant amount of the differences between girls' and boys' performances on physical tests such as sit-ups, timed runs, and the standing broad jump. In comparisons of obese girls and boys, extra fat hindered both boys and girls to the same degree. Other factors that tend to have an effect on girls' poorer performance in Western culture include a fear of appearing too masculine, too strong, or of injuring female internal organs, a lack of environmental/school/parental reinforcement for sports participation, and a lack of overall motivation.

Effects of Practice on Motor Skill Development

Many adult sports are not ideal for children because they require fast reaction time, power or judgment of speed. However, physical activity is very beneficial for children, since it helps them improve their rapidly developing motor skills and their sense of balance as well as increase their self-confidence. Appropriate physical activities for those in the school years are running, jumping, catching, cycling, and climbing.

Another important influence on games and the development of physical ability is the reluctance of middle school-aged girls to compete with boys. Many times in mixed-sex games like dodge ball, the girls let the boys win. This occurs although some of the girls independently were rated as having much higher game skills than a significant number of the boys. These results were noted in African-American children in a Midwestern city and also in Hopi Indian children from a reservation in Arizona. Girls become much less competitive when playing against boys as compared to playing with other girls. Such indicators have also been found in adolescence, when girls are apt to be unwilling to compete against boys. This gives the appearance that girls' games and physical skills are inferior to those of boys.

Handedness

Ten percent of the population is left-handed. This varies in some societies. People in Islamic societies use the left to wash the private areas, and it is considered an offense against decency to use this same hand to write or serve food. Some Japanese parents attempt to force their children to use the right hand, going to such extremes as binding the left hand with tape in order to restrict its use as the dominant hand. Even in Western culture, children who favor the left hands are sometimes actively encouraged to use the right hand instead. Signs of hand preference appear in early infancy; this preference becomes distinct by age five. It is in the beginning of the school years, when a child enters school, that left-handedness becomes distinctive, for better or worse. In the school years, left-handed children may be discriminated against because of the lack of school materials appropriate for left-handed children. On the other hand, left-handedness in young athletes may be encouraged because the way they throw or catch a ball may confuse the opposing team.

HEALTH AND ILLNESS

Many diseases show up during the school years: mumps, measles, chicken pox, rubella, scarlet fever, chronic ear infections, and so on. Many of these illnesses have become less common through the use of antibiotics or even been prevented through immunizations. Although the common cold is widespread, middle school-aged children get fewer colds than preschoolers. Bedwetting dramatically decreases. The most frequent cause of childhood deaths is accidents, especially car accidents.

Physical fitness has numerous benefits for school-aged children. Increased physical activity encourages normal growth and bone development. Children who are physically fit have higher self-esteem than children low in fitness. Exercise can be entertaining, and it encourages socialization among children. Academic performance improves. Children become more resistant to stress, appear happier, and have an improved attitude toward schoolwork when physical activity is part of the everyday routine.

Nutrition has an important role in the physical and mental development of children. Foods high in fats, salts, sugar, and preservatives account for about one-third of the average child's total caloric intake. The number of hours children watch television correlates positively with the amount of snack foods children consume and with how overweight they are. Poor nutrition contributes to a slower rate of growth, and malnourished children are shorter and less healthy than their well-nourished classmates. Malnourished infants have been shown to grow up to be more passive, more dependent, and more anxious than other children. A study from Guatemala postulates that if an infant is malnourished and lacks the energy to engage its mother's attention, this infant develops poor interpersonal skills and a pattern of passive sociability. As the malnourished child grows, his or her self-esteem suffers along with physical development. Malnutrition appears to hinder growth as well as personality development.

School-age children show distinctive growth and activity patterns; however, the rate of growth during this time is slower than that during infancy and adolescence. Girls are generally heavier than boys and have more fat tissue. A child's size varies significantly according to nutritional quality of her or his diet. Genetics also plays a role in size, with the shortest children coming from Southeast Asia and South America, and the tallest from the United States, eastern Australia, and North Central Europe.

Deciduous teeth, begin falling out around age 6 and are generally gone by age 12. It is important to keep deciduous teeth healthy, because if these teeth are lost too early, then dental problems will be common in adulthood. Also, a fear of dentists will develop in this age range despite good dental visits during the preschool years. This fear may be the result of imitating adult fears about dentists.

Strength, physical ability, and performance in sports are significantly influenced by cultural edicts that girls are less physically skilled than boys. Also, in some cultures (Hopi Indian, African-American), girls become much less competitive when playing against boys compared with playing against other girls. Another strong factor in physical performance is the amount of fat tissue the person has, regardless of his or her gender. Finally, self-esteem is significantly affected by physical fitness and good nutrition.

Selected Readings

Albinson, J. G., and G. M. Andrew. (1976). *Child in sport and physical activity.* Baltimore: University Park Press.

Eveleth, P. B., and J. M. Tanner. (1976). *Worldwide variation in human growth.* Cambridge, England: Cambridge University Press.

Gesell, A., L. B. Ames, and F. L. Ilg. (1977). *The child from five to ten.* NY: Harper & Row.

Lowery, G. H. (1986). *Growth and development of children.* 8th ed. Chicago: Year Book Medical Publishers.

Wolraich, M., and D. K. Routh. (1985). *Advances in developmental and behavioral pediatrics.* Greenwich, CT: JAI Press.

16

The Elementary School Years: Cognitive Development

Cognitive development during the elementary school years is marked by a reduction in the problems related to thinking found in the preschool era. Piaget described this stage as being similar to that of adulthood in that it involves an establishment of logical reasoning ability and the removal of egocentrism. The psychometric and information-processing approaches are important in describing the necessary underlying maturational processes that make the Piaget concepts possible.

Language development expands even more now that the child has the ability to read. As symbols of the changing cognitive abilities of the child, the child's understanding of jokes and the use of pragmatics clearly demonstrate through language the loss of egocentrism.

The school experience, finally, is the one that helps break the ties between a parent and child because much of the social and personal feedback that came from the home now can come from the teacher and peers. This chapter will cover some of the school experiences that most aid or inhibit the development of a child.

THEORETICAL APPROACHES

Piaget and Concrete Operational Stage

The concrete operational stage in Piaget's theory of cognitive development is so named because during this stage the child acquires and masters the "concrete" intellectual skills needed to be fully functional. At this point the child's brain has matured sufficiently, and he or she has had the environmental experiences needed to understand how the world works without making the cognitive errors that are ever present during the first two stages. In other words, the child can understand logically almost anything he or she perceives. To understand how far the child has come one need only note the directions for many board games that say: "For children eight and above." This means that the concrete operational child should be able to understand the rules by which the game is played, just as an adult would.

CHARACTERISTICS

The Five to Seven Shift. The preoperational stage does not automatically become the concrete operational stage overnight. There is a transition phase (usually between the ages of five and seven) during which the child functions with some preoperational factors and some concrete operational factors. For example, a six-year-old can watch his or her mother pour water from a one-gallon jug into a one-gallon pot. As a four-year-old, that child would not have understood the concept of conservation and would have assumed that there were different amounts of water in each container. An eight-year-old could tell you that the amounts of water were the same even though the containers were different and that the different visual components did not change the amount of liquid. The six-year-old would tell you that the amounts of water were the same but not know why.

Logical Operations. Fully concrete-operational children can view pictures of themselves as babies and know it is the same person. They are able to "decenter" or look at more than one aspect of an object or person. In the preoperational stage, this could not have happened because the children could see only one identity in a person. For example, they could not think of their mothers as their grandmothers' daughters at the same time. Now, however, it is possible for them to recognize more than one identity.

Reversibility is also possible now; a boy may have a sister and understand that the sister has a brother (the original boy). By such thinking, the boy has moved away from the original object and returned, a process the preoperational child could not do. This is similar to the principle of reciprocity: changes in one dimension can result in changes in another dimension. For instance, a 7-inch-by-6-inch rectangle has the same area as a 2-inch-by-21-inch rectangle. The preoperational child would assume that the later rectangle has more area because it looks longer.

Placing objects into different classifications is also possible now. A girl's sister, mother, and grandmother could be in the classifications of relatives, or family, or women all at the same time. The difference in classification abilities can be seen in the game "Twenty Questions." Here a child can ask only twenty questions in order to gather enough information to correctly identify some hidden object or identity. The preoperational child will most often ask "hypothesis" questions, that is, specific guesses as to the identity of the object. The concrete-operational child, on the other hand, will use a "constraint scanning" series of questions, that is, the majority of questions will whittle down the possible classifications the object could belong in.

Seriation. This child can now arrange objects or items in a series, such as biggest to smallest or tallest to shortest. The child understands the conceptual dimension underlying the arrangement and thus can arrange things from one direction to another (such as pencils from tallest to shortest), disarrange them, and then rearrange them in the reverse order (again using the concept of reversibility). This also indicates that the child is able to manipulate the dimension internally. The preoperational child could do the same task if only a few objects were involved but only through a trial-and-error method.

Mathematics. With seriation as a basis, mathematical principles can now be acquired and manipulated. Seriation allows an understanding of the number system and of the relationships between numbers. Reversibility allows this child to add to a starting number and then to subtract. Classification allows the child to comprehend mathematical processes: addition (more of something), subtraction (less of something), multiplication (numbers belong in more than one category), and division (numbers have logical relationships with each other). These same processes also work together to help children comprehend principles and logical relationships necessary for understanding science.

Loss of Egocentrism. With reciprocity, reversibility, conservation, and decentering comes the knowledge that other people and objects have different perspectives. For example, two people looking into the same house through two different windows will not see the same things the same way. The preoperational child would assume that each observer sees the same things he or she sees; the concrete-operational child realizes that each person's perspective is different. This is important because now the child can be aware of the different perspectives of another's personality. This can be most clearly seen in the area of jokes. For the preoperational child, a joke is anything that sounds silly. That child does not understand why people laugh at some jokes and not at others. The concrete-operational child understands not only the humor of the joke but also why it is funny to some people and not others, that is, the appropriateness of the joke to the audience.

PIAGET IN REVIEW

As with the sensorimotor and preoperational stages of Piagetian theory, the actual abilities or lack thereof are rarely in question. That is, there appears to be a shift from preoperational to concrete operational abilities that takes a period of years to fully complete. Also, the fully concrete-operational child does indeed appear to have all the abilities listed above enabling the child to think logically with an understanding of relationships outside of himself or herself. What appears to be in question is the state of the abilities across children at any particular age. Essentially, concrete operational abilities are very inconsistent between children. All eight-year-olds do not have the same capabilities in logical reasoning, for example. The reason may lie in differences in genetics or in children's environments or in some combination of the two.

It is clear that the elementary schooler approaches the world with a better sense of logic and a solid grasp of the progression of rational thought. This knowledge may occur because the loss of egocentrism makes the child a more active listener and learner. Because he or she realizes that others may have important perspectives, the concrete operational child pays attention to the thoughts, feelings, deductions, and experiences of others.

Psychometric

As mentioned previously (see chapters 8 and 12), the psychometric approaches to understanding cognitive development are much more individualistic because they look at the intellectual powers of children. These powers are usually measured as intelligence quotients (IQs). Children with higher IQs have more intelligence, as measured by intelligence tests, than children with lower IQs.

What we see now in terms of IQ is that it is more stable over time, less subject to variability, and a stronger predictor of future intelligence levels than at any time previously. The relationship between IQ scores late in elementary school years and adult IQ scores has run as high as +.80 for some researchers. This means that we can predict with considerable certainty the intelligence scores of adults by their intelligence scores as sixth graders.

It is at this stage that IQ scores can be most useful. They can be used to help predict school performance. Keeping in mind that performance is related to other variables as well (for example, a high IQ coupled with low motivation will probably result in poor performance), IQ scores can be used to predict current and future grades. That is, third graders with high IQ scores are likely to continue to do well in third grade and to do well in high school. In addition, IQ scores can be used to predict the number of years a child is likely to stay in school: a higher score is related to more years in school.

Intelligence tests are examples of what are known as aptitude tests; that is, they measure a child's potential. Aptitude tests (in the form of intelligence tests) are not achievement tests, or measures of what has been accomplished or learned in a particular area. The Iowa Tests of Basic Skills and the California Achievement Tests are two examples of achievement tests. They are designed to measure knowledge and weaknesses in specific areas like math, science, and reading. Presumably, then, the results can be used to correct deficiencies in a child's education.

Of importance in understanding aptitude and achievement tests, is knowing how to use the results. This relates to the discussion of self-concept. Specifically, school-age children are a great deal more self-critical because they compare themselves and their abilities with other children and their abilities. The preschooler does not do this as much because of the ego-centrism inherent in that age group. But with the loss of egocentrism, the school-age child is more aware of the differences between children. Hence, information on poor performance needs to be explained to the child so that he or she does not stop trying tasks he is unable to do at present.

Information Processing

As we saw in chapter 12, the information-processing abilities of the preschool child improved over the course of that age range. This stage is no different. Children in the elementary school years become better at selective attention, and are more able to distinguish the relevant from the irrelevant in any particular situation and then to keep their attention on the problem at hand until it is solved.

We also now see improvement in memory skills, especially in the storage and retrieval of information. For example, preschoolers use a "sink-in" type of memory strategy. If they look at items long enough, the items will basically "sink in" to their memory. It is a very inefficient approach to memorization. This explains how and why preschoolers have a difficult time remembering the associations between the sight and sound of letters of the alphabet. However, the school-aged child uses specific strategies for storage and remembering of information, e.g., mental or vocal stimulation.

We also see an increase in the memory capacity of school-age children over the preschooler. Children in this age group can hold and process more information in their "working" memory, where thinking actually occurs. This means that a child is able to process more information about a problem or object, enabling him or her to comprehend reversibility and reciprocity. This memory expansion may not actually be a physical increase but rather an improvement in strategies that perhaps operate involuntarily. The child needs to spend less time organizing how to attack a problem and can simply go ahead and attack it. In like fashion, the changes or improvements in the information-processing capabilities occur concurrently with an improvement in preoperational thinking. As the child is able to handle more and different information, the child also decenters (becomes less egocentric) and grasps the concepts of conservation and classification.

One aspect of the information-processing approach puts the Piagetian approach into question: the application of knowledge. Basically, more specific knowledge about a topic appears to make thinking about the topic more efficient. Better memory skills seem to follow. That is, differences between an adult's and a schoolchild's memory may be related more to the adult's increased amount of knowledge of the area. In experiments where schoolchildren had more expertise on a given topic, they showed better memorization and learning skills than novice adults in the same area.

In summary, the information-processing abilities of the school-age child are equivalent to those of an adult by the end of this period. Memory capacity, selective attention skills, and storage and retrieval strategies are all essentially equivalent. Differences that do exist are in the areas of knowledge (adults usually have more knowledge about any given topic), which influences speed and efficiency of learning and memorization, and in the amount of practice: the more practice a person has, the more automatically and efficiently the cognitive processes function. Therefore, adolescence can be viewed as a time for practicing the skills that became functional during the school-age years and that will be needed during the adult years.

LANGUAGE

General Vocabulary

The vocabulary of the school-age child continues to increase, especially after the child learns to read. Whereas new words became a part of the preschooler's vocabulary only as they were heard and memorized, the school-age child adds to that the ability to read new words, look up their definitions or discern the definitions from the usage in the text, and then utilize the word—all without having contact with the word in conversation. The ability to expand this vocabulary-learning process is probably directly related to the advances in the information-processing capabilities seen during this time. Likewise, words become less bound to context in terms of their meanings. Specifically, children decenter in their language usage, allowing classifications of words into more than one category. For example, a preschooler can describe an orange within its immediate context, that is, orange color, round, easy to peel, whereas the school-age child can describe the orange in terms of its classification ("fruit") or function ("source of vitamin C"). Finally, better cognitive functioning allows school-age children to differentiate between similar words like *tiny, small,* and *minuscule.*

Grammar

Children continue to learn about grammar throughout this period and are less prone to hold onto their mistakes. The preschooler regularly overregularizes and will continue to do so even if taught otherwise. The school-age child knows and uses correct grammar when asked, even if he or she does not speak grammatically among friends. He or she understands the figurative meanings of metaphors ("You eat like a pig"), the correct usage of comparatives, and the correct use of past tense (which corresponds with a knowledge of how to tell time). By the end of this period, school-age children will possess the fundamentals of correct grammar and lack only practice in using them.

Pragmatics

The ability to adjust one's speech to the listener (and his or her perspective) describes the concept of pragmatics. This ability is prevalent in the concrete operational child, largely because of the lack of egocentrism and the ability to decenter. Pragmatics, which was seen in rudimentary form in the preschooler and can be seen in expanded form in the school-age child, is a necessary prerequisite for clear communication between different peoples.

The best example of pragmatics is in the joke-telling abilities of children in this age group. The following joke was found to be funny by a preschooler: "How do you keep a dog from crossing the street?" "Put him in a barking lot." The preschooler retold the joke several times, yet did not understand why it was funny. That lack of knowledge was demonstrated by his telling the joke repeatedly using different animals in place of the dog. The preschooler did not understand the pun. A school-age child, however, would understand the joke and be able to retell it to others correctly.

Another example of pragmatics is in the use of code-switching, that is, changing from one form of speech to another depending on the audience. Within a classroom children often use an "elaborated" code with teachers (long sentences, correct syntax, and a large vocabulary) and a "restricted" code with their friends (limited vocabulary and syntax and more gestures). To a teacher, one student may describe someone else's clothes as "appropriate for the weather today" but to a friend the same clothes may be described as "right on."

The ability to code-switch may be of growing importance among immigrants within different cultures. For example, even though English is the dominant language within the school systems of the United States, many immigrant populations still use their restricted codes in order to maintain a sense of heritage and group affiliation.

CHILDREN IN SCHOOLS

For the first six years of life, a child's sense of fulfillment, self-esteem, morality, and values are influenced to the greatest extent by the child's strongest role models (parents) in the child's most consistently influential environment (home). However, with the beginning of school, the blossoming of different cognitive abilities and consistent affiliation and competition with one's peers, the earlier models and influences change. The importance of school as a force for physical, cognitive, and psychosocial change cannot be overemphasized. Testimony to that fact comes from Erik Erikson's theory of personality development, which ties the onset of the stage of industry versus inferiority to entrance into elementary school. For students in the United States that would correspond to the age of six. Elsewhere, that stage could start either earlier or later.

Teachers as Important Cognitive Influences

The influence of teachers is probably greatest during this period. At this time they take on a surrogate parenting role, becoming an imparter of values and morals in a new social context, as well as the first source of information relating to a child's sense of self-esteem outside the home. With even a moderate amount of courtesy and respect for each child and by treating all children as though they are indeed capable of accomplishing what they set out to do, teachers encourage cognitive stimulation and growth. This is why, years later, many people remember their elementary school teachers with respect and with fondness.

On the other hand, teachers also have the ability to make the school experience unbearable for children. Teachers may use self-fulfilling prophesies when interacting with their students. In one experiment, teachers were told at the beginning of the school year that one group of students had scored high on IQ tests and should therefore perform well in class ("high" group), that another group had scored low on the same test and therefore should perform poorly in class ("low" group), and that still another group had scored about average ("average" group). In reality, there were no significant IQ differences between the students in any of the groups at the beginning of the experiment, and all students had been chosen at random for group assignment (see chapter 2 for a further discussion on setting up experiments).

Six months later, the experimenters gave the same IQ tests to all the children and found that the "high" group showed significantly higher IQ scores than the "low" group, with the "average" group falling in between. In effect, the teachers had expected better performance from the "high" group and had given them more individual attention and access to a more personalized learning environment. The "low" group, on the other hand, was not expected to do well, so the teachers had spent less time with them—and it showed. They did poorly, a performance standard consistent with the teacher's expectations. In effect, the teachers inadvertently had treated the students according to their incorrect perceptions and expectations and the students lived either up or down to those expectations.

Effect of School Failure

The exuberant positive attitude with which the preschooler approaches all situations changes in the school-age child largely because of the changes in the cognitive skills that are being mastered. Since the child is decentering and is looking to others for information for evaluating self-esteem, the cost of failure is different than it was just a few short years ago. When the preschool child fails at a certain task, he or she will simply try again later and not take the loss as a measure of self-worth. However, the school-age child's failures inhibit attempts at mastering newly acquired skills.

Specifically, a past failure can influence a child to believe success is not possible, a condition known as *learned helplessness*. If failures are especially public so that the child is reminded of them repeatedly, then the learned helplessness may be even more devastating. Generally, older children and girls are more susceptible to this problem than any other subgroup, but no one in this age range is immune. This condition continues to build on itself unless the child receives help from parents and teachers on how to understand successes and failures—as reflections of effort or knowledge and not of competence or worth.

Creativity

Many positive experiences can also exist in the school environment. The opportunities for creative expression in art, music, physical activities, and classwork abound in school. Creative expression here refers to reorganization of the environment so that a new perspective becomes available and causes others to think or feel or experience in ways they did not previously. Schools provide many opportunities for creative expression, but the school is not the sole influence. A number of family influences encourage creativity: being unconcerned about what others think; treating children with respect and confidence; and allowing them to decide for themselves how they want to be creative.

*P*iaget observed that the attainment of concrete operational thought was not instantaneous; there is a transition period of at least two years. This stage of thinking, however, is distinctly different from the preoperational stage of the preschooler. The concrete-operational child has the ability to logically reason, understand the perspectives of others (even in social relationships), decenter, grasp the concepts of conservation and mathematics, and de-emphasize their egocentric view of the world. In essence, at the end of this period the child is similar to the adult in terms of logical thinking. The main differences between the two fall into the areas of knowledge and practice.

The psychometric approach is much more reliable now for predicting the IQ scores and performance of the school-age child. The reliability of IQ scores is also improved over what it was during the previous stages. The information-

processing approach outlines the simple attention and memory skills necessary for many of the suppositions and abilities outlined by Piaget.

Language skills blossom during this age to a large extent because the child now has the ability to read. Therefore, the child is not restricted to verbal communication in order to learn vocabulary, syntax, grammar, and the like. Language use demonstrates the child's taking the perspectives of others, as is evidenced by the child's ability to tell jokes, use pragmatics, and speak in elaborate or restricted codes.

Finally, a child's school experiences are important in reaffirming and reestablishing a sense of self-worth outside of the home. In that sense, the teacher takes on many roles, from surrogate parent to morality teacher. The teacher's perceptions and expectations greatly influence the performance of the elementary school-aged child. This occurs regardless of whether those expectations are positive or negative (an effect known as the self-fulfilling prophesy).

Selected Readings

Chomsky, N. (1969). *The acquisition of syntax in children from five to ten.* Cambridge, MA: MIT Press.

Damon, W. (1984). *Morality, moral behavior, and moral development.* NY: Wiley.

Gardner, H. (1982). *Art, mind and brain: A cognitive approach to creativity.* NY: Basic Books.

Gardner, W. I. (1977). *Learning and behavior characteristics of exceptional children and youth: A humanistic behavioral approach.* Boston: Allyn & Bacon.

Hirschi, T. (1969). *Causes of delinquency.* Berkeley, CA: University of California Press.

Kohlberg, L. (1981). *The philosophy of moral development.* NY: Harper & Row.

17

The Elementary School Years: Psychosocial Development

*C*hildren in elementary school undergo a period of latent personality development. They also expand their intellectual processing and self-control. The school years also mark the advent of peers and school as influences on emotional development.

Although the family is still the major influence, the child's social learning extends into other realms: the classroom, organized clubs, and peer social groups. Friendships become an integral part of his or her social world. All of this social interaction appears to generate higher rates of prosocial behavior. However, stress also is a by-product of many social interactions and therefore must be dealt with.

Self-esteem develops under these new influences, and ideas about sex roles and sexuality are solidified. The child's social world is expanding as influences beyond the family exert their impact.

PERSONALITY THEORIES

Psychoanalytic Theories

SIGMUND FREUD

Freud called the elementary school years "the latency period," a time of relative sexual calm between the stormy preschool years and turbulent adolescence. By this latency stage, according to Freud, the child has arrived at some resolution of the Oedipus or Electra conflict. Peer interactions tend to be exclusively with members of the same sex. Sexuality is hidden, and gender segregation of children becomes stronger. Freud explained this phenomenon by stating that children repress their feelings toward the opposite sex in order to resolve their Oedipal conflicts, and they stay away from the opposite sex in order not to reawaken these disturbing emotions.

Although Freud assumed that children during this stage were free of sexual feelings and generally directed their emphasis toward socializing with other children, many child development theorists disagree. That is, even though children in elementary school do not appear to be sexual, much latency-age sexuality seems to be hidden because the adult world does not approve of sexuality in children. During this time, however, children do engage in sex play and masturbation and question each other about sex. Bathroom and bosom humor is common. During this time also, children learn and are intrigued by four-letter words and obscene hand gestures.

ERIK ERIKSON

Erikson concurs somewhat with Freud and sees this period as a time of sexual and physical latency. The crisis Erikson postulates for this developmental period is "industry versus inferiority." By the time they reach this stage, children have generally developed a sense of trust, autonomy, and initiative. With the advent of the school years, children no longer are content to play; they begin to work. In primitive societies children at this age become industrious. They start to help their parents in the daily gathering of grain or with other necessary tasks. Many become responsible for younger siblings. In industrialized countries, children attend school and learn how to read and write.

The latency child's task is to develop the abilities society demands and to get approval for his or her actions through competence. Children now begin to form a positive self-concept and to develop self-esteem. They judge their performance by the performance of their peers. As youngsters master skills valued by their culture, they develop views of themselves as either competent or incompetent. If the child is unable to develop the expected skills, he or she will instead develop a basic sense of inferiority. If too much emphasis is placed on achievement, the child becomes a "workaholic."

COGNITIVE AND LEARNING THEORIES

Two other orientations attempt to explain the nature of children and the impact of society on them: cognitive and learning approaches. Cognitive theory explains that children begin to think more systematically during the school years. Vulnerability to the opinions of peers becomes an important factor in determining behavior. Also during this time they are more able to understand someone else's point of view; that is, egocentrism is reduced.

Learning theory postulates that children become more able to control themselves and increase their ability to learn. They do this by getting a better understanding of cause-effect relationships. Intrinsic motivation becomes important; children complete tasks because the task or process has inherent reinforcement. For example, a child may take pride in completing a science project regardless of the grade he or she receives from the teacher. This means, then, that a wider variety of reinforcers is now available than was in earlier years.

SELF-CONCEPT OF SCHOOLCHILDREN

During these school years a child's self-concept develops from mainly two sources: feedback from many different people and his or her own evaluation of personal experiences. Prior to age seven, children tend to define themselves in physical terms. When asked about themselves, they describe concrete observable features, such as height, weight, and hair color. Around age seven, children begin to see themselves in more abstract terms. They start to attribute psychological traits to themselves; for example, "I'm a nice person."

During this time children evaluate the feedback they get from parents, peers, and others. They compare their own experiences with the standards set by society and their own standards. They seem to be particularly concerned with their own competencies, especially when compared with those of others; for example, "I can dance better than Susie." The development of a self-concept becomes complicated because children receive feedback from many sources, some of which are contradictory. A child who has been the center of attention at home will experience a different situation at school, where he or she must share attention with others. Because logical reasoning develops during this age (concrete-operational stage), children can test and verify their thoughts and opinions of themselves with reality.

Importance of Self-Esteem   Self-esteem refers to a child's evaluation of his or her own qualities. With children under age seven it is difficult to measure self-esteem accurately. Preschool children generally report satisfaction and happiness with themselves and their abilities. However, by age nine or ten, low self-evaluations occur frequently; children begin to be judgmental about their attributes.

An important study on self-esteem in children was conducted in 1967. Stanley Coopersmith gave a questionnaire on self-esteem to hundreds of fifth- and sixth-grade children. He found that children with high self-esteem were more popular and did better in school. Those with low self-esteem were more likely to be loners and have behavioral problems, such as bedwetting and poor grades. Self-esteem didn't seem to correlate with height, physical attractiveness, family size or social status. The most important factor in influencing self-esteem was how children were treated by significant others. Only and first-born children, boys with dominant mothers, and children with warm parents showed higher self-esteem.

Coopersmith also found that parents who were both strict and democratic had children with higher self-esteem. Children who had parents who were permissive or very authoritarian showed, overall, lower self-esteem. Firm but reasoned control, encouragement of independence, and a loving and warm atmosphere appeared to encourage higher self-esteem in children.

SOCIAL COGNITION

Peer Groups and the Society of Childhood

In middle childhood, people outside the family (other children, teachers, and so on) become an important influence on the child. By age five or six, children are generally attending school and spending a significant amount of time with peers. Children turn to their peer group when they want companionship. Same-sex friendships flourish in this age group. Children during this stage normally have more than one "best friend." Small informal groups in classrooms occur, each of which has standards and social rules. At this age children begin to gossip. This form of communication serves to affirm group norms and values. Adults and older children are seen as helpful, but peers are turned to for play and companionship. By age 10 to 11, children frequently spend 50 percent of their social interaction time with their peers.

The rules of the school-age subculture cover slang words, special vocabularies, dress codes, and rules of behavior. Children in this age group begin to spontaneously organize clubs, paying much attention to details regarding rules, dress, elected officers, and establishing a meeting place or clubhouse. These clubs may have no announced purpose and may appear to serve only to exclude adults and/or other same-sex children. In reality, these clubs also help facilitate the development of social skills, teaching acceptable codes of behavior and building self-esteem.

Popularity and unpopularity are critical issues during this time. Low achievers and drop-outs tend to be less popular. Popular children are generally physically attractive, friendly, outgoing, enthusiastic, and have good interpersonal skills. Aggressive children tend to play with other aggressive or unpopular children. These aggressive peer clusters tend to persist throughout elementary school. Children who are less popular tend to feel sad and rejected, have low self-esteem, and have more trouble in school.

Unpopular children are more likely to have problems with mental health, to drop out of school, and to become delinquent. The situation for unpopular children can improve if they are taught social skills. When these children are taught how to work with others and are given feedback about their own behavior through structured experiences involving peers, they learn how to share information about themselves, to show interest in others by asking questions, and to give appropriate suggestions and feedback to others.

Friendships

Friendships become increasingly important as children get older. The complexity of friendships also increases with age. The older the child, the more likely it is that self-disclosure and reciprocal intimacy will be important. As children grow older, friendship circles become smaller. By age ten, children are often able to describe one "best friend" to the exclusion of others. Children tend to choose friends who are of the same sex, race, and economic background as themselves. During these elementary school years same-sex friendships tend to be most common. Boy/girl relationships usually lack intimacy.

Robert Selman has outlined a useful model of the development of friendships as children grow up. He sees children as developing their ideas of friendships in stages. The most primitive style of friendships (stage 0) starts with momentary encounters with a playmate that are based on physical proximity. This stage could more accurately be described as playmateship. In stage 1, the friendship is based on what the other person can do for the child: if the friend can meet the child's requirements, then the friendship continues. During stage 2, the child discovers that meeting needs is a two-way street. The cooperation that results, however, is not usually sufficient to carry the friendship over rough times or conflicts. In stage 3, the friends achieve some continuity of the friendship over time usually because of an underlying emotional bond between them. At this stage the underlying connection between the friends can help them overcome any conflicts that may arise. Lastly, in stage 4, friendships blossom because there is a realization that each person needs to put his or her own feelings of dependence and independence aside so that no one will be jealous, for example, if other friendships also exist. Friends gain strength and closeness from such a relationship but are also able to retain a sense of independence from it.

Prosocial Behavior

During the early childhood years, selfish and aggressive responses outnumber by far prosocial altruistic behaviors—those actions that are performed to help someone else without expecting any reward for oneself. However, during the elementary school years helping, sharing, sympathy, and empathy increase dramatically. The increase of such behavior is influenced by several factors:

CULTURE

A number of international studies found that Kenyans and Mexicans show many more prosocial behaviors than average American children. This difference appears to be influenced by cultural phenomena. In Kenya, Mexico, and the Philippines the children studied lived in extended families, had greater responsibilities, and experienced a much simpler social structure. Rural children are generally found to be more cooperative and less competitive than urban children.

AGE

Age trends are not always clear-cut. Nursery school children are more likely to be generous in their sharing compared with older school-age children. Overall, however, prosocial behavior increases with age. As a child gets older, he or she is more able to feel empathy with another child's situation and feelings.

CHILDREARING METHODS

Parents who display more prosocial behavior raise children who display prosocial behavior.

TELEVISION

Children exposed to prosocial and empathic behaviors on television, through such films as Lassie and "Mr. Rogers' Neighborhood," tend to display more prosocial behavior towards others compared with children viewing more aggressive content on television. Although it is only one influence among many, prosocial television may help foster prosocial development and behaviors.

Social Learning in the Home

Although peers become an increasingly important influence during the school years, the family continues to be the most powerful influence on the school-age child's personality. Some specific family factors that influence the child's psychological health include divorce, having only one parent, childrearing strategies, siblings, and so on. Some of these factors have been covered in other chapters.

One of the most important events during the school years is the development of enduring relationships between siblings. Relationships between friends are more ephemeral, with best friends and "cliques" changing frequently in contrast to sibling relationships. Siblings learn how to resolve conflicts and how to deal with anger within close relationships. Siblings can't avoid interacting with each other on a daily basis, so they must learn to get along somehow.

Other phenomena relating to siblings are: (1) culture determines the amount of active caretaking of younger by older siblings (especially girls), e.g., in American society, there is much less demand for sibling caretaking than in less industrialized cultures; (2) eldest children tend to be the most bossy; (3) the most argumentative combination is two brothers; (4) siblings do not suffer from inadequate attention from parents because of an added child, e.g., studies with handicapped children have found that the siblings of these children, who need much more attention than the average child, have no more psychological problems than the average child (apparently parents are able to remain sensitive even in the face of high demands for attention); and (5) the closer they are in age, the more ambivalent but also the closer the relationship is between the siblings.

The effect of a working mother on school-age children seems to be mostly beneficial. Children of working mothers generally tend to be more independent, score higher on tests of personal and social adjustment, and show fewer stereotypic ideas about sex roles. Daughters of working mothers have higher self-esteem than daughters of homemakers. A few studies have shown a slight decrease in academic and cognitive achievement of sons of working mothers. However, these effects are small, and the findings are inconsistent.

Stress

Although children are resilient, stressful events are part of every childhood: working or absent parents, the birth of a new sibling, and the demands of school are some examples. Boys are more vulnerable to environmental challenges. Also, the older the child, the more resilient he or she is. Academic success is correlated with a good response to stress. It is not clear whether academically successful children are innately better at problem solving or if an increase in self-esteem due to school achievement "inoculates" them somewhat to trauma.

However, many children appear to be innately resilient; they seem to bounce back and succeed despite overwhelming stressors. These are the children who achieve professional mastery despite being raised in the ghetto, or who rise to the top of a corporate structure despite severely disadvantaged childhoods. They may have been abused or neglected but grow up to lead lives of fulfillment and are able to establish rewarding, intimate relationships.

Michael Rutter and other researchers have outlined a number of factors that appear to reduce the impact of stressors on children:

FAMILY

The stress-resilient child is likely to have intimate, supportive relationships with parents and/or other relatives. A trusting, caring, and enduring relationship with even just one adult can be a critical protective influence. Additionally, such a child has frequently been involved in caring for another, most frequently a younger sibling. Helping another tends to increase coping skills and morale.

PERSONALITY

Stress-resilient children tend to be more adaptable, socially sensitive, friendly, and independent, and have high levels of self-esteem. These children are less likely to have negative reactions and more likely to focus on the positive aspects of a situation.

POSITIVE EXPERIENCES

Resilient children tend to have experienced success in sports, music, hobbies or outside experiences. These activities may function to keep them away from an inadequate home environment.

EXPERIENCES OF ENVIRONMENTAL CONTROL

Either through modeling by a parent or significant other or through their own learning, resilient children have experienced positive results in problem-solving situations. These children have learned that they can be successful and exert control over their own lives.

At the same time, Rutter found six factors that strongly correlate with childhood psychopathology. Although the occurrence of just one of these factors has no significant influence on emotional functioning, the occurrence of two or more together dramatically increases the risk for psychopathology. The factors include: severe marital discord; low social status; large family size or overcrowded environment; history of paternal criminality; history of maternal psychiatric disorder; and custodial care of child by a governmental or social service agency.

Gender Differentiation in the School Years

At about age two and a half to three, most children accurately label the sex of another. By age four, children understand that a person stays the same gender throughout life. But by age five to six, at the same time the concept of conservation of mass, weight, and number begins to be understood, the idea of gender constancy develops. At this age, a child understands that someone stays the same gender even if he or she puts on opposite-sex clothes or has hair of an unconventional length. Studies have shown the same sequence to occur even in widely varying cultures such as the United States, Kenya, Nepal, and Belize.

Although gender schema (a child's understanding of sex roles) has been developing through the early years, at the beginning of this age range children search for and adapt "rules" about how boys and girls behave. Initially, children treat these rules as absolute moral dogma, for example, "boys don't cry," "girls always play with dolls." By about age seven to nine, children understand the ideas of social conventions, and sex stereotyping tends to lessen somewhat as sex-role concepts become more flexible.

Overall, however, during the school years children show significantly sex-stereotyped attitudes. Kindergarten and first grade children associate aggression with boys. Boys tend to be more rigid about gender-role views than girls. Fourth and fifth grade children in the United States, England, and Ireland see girls as emotional, weak, affectionate, and sophisticated. Boys are seen as strong, aggressive, cruel, ambitious, and dominant.

In this age group, the school becomes an important ingredient in developing gender schema. Elementary school teachers tend to have more interaction with boys than with girls; however, this interaction is generally negative. Boys tend to get harsher reprimands, more attention, and more nurturing than girls. Stereotypic feminine behaviors (passivity, conformity, and obedience) are reinforced by elementary school teachers. School materials tend to portray females in less important roles than men. Girls may be encouraged to minimize the importance of physical education, science, and mathematics. Also, school role models are generally skewed; that is, most elementary school principals are men and most teachers are women.

Childhood during the elementary school years is a time when personality development is moderately dormant from psychoanalytic viewpoints. However, cognitive theory assumes that thinking skills are significantly improving because of the interaction within a competitive schoolroom environment. Learning theory assumes that the repertoire of skills expands through reinforcement by the internal reward that can come from a "job well done."

The self-concept of these children begins to include abstract qualities as well as comparisons with other children. Given that environmental feedback about the child's abilities may be contradictory, he or she now has the logical ability to test his or her self-concept against reality. In this regard, the self-esteem of the child will affect the child's social interactions (e.g., high self-esteem is related to high popularity).

Influences outside the family become important. Children at this age develop their social groups and friendships. School opportunities and challenges foster the development of social subgroups with unique rules, values, language, and codes of behavior. Prosocial behavior develops and is influenced by prosocial behavior in the environment. Likewise, factors such as culture, age of the child, parenting style, and the amount and kind of television watched significantly influence the development of prosocial behavior.

Sibling influences are strong and provide the child with an opportunity for intimacy in the face of daily conflict. With regard to conflict in general, the amount of stress experienced by the school-age child is handled differently by different children, with some being more resilient than others. Good experiences and a supportive family increase that resilience: children can be "inoculated" by positive experiences with significant others. Socially and emotionally, middle childhood is a complex age when children become less dependent upon their parents and more enculturated by society.

Selected Readings

Aboud, F. (1985). Children's application of attribution principles to social comparisons. *Child development*, 56.

Dunn, J. (1985). *Sisters and brothers*. Cambridge, MA: Harvard University Press.

Erikson, E. H. (1963). *Childhood and society*. NY: Norton.

Flavell, J. H., and L. Ross. (1981). *Social cognitive development: Frontiers and possible futures*. Cambridge, England: Cambridge University Press.

Freud, S. (1938). *The basic writings of Sigmund Freud*. NY: Modern Library.

Lamb, M. E., and B. Sutton-Smith. (1982). *Sibling relationships*. Hillsdale, NJ: Erlbaum.

Rutter, M. (1980). *Changing youth in a changing society: Patterns of development and disorder*. Cambridge, MA: Harvard University Press.

Yussen, S. R., ed. (1985). *The growth of reflection in children*. NY: Academic Press.

18

The Elementary School Years: Special Issues

*T*he beginning of formal schooling is one of the strongest influences in middle childhood. With the start of school, peer group influences and education issues become paramount. The child is constantly being evaluated socially by peers and formally by teachers. This puts the child under new pressures and performance edicts. Some children do worse than others in school because of the effects of Attention Deficit-Hyperactivity Disorder or a specific learning disability. These children and those who are overweight may experience a drop in self-esteem because of being different from their classmates. Issues concerning the best way to educate special children also arise: should the handicapped child be educated in the classroom (mainstreamed) with the nonhandicapped child? How should the gifted child be incorporated into the educational system?

School, peer, and family pressures may also engender psychological problems (psychopathologies) during middle childhood. Depression and conduct disorders appear in school-age children. Bedwetting and soiling also occur. School phobias may develop in the child with social anxiety. Stressors on the school-age child include dual-earner families, the "latch-key" child phenomenon, divorce, and the blended family. The following chapter examines the impact of special issues on middle childhood.

THE IMPACT OF SCHOOL

Many important developmental issues stem from the child's entrance into the structure and challenge of formal education.

Learning Disabilities

A child with a learning disability has difficulty achieving at his or her age and ability level in a basic skill such as reading, writing or mathematics. Children with learning disabilities have average or better than average intelligence as measured by an IQ test but are one to two years behind the average achievement in a specific area. Learning disabilities do not result from either speech or hearing. There are three major types of learning disabilities: (1) dyslexia (a great difficulty in reading); (2) dyscalcula (disability in mathematics); and (3) dysgraphia (problems in handwriting and printing that produce large, awkward letters generally characteristic of much younger children).

It is generally agreed by professionals that some physiological cause lies at the root of learning disabilities. Brain damage, either at birth or prenatally, is thought to affect the functioning of learning disabled children. Adults with problems due to tumors often show the same types of cognitive difficulties as learning disabled children. A second physiological influence may be an inherited difficulty in brain functioning. Significant anecdotal evidence exists that siblings and other relatives of children with learning disabilities often have some type of learning problems themselves. That is, learning disabilities may tend to run in families.

The problems as well as the treatments for children with learning disabilities are both academic and psychological. Academic problems generally surface in the early school years, resulting in poor grades and low self-esteem. Children with learning disabilities also may not interpret verbal communications correctly, thus responding to peers and adults insensitively or inappropriately. This may result in a lowering of self-concept and self-esteem. Academic interventions include special classes in the areas of the learning disability that help with individualized learning strategies. Psychotherapy is used to help the child learn how to interpret social cues appropriately and to raise self-concept and self-esteem.

Attention-Deficit Hyperactivity Disorder

One major factor that may influence academic performance is Attention-Deficit Hyperactivity Disorder (ADHD). Children with ADHD have difficulty focusing on a task, sitting still, and paying attention. Such children also have difficulty in their peer relationships, in their relationships with teachers, and with achievement. These children are often seen as aggressive, annoying, and easily frustrated. The American Psychiatric Association has defined ADHD as encompassing the following symptoms:

1. fidgeting or squirming in seat
2. difficulty in remaining seated
3. being easily distracted by extraneous stimuli
4. problems in turn taking and games or group activities
5. blurting out answers to questions
6. problems with following directions from others, such as finishing chores
7. problems in maintaining attention in school tasks or play activities
8. shifting frequently from one activity to another
9. problems in playing quietly
10. talking excessively
11. inappropriately interrupting others' activities, such as children's games
12. problems with listening to what is said to him or her
13. problems with losing things necessary for school or home activities
14. engaging in activities that would be considered physically dangerous, such as running into the street without looking in both directions
15. these symptoms occurring before the age of seven.

Eighty percent of ADHD children carry some of the above symptoms of hyperactivity to adulthood; for example, poor grades are common throughout the school years. ADHD is estimated to occur in as many as 3 percent of all children and occurs six to nine times more frequently in males than in females.

The exact causes of ADHD are unknown. It is likely that this disorder is actually a group of disorders clustered together because of similar symptoms. Thus, there may exist multiple causes for these multiple symptoms. The following causes have been varyingly associated with ADHD symptoms: premature birth, trauma to the head, infections, genetic differences, lead poisoning, prenatal damage, diet, family stress, and the environment

Current treatments for hyperactivity are as varied as the proposed causes. Even though there is no cure for ADHD, medication and psychological therapy have been found to be effective. Frequently, children with ADHD are medicated with Ritalin (methylphenidate), an amphetamine derivative, which is a strong nervous system stimulant. Its effect on ADHD children is to calm them, which is the opposite of the stimulating effect it has on children or adults without ADHD.

One theory has recently been proposed to explain this paradox. In essence, the human brain may require a certain amount of stimulation in order to work properly and efficiently. If the particular level of optimal stimulation for an individual child is not present, then that child may become more active in order to create the amount of stimulation for himself or herself to meet a biological or central nervous system need. The effect of Ritalin, like that of most amphetamines, is to stimulate brain activity. It is likely that Ritalin would raise the brain activity in both ADHD and normal children equally but with decidedly different behavioral effects. That is, in normal children or adults it would stimulate their brains so they would become "overloaded," losing control over their thoughts and behaviors. On the other hand, the ADHD child would calm down because the brain's activity level has been raised so that hyperactive behaviors are no longer needed. Following this line of thinking, some physicians feel that a positive response (reduction in hyperactive behaviors) to Ritalin is a diagnostic tool in assessing a child for ADHD.

Another treatment for the symptoms of ADHD includes psychological therapy to help the child focus his or her attention and control his or her temper by developing patience. Psychotherapy can also help parents cope with a child who has these challenging symptoms. A controversial treatment has been to limit the child's dietary intake of food additives, preservatives, artificial colors, flavors, and other chemicals. Some support for this dietary manipulation has been found; however, many studies also show few children responding to such dietary changes.

Mainstreaming

Mainstreaming is a controversial issue. In the late 1960s educators advocated the integration of children with special needs with normal children as much and as early as possible. Such a practice is called mainstreaming. In 1975 federal law mandated that all children, regardless of their limitations, receive public education in the "least restrictive" environment that is educationally sound. The results of these mainstreaming efforts have been mixed.

Such an integration is supported by common sense. It encourages handicapped children to grow up and function in nonhandicapped society. It also encourages handicapped and nonhandicapped children to associate with one another in the formative childhood years and to learn social skills necessary for dealing with one another. Theoretically, prejudices are then dispelled.

However, there have been significant problems. Recently, money for education has been cut back, and school resources for all special programs have been limited. Handicapped children generally require special programs where they can get the individual attention they need. Thus, without adequate support in the classroom, teachers are overburdened and neither handicapped nor nonhadicapped children get the attention they need.

Although acceptance of mainstreamed handicapped children by their nonhandicapped classmates does happen, it is not the norm. The integration of handicapped children into the normal classroom appears not to be as effective as originally envisioned. Some studies have shown that the self-esteem of handicapped children does not necessarily improve in mainstream classes. In addition, handicapped children often feel less competent in classes with normal children than they do in special placement classes. Experience with mainstreaming has shown that this process requires additional teacher training on how to meet the special needs of such children, additional resources, and special training in social skills for both the handicapped and nonhandicapped children. It seems that the mainstreaming process is not for every handicapped child, but where such programs are in place, the measures given above help them succeed.

The Gifted Child

Having special talents, or giftedness, is another special circumstance that influences the child's emotional, social, and educational development. These special talents may include some or all of the following: musical or artistic skills, special mathematical ability, and a high IQ. In the school system, giftedness is most commonly ascertained by scores on an intelligence test. About 2 percent of all children are significantly brighter than their peers. Approximately one child in every thousand is considered extremely gifted, with an IQ of 180 or above.

In a major longitudinal study, 1,500 gifted children were followed from the 1920s throughout their lives. On the whole, these children were found to be physically healthier, taller, more successful, of higher self-esteem, and better adjusted psychologically and socially than their nongifted childhood and adult peers. This evidence would seem to lay to rest the myth that smart kids are socially backward. However, other researchers have shown that extremely gifted children (IQ greater than 170) may indeed be seen by others as "odd" or "weird" and may be less well adjusted than their peers. To reconcile this conflict, one need only look at the environmental experiences of gifted children. That is, they appear to adjust better when they are given early social and intellectual encouragement and enrichment in their particular "gift" as well as an opportunity to accelerate through the classroom environment. The results are a better development of self-esteem, self-concept, and social interaction skills along with improvement in their individual talents. Placing excessive emotional and intellectual pressure on the gifted child at home and at school has the opposite effect.

With respect to educating gifted children, two approaches have been used: "skipping" and enrichment. Acceleration, or skipping classes or grades, allows a child with special talents to work at his or her own pace, avoiding the boredom and frustration that many cognitively gifted children experience in regular classes. Enrichment, on the other hand, entails keeping the student at his or her grade level for psychosocial continuity with their same-age peers yet providing for additional stimulation, more challenging instruction, and perhaps even a separate classroom.

Bilingualism

In most countries one or more significant minorities speak a language or a dialect different from the official national language: for example, French vs. English in Canada; black English and Spanish vs. English in the United States. The emotional controversy of how and when to introduce children to the rules of language in school has raged for decades. Immigrants feel strongly about instructing their children in the language of their homeland. Dialectic minorities (such as black Americans) strive to protect their children from being disadvantaged in the schools. How and when to teach children a second non-native language has also been argued. Although this area is still controversial, several conclusions have emerged from research:

1. There is no evidence of harm if children learn two or more languages in early childhood. There may be some temporary decrease in IQ scores in the initial stage of learning both languages, but the effect is transitory.

2. Children learn language pronunciation more easily than adults.

3. There is no clear answer to the question of how to teach language in school. Methods have varied from total immersion in the second language from an early age to delaying new language learning until adolescence. Researchers disagree on the effectiveness of these different methods.

PSYCHOPATHOLOGY IN THE ELEMENTARY SCHOOL YEARS

When children reach this period in development, school and peer groups become important factors in the emotional distress of children. The following syndromes are the primary emotional disturbances during the elementary school years.

School Phobia

Most professionals studying this phenomenon agree that children who display an unrealistic fear of attending school actually fear leaving their mothers (separation anxiety). Such children are not truants but are generally good students between the ages of five and fifteen. They tend to be timid and shy away from home but stubborn and demanding when with their parents. They also tend to have low self-esteem. Initial symptoms include some physical ailment (e.g., stomachache, nausea, headache) on a school morning (especially on Monday), which quickly disappears when the child is allowed to stay home. The longer the child stays out of school, the harder it is to go back. Many parents resort to homeschooling for such children after trying many ways to get the child back to school. They fear forcing such a "sensitive" child to face such a trauma. The best treatment is to get the child physically back in school. This is sometimes accomplished gradually, beginning with an initial short visit to the school building and increasing the length of the visits over time. Other methods of treatment advocate physically carrying the child into the classroom if the child refuses to go. After the child returns to school, psychotherapy can aid the child with resulting anger and social fears of the school environment.

Depression

Although depression does occur prior to age five and has even been described in infants, it becomes significantly more easily recognizable in the school years. The symptoms range from sadness and a sense of hopelessness to a suicide attempt. Children who are depressed may have problems sleeping (too much or too little), weight loss or gain, crying spells, negative thoughts about themselves, and low self-esteem. Generally, depression occurs after a period of increased stress.

Suicide attempts in young children are not rare. Many such attempts are disguised as accidents or are concealed by parents. Suicidal children are more likely to have been unwanted, neglected or abused by their parents. Treatment for depression and suicide prevention entails individual and family therapy, social skills training, and perhaps medication.

Childhood Obesity

Although obesity is not strictly classified as a psychopathology, being physically overweight influences the psychosocial functioning of children and can be caused by emotional factors. During the school-age years at least 10 percent of American children are sufficiently overweight to be classified as obese: that is, weighing more than 20 percent more than average for a child's age, sex, and body size. Weight problems at this age significantly affect the self-concepts of children. Children of this age group perceived as "fat" by their schoolmates are more likely to be teased, picked on, and rejected. Their self-esteem is likely to be diminished, and depression or behavior problems may result. These children generally are given nicknames such as "Fatty" or "Thunderthighs" and thereby suffer teasing and joking.

The causative factors of obesity for each child are complex and perhaps numerous.

Genetics. Heredity is an important influence in determining fat distribution, height, weight, bone structure, and metabolic rate.

Activity Level. Overweight children are less active than their average-weight peers. It is not clear whether the child is less active because he or she is obese or obese because he or she is less active.

Amount of Food Eaten. Eating patterns differ across cultures and families, influencing the food consumption of children.

Television. Recent studies have reported that body weight tends to rise 2 percent for each hour of regular television viewing. Hence the more television a child watches, the more likely it is that he or she will be overweight. Factors influencing this are lower activity levels, consumption of fattening foods, and commercials that influence children to eat junk food.

Treatment for obese children is somewhat different than for obese adults. In order to avoid hindering a child's development, heavy dieting is not recommended. A child's activity level is increased and good nutrition is promoted so that a child maintains constant weight as he or she grows. Ultimately this causes a reduction in accumulated body fat. Psychotherapy also helps the child cope with self-esteem and any other psychological problems that cause increased food consumption.

Other Psychopathologies of the Elementary School Years

CONDUCT DISORDERS

Parents frequently bring children into psychotherapy because of behavior disorders. Symptoms include lying, stealing, refusing to follow directions, aggression, and other mild to serious antisocial behaviors. These are a common result of severe family problems, such as parental separation or divorce. Divorce, for example, appears to occur without the children's permission or control, and they become angry, hurt, and even guilt-ridden. The situation may worsen when the custodial parent remarries. In both scenarios, children may start conduct disorders as a response to a situation that they do not understand and are powerless to stop. Family psychotherapy holds the best chance of improving the situation not only for the child but also for the family.

BEDWETTING AND SOILING (ENURESIS AND ENCOPRESIS)

These behavior patterns occur less frequently after age five but are still a problem for some schoolchildren. Generally, they are not the result of a biological problem, although with younger children this possibility should always be checked first. In most cases, these problems are the result of anger and hostility toward the family or the parents or because the child has massive anxiety over some unresolved problem at school or in the home. Whatever the cause, individual and family psychotherapy usually works to solve the condition.

TICS

These are repetitive, involuntary muscular movements such as head-bobbing, lip-smacking, and eye-blinking. They generally stem from emotional causes and disappear before adolescence, although they may reappear during times of stress. The most severe, and one of the most rare, of the tic disorders is Tourette's syndrome, which is characterized by involuntary muscular movements and vocal sounds (such as grunts, snorts, and swearing). Tourette's syndrome is thought to have a neurological basis and generally is controlled by medication.

STUTTERING

This syndrome appears four times more frequently in boys than in girls and occurs between the ages of two and seven. Again, the problem is thought to be related to emotional causes, and the symptoms generally disappear by adolescence. More persistent stuttering is remediated by psychotherapy, medication, speech therapy, and computer-assisted therapy.

FAMILY INFLUENCES

Divorce

Because of the increased frequency of divorce (50 percent of all marriages end in divorce) in our society, today, the effect of this stressor is seen in many school-age children. The influence of divorce on children depends on the individual child, but there are some common patterns. Initially, children respond to divorce with anger, shock, guilt, and fear. Frequently children blame themselves and attempt to reunite their parents. There is a tendency to become withdrawn and depressed. School performance may be disrupted, and some children may display behavioral problems. The worst of these symptoms occur during the first year after the divorce, and most children gradually adjust. However, significant developmental disruptions can occur if other stressors are added to the child's burden.

Through several longitudinal studies, a number of factors have emerged as influencing the child's adjustment to the disruption of divorce. Boys tend to have more difficulty in adjusting to their parents' divorce than girls, and boys adjust better when the father is the custodial parent. Divorce is disruptive no matter what age the child. However, its effect appears to be strongest when the child is at a transitional age, such as beginning adolescence or beginning elementary school. The more conflict between the parents during the divorce process, the worse the effect on the child and the child's relationship with his or her siblings. Joint custody and frequent, regular home switching can be increasingly detrimental to the child's emotional well-being if relations between the parents are bitter and hostile. Although the involvement and contact of both parents with the child is optimal, if the child is involved in the conflict, anxiety and depression are likely to increase.

Divorce may result in a child living at home with one parent. Children of single-parent families fare worse academically, socially, and emotionally than children living in a two-parent household. Single parents have increased logistical and financial responsibilities and may become more strict and less playful with their children.

Most recent research has shown that divorce has long-term effects on children. Even ten years later, children express sadness at the loss of their intact family and express fears of being betrayed in relationships.

Blended Families

Because of the high divorce rate, families made up of stepparents, stepsiblings and halfsiblings living under one roof are common. Contrary to long-standing myths, living in a blended family can be a positive experience. Shortly after the remarriage, children may display more problem behaviors (such as the conduct disorders mentioned above) but with patience and time for readjustment, the stepparent and children can enter into positive relationships with each other.

"Latch-Key Children"

Because of divorces, financial strains on two-parent families or other reasons, the number of children who come home from school to an empty house has dramatically increased. Studies have shown that "latch-key children" who spend after-school time alone suffer no ill effects if they are taught how to manage their time while alone, are monitored by their parents over the telephone, are taught what dangers to avoid, and come home right after school. Their self-esteem, social adjustment, and school achievement have been shown to be comparable to those of children who receive after-school care from adults. On the other hand, a lack of parental monitoring through structure and phone calls, as well as not coming directly home after school, has been associated with antisocial behaviors such as stealing and aggression.

Children are exposed to new and varied problems during the elementary school years. For example, the presence of specific learning disabilities becomes apparent when a child enters a full-time school environment. These disabilities can cause both problems in learning school material and emotional difficulties for the affected child. Academic and psychotherapeutic intervention, such as special classes, can improve a child's school standing and raise his or her self-concept and self-esteem.

Attention-Deficit Hyperactivity Disorder (ADHD) manifests itself through an inability to focus on tasks and to control attention. Aggression and poor peer/teacher relationships are also common. The most visible symptom is hyperactive behavior in the classroom. Even though the direct causes of ADHD are unknown, the most effective treatments to date appear to be some form of medication such as Ritalin and psychotherapy.

Often children in elementary school have their first contacts with special-needs children (those with a physical or mental handicap). The integration of these children with "normal" children in school is called mainstreaming. In theory, this process should improve the psychological well-being of the handicapped child and dispel myths about the handicapped held by the nonhandicapped. In practice, this process requires extra teacher training, more resources, and social skills training for both groups of children.

Gifted children (those with special talents, mathematical skills or high IQ) are mistakenly thought to be socially and emotionally inept. With adequate social and intellectual support at home and in school, they display normal social/emotional development and also get enrichment in their particular gift and an opportunity to accelerate through schooling. Similar social and emotional support can also help the child who is attempting to learn a second language (bilingualism).

Different problems in psychological functioning may appear during this stage of development: school phobias, depression, and obesity. Each is most often caused by fear of the school environment, shyness, initial failures in school combined with pressures from home to succeed or some other factors that lower self-esteem and self-concept. Treatment for these conditions include psychotherapy and stronger parental involvement in the child's school life. Less frequently occurring psychological problems (conduct disorders, bedwetting, soiling, tics, and stuttering) can occur through emotional upset brought on by family dysfunctions (separation or divorce) and are mainly dealt with through family psychotherapy.

Finally, family influences are still significant through the elementary school years. Divorce and the resultant emotional feelings of anger, shock, guilt, and fear can result in major emotional disturbances and disruptions in the school-age child. Divorce is a situation that is difficult for children to understand and one that they feel powerless to stop. As well as becoming withdrawn and depressed, the child of divorced parents may also show significant behavioral and performance problems in school. If the divorced parents communicate and provide consistent support to the child, these emotional problems can be dealt with over time. Similar disturbances can occur in blended families, but in the long run the renewal of a complete family structure is a positive experience. Some children ("latch-key children") find themselves at home alone after school. As with the other family influences, parental support, monitoring, and guidance in time management help these children maintain high levels of social adjustment, school performance, and self-esteem.

Selected Readings

Emory, R. E. (1988). *Marriage, divorce, and children's adjustment.* Newbury Park, CA: Sage.

Farnham-Diggory, S. (1978). *Learning disabilities.* Cambridge, MA: Harvard University Press.

Janos, P. M., and N. M. Robinson. (1985). *The gifted and talented: Developmental perspectives.* Washington, DC: American Psychological Association.

Johnson, C., and M. E. Conners. *The etiology and treatment of bulimia nervosa: A biopsychosocial perspective.* NY: Basic Books.

Lamb, M. E. (1982). *Non-traditional families: Parenting in child development.* Hillsdale, NJ: Erlbaum.

Meisel, C. J. (1986). *Mainstreaming handicapped children: Outcomes, controversies, and new directions.* Hillsdale, NJ: Erlbaum.

Ross, D. M., and Ross, S. A. (1982). *Hyperactivity: Current issues, research, and theory.* 2d ed. NY: Wiley.

19

Adolescence: Physical Development

*A*dolescence begins somewhere between the ages of 10 and 12 for most children and lasts until about age 20 in industrialized societies. This stage begins with a prescribed set of gender-specific physical changes termed puberty. These changes bring the child's body to sexual maturity. The puberty process begins when the brain signals the body to begin releasing gender-specific sex hormones. These in turn begin the development of the primary and secondary sex characteristics. The specific age at which this process begins is influenced by such genetic and environmental factors as family history and nutrition. The process nears completion when males achieve their first ejaculation and females their first menstruation (menarche), even though the ability to conceive children may not be possible yet.

Many psychological issues are related to puberty. One is the importance of teenagers' own body image, that is, how they see themselves in relation to their concepts of femininity and masculinity. A second is the influence of the timing of the onset of puberty, that is, whether it is early or late relative to the average age for that gender.

There are also many health-related issues in adolescence. The importance of proper nutrition, as opposed to fad or deficient diets, is clear when one considers the bodily growth that takes place during this time. It is second only to that which took place during the period from conception to age two. In addition, even though diseases and illnesses during adolescence are uncommon, this age is marked by lifestyle behaviors that can result in accidental death in the short term or by bodily deterioration in the long term.

ADOLESCENCE VS. PUBERTY

As mentioned in chapter 1, adolescence was first defined as a stage in human development by G. Stanley Hall, the first developmental psychologist. Although the time between childhood and adulthood was considered different from each other, it was often viewed as a kind of apprenticeship to adulthood. That is, the person was no longer a child but rather an adult that simply lacked the experience or practice with adult skills. This period was not seen as qualitatively different from adulthood. Hence, late childhood and early "apprenticeshiphood" often found children working long hours under conditions that did not recognize (either emotionally or physically) the changes that the child was undergoing.

With Hall's work, psychologists began to realize that the time between the ages of 10 and 20 (approximately) presented a missing link in the development of children into adults. Specifically, this 10-year period is indeed a qualitatively different stage from both childhood and adulthood, one that has its own characteristics and patterns. It is influenced not only by the events of childhood that precede it but also by its own particular set of hereditary and environmental events. Today, psychologists generally refer to adolescence as the total set of changes that occur between the ages of 10 and 20. The physical changes that turn a child's body into a basic adult body are termed *puberty*.

Puberty

Puberty occurs during the early years of adolescence. At this time the child's body (particularly the sexual organs) is developing rapidly. The word *puberty* has generally been used in two ways. First, and more narrowly, it is sometimes defined as a specific time when an individual becomes capable of having offspring. By this definition, puberty occurs in boys when they have their first ejaculation, usually as a nocturnal emission or "wet dream." (Sexual intercourse and masturbation may also result in a first ejaculation.) When ejaculation first occurs, the number of live sperm are usually too few to enable the boy to father a child. For girls, puberty is marked by the day that they have their first menstrual period, or menarche. In many cases, the first few menstrual cycles are anovulatory, meaning that they occur without an ovum being released from the ovaries. This means that the girl would be unable to conceive a child. (As will be discussed in chapters 20 and 22, this information may lead many adolescents to think that early sexual activity is safe. The contrary is true because males and females may produce active sex cells right from the very beginning of puberty, making conception possible.) Fertility in both sexes increases over time.

Another way the term *puberty* has been used is to more generally refer to the entire period of sexual maturation in early adolescence. This is the period that ends childhood and transports the individual into adult size, shape, and reproductive capability. This definition covers both the maturation of the reproductive system and the development of secondary sex characteristics, during which most of the tissues in the body are affected. The main difference between the two definitions of puberty has to do with the starting point. Both definitions use the same endpoint.

Following the more global interpretation, puberty begins with pubescence when the hypothalamus (in the brain) signals the pituitary gland to secrete gonadatrophins, which will stimulate the ovaries (female) or testes (male) to increase production of the sex hormone estradiol (an estrogen precursor) or testosterone, respectively. Pubescence begins approximately one year before teenagers notice changes in their bodies, such as enlarged breasts or testes. This second set of bodily changes will also occur, approximately one year before the beginning of the growth spurt. At that time, the hypothalamus is stimulating the pituitary gland to secrete increased amounts of human growth hormone (somatotrophic hormone), which causes rapid changes in physical growth. Along with this growth spurt, higher amounts of adrenaline and thyroxine are produced in order to match the increase in the number of cells and body weight. (This entire process is diagramed in Fig. 19.1.)

The sex hormones stimulate the development of the primary and secondary sex characteristics for their respective gender (see Table 19.1). A review of Table 19.2 will give the reader a general sequence of the pubescent and pubertal changes of adolescence. Progesterone, another female sex hormone, is also secreted, making puberty possible. It promotes development of the uterine wall, preparing it for the implantation of a blastocyst following conception, and of the placenta after implantation has taken place. In addition, it aids breast development during pregnancy.

PRIMARY VS. SECONDARY SEX CHARACTERISTICS

The primary sex characteristics (Table 19.1) show changes at the onset of pubescence with the secretion of the gonadotrophins. These characteristics are those that are directly involved in reproduction. Both males and females experience an increase in the size of sex organs. In females, the vaginal lining thickens and the uterus begins to grow. In males, puberty causes a growth of the testes and, approximately a year later, a lengthening of the penis and an enlargement of the scrotal sack.

The secondary sex characteristics (Table 19.1) are those changes taking place in other parts of the adolescent's body as a result of the onset of puberty. For example, body shape begins to take on sex-distinctive patterns. Females widen at the hips and males widen at the shoulders. Males grow taller than girls. A pubescent girl's breasts begin to "bud," the first stage of breast development,

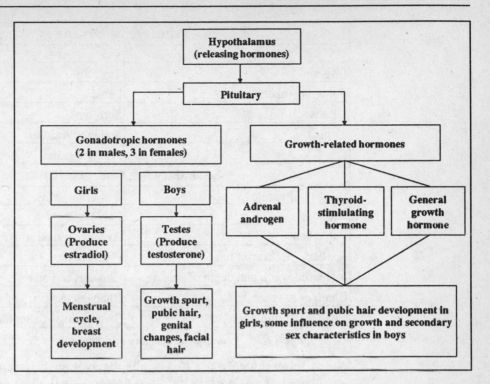

Fig. 19.1 The action of the various hormones at puberty is exceedingly complex. This figure oversimplifies the process but gives you some sense of the sequence and the differences between the patterns for boys and girls.

when a small accumulation of fat around the nipples causes a slight bulging. Full breast growth is not complete until the end of puberty.

Other distinctive secondary sex characteristics include an increase in the diameter of the areola (the dark area around the nipple) for boys. Over half of all adolescent boys show some breast enlargement; however, this generally disappears by age 16. Voice changes occur with puberty: girls develop lower voices and boys develop much lower voices, with occasional loss of control that may result in a high squeaking. Pubic hair begins to appear for both sexes. New hair growth occurs under the arms and on the face, most noticeably on young males. Although facial hair for an adolescent boy is usually the last secondary sex characteristic to appear, the quality is generally determined by genetic influences. Hair on arms increases in darkness, and pubic hair becomes curlier, darker, and thicker, covering a wider area as puberty progresses.

DIFFERENCES IN PUBERTY ONSET

Differences in the timing of the onset of puberty are the result of such factors as gender, heredity, body weight, fat proportion, nutrition, medical care, and culture. In industrialized societies, the average girl reaches menar-

Primary Sex Organs	
Female	**Male**
Ovaries	Testes
Fallopian tubes	Penis
Uterus	Scrotum
Vagina	Seminal vesicles
	Prostate gland
Secondary Sex Characteristics	
Female	**Male**
Breasts	Pubic hair
Pubic hair	Axillary (underarm) hair
Axillary (underarm) hair	Facial hair
Increased width and depth of pelvis	Changes in voice
Changes in voice	Changes in skin
Changes in skin	Broadening of shoulders

Table 19.1   Primary Sex Organs and Secondary Sex Characteristics

che at approximately age 12.5, while the average boy experiences his first ejaculation at age 13.5 to 14. The difference for identical (monozygotic) twins in menarche averages approximately 2.8 months, while variability between girls in general for the age of menarche varies from nine to 18 years of age. Children whose body weight and proportion of fat are high tend to experience puberty earlier than those children who are taller and thinner. Menarche in particular seems to be influenced by the proportion of body fat. Athletic girls, such as runners and dancers, tend to have little body fat and menstruate significantly later as well as more regularly than the average adolescent girl. Inactivity also seems to influence an earlier menarche. Blind girls (less active than sighted girls) generally have their first menstruation earlier than girls with sight. Also, menarche is more likely to occur in winter than in spring or summer, probably because of the lower activity rate in winter.

Better nutrition and medical care have allowed genetic gender influences to have a significantly larger impact on the onset of puberty. This is commonly referred to as the secular trend. Specifically, over the last a hundred years, industrialized societies have witnessed a gradual decrease in the average age of menarche because of better diet and the availability of health care. Hence, the ages that are referred to in Table 19.2 for first appearance of different characteristics were much higher a hundred years ago. For example, since approximately 1900, children have been increasing in height by approximately 1 centimeter and ½ kilogram (1 pound) each

Girls' Characteristics	Age At First Appearance
Growth of breasts	8–13
Growth of pubic hair	8–14
Body growth	9½–14½(average peak, 12)
Menarche	10–16½(average, 12½)
Underarm hair	About 2 years after appearance of pubic hair
Oil- and sweat-producing glands (acne)	About same time as appearance of underarm hair
Boys' Characteristics	**Age At First Appearance**
Growth of testes, scrotal sac	10–13½
Growth of pubic hair	10–15
Body growth	10½–16 (average peak, 14)
Growth of penis, prostate gland, seminal vesicles	11–14½(average, 12½)
Change in voice	About same time as growth of penis
First ejaculation of seminal fluid	About 1 year after beginning of growth of penis
Facial and underarm hair	About 2 years after appearance of pubic hair
Oil- and sweat-producing glands (acne)	About same time as appearance of underarm hair

Table 19.2   Usual Sequence of Physiological Changes of Adolescence

decade. The secular trend may have bottomed out, as there have been no significant changes in these ages in the last 25 years.

The age at which puberty begins varies not only from adolescent to adolescent but also from culture to culture. Children in the United States mature up to a year earlier than those in European countries. Within the United States, African-American girls have their menarche at 12.5 years while Caucasian American girls menstruate for the first time at approximately 12.8 years. Elsewhere in the world, Czechoslovakian girls experience menarche at about 14 years, New Guinean girls at about age 18, and girls in Kenya at about age 16.

CULTURAL VIEWS OF MENARCHE

Menarche is a dramatic and significant event for pubescent girls in most cultures around the world. Many cultures have elaborate rituals regarding menstruation. Strict Orthodox Jewish women must take a ritual bath after menstruation prior to having sexual relations with their husbands. Many societal customs and laws clearly delineate what may and may not be done during menstruation. At menarche young girls in Borneo are confined for significant periods of time to dark cells suspended by poles. After the cessation of this first menstrual period, they are allowed to rejoin the tribe. Members of a South African tribe believe that cattle will die in an instant if they walk on ground on which menstrual blood has been dropped. During menstruation, women must use special paths so that they have no contact with the ground that cattle walk upon. Even in Western society, cultural edicts have discouraged girls and women from swimming, going barefoot, participating in sports, or informing others that they are menstruating. Overall, Western society has improved in the preparation of young girls for menstruation, and helpful information has become more available. This helps prevent shock, confusion, and embarrassment when menarche occurs.

EARLY AND LATE MATURATION

During puberty, individual variations in growth rate are not uncommon. Some adolescents reach puberty significantly earlier or later than their peers. There are certain advantages and disadvantages to the timing of maturation; this timing has significant psychological effects on the pubescent teenager.

Girls. The early maturing girl may experience breast development at the age of eight or nine, a height spurt at age nine or ten, and menarche at age ten. This girl will be more womanly in appearance than her age-mates (i.e., taller, heavier, and more shapely). She will also have an athletic advantage over other girls in her class because of her strength, size, and stamina. She is also more likely to be approached by older adolescent boys interested in her because of her budding femininity. Overall, she is likely to receive a greater amount of male attention and have more male/female social opportunities than other girls. Because of her increase in social status among boys she is likely to feel an equal increase in her social status among her female peers.

There are a number of drawbacks, however, for the early maturing girl. She often feels conspicuous and self-conscious because of the differences between her and her friends and the increased attention paid to her, resulting in problems with her self-esteem and body image. (See chapter 21 for a discussion of psychosocial influences in adolescence.) She will likely be called "boy crazy" by peers and adults because of their focus on her developing body. Her dates will likely be with boys who are older, thereby confronting her with situations that she might not be mature enough to handle. There is usually more pressure from older dates to be sexually active. Because of this pressure, she is more likely to have sexual intercourse before high school is over and less likely to use contraception. Although most early maturing girls do not follow this path of premature sexual experience, early physical development does increase the amount of stress on adolescent girls. On the other hand, early maturation may be advantageous. Compared with late maturing girls, early maturing girls have been found to make better adjustments in adulthood.

The late maturing teenage girl may be 14 or 15 before she experiences a height spurt and nearly 16 when she experiences menarche. Because she will develop "late" compared with her peers, she is likely to suffer anxiety about her body image. Teenage boys will tend to pay less attention to the late developer than to the early or even average developer, making her social development lag behind. However, research in this area does not make clear whether early or late maturing adolescent girls have the bigger emotional disadvantage. In any event, parental support and understanding help mitigate the effects of variations in the timing of puberty. Differences appear to exist, but they are less clear and their influences are more transient than those found in male adolescents.

Boys. Although the consequences of early and late maturation in adolescent boys appear mixed, there is an advantage to early maturation. Specifically, late maturity appears to be a significant handicap for the teenage boy. The early maturing adolescent boy will notice his testicles develop at about age 10 and his penis start growing about a year later. His growth spurt may also start when he is about 10, making him athletically superior to his peers. That is, because he is bigger and stronger, he can jump higher and run faster. A social benefit of this size change is that he is now more attractive to the opposite sex. He will usually experience increases in self-confidence and social maturity because of his increased social experience, making him more popular and more assertive in social situations. Because of his older appearance alone, adults will tend to entrust him with more responsibilities.

Even though some studies have found negative effects of early maturation (e.g., excessive worry and concern with body image), early maturing boys overall tend to do significantly better psychologically than their late maturing peers. The average male adolescent finds his body starting to appear masculine and more adult during his mid- to late teens; the late maturing boy is the last to develop. He is even behind late maturing girls. Because of these physical differences, he is viewed by his peers and adults as less physically attractive, less athletic, and less likely to be a leader. He tends to be more intense or restless, less poised, and more talkative than early maturing boys. Some studies have found an increase in juvenile delinquency for this group. These personality characteristics tend to persist, with late maturing boys being less independent, less dominant, and less responsible even in their adult years.

Some studies, however, have found advantages to late maturation in boys. They are more likely to have a better sense of humor and to be more perceptive and more compassionate than their earlier maturing peers. Differences continue to exist when early and late maturers are tracked longitudinally into their forties. Early maturers tend to be more rigid and conforming, whereas late maturers are more creative, flexible, and insightful.

BODY IMAGE

Because of the combined cognitive factors (see chapter 20) and physiological events occurring at this time, adolescents are challenged with the major task of revising their body images. At this stage they tend to be quite dissatisfied with how they appear. What their body image "should" reflect is often dictated by a mixture of media images and what they think the opposite sex is looking for. Nonetheless, a psychologically healthy body image is a critical part of becoming an adult. Girls spend hours examining themselves in front of a mirror worrying about their complexions, and boys tend to worry about beard growth and muscle development. Generally, girls tend to be more dissatisfied with their appearance than boys. This intense self-preoccupation with body image lessens over time. In some adolescents, however, preoccupation with body image may cause or result in depression and/or eating disorders. (see chapter 22).

Nutrition

When children reach adolescence, the body changes rapidly, requiring additional vitamins, minerals, and calories. The average boy and girl need about 2,800 and 2,200 calories per day, respectively. During the growth spurt of puberty, the requirements of vitamin D, iron, zinc (for sexual maturation), and calcium (for bone growth) increase by more than 50 percent.

The typical diets of teenagers, however, tend to result in nutritional and health problems. Although there is no single eating pattern during adolescence, many teenage diets are deficient. For example, almost half of all college students skip breakfast half the time. The average adolescent also tends to be influenced by food fads and unusual diets. For example, teenagers tend to gravitate toward junk foods like french fries, soft drinks, ice cream, and candy. These are particularly harmful at puberty because of the rapid growth of the adolescent body and organ systems. Adolescents who do not have proper nutrition will be shorter and less well-formed adults.

In addition, deficient diets may result in specific problems. Teenage girls may become apathetic and lethargic if they suffer from iron deficiency anemia, and they are also especially prone to calcium deficiency. Eating disorders and obesity are particular risks in this age group. Many teenagers are significantly overweight while others tend toward anorexia and bulimia (see chapter 22).

Health and Illness

Adolescence is a comparatively healthy time. Adolescents have low rates of debility, chronic disease, and hospitalization. Their mortality rate is also low compared to that of all other age groups; however, other factors impact the bodies and lives of teenagers. The leading cause of death during the teenage years is violence. in 1980 eighty percent of all deaths during the teenage years were due to accidents, homicides, and suicides. Thus while the overall health of teenagers is good, lifestyle behaviors may represent major health-related problems. The greatest cause of death for black teenagers is homicide. Suicide is also a major cause of death for teenagers. In 1984 6,000 teenagers in the United States committed suicide. The teenagers who succeed at suicide tend to be socially isolated, to have behavior or discipline problems, and to be doing very poorly in school. The majority of these teenagers at one time or another were diagnosed with Attention Deficit Disorder. In addition, significant family problems often contribute to suicide.

Some teenage lifestyle behaviors have less immediate effect than suicide but are cumulative and detrimental. For example, many teenagers begin to smoke, develop low activity levels, and poor eating patterns. Television watching becomes a major pastime, and overall stress levels are generally high. (Further discussion on the effects of some specific lifestyle behaviors, such as drug abuse, pregnancy, and sexually transmitted diseases, is found in chapter 22.)

Comparatively, international studies indicate that adolescents in the United States tend to be heavier and taller and have lower cholesterol levels than teenagers in other nations. Teenagers in the Netherlands tend to be the tallest, and those in Thailand the shortest. American teenage boys average 5 feet 2 inches, ranking sixth in world, and American girls ranked seventh, also at 5 feet 2 inches. The lightest adolescents were from Thailand and the heaviest from Greece. U.S. teenagers ranked third in weight with the average weight for girls 108 pounds and for boys 110 pounds. Nigerian teenagers have the lowest cholesterol rates, and Finnish teenagers the highest.

*A*dolescence generally refers to the total amount and kinds of changes that occur during the ages of 10 to 20, with puberty specifically referring to the physical changes that occur during the early portion of adolescence. These changes bring the child's body to a state of reproductive capability (primary sex characteristics) and make the body look more like that of an adult (secondary sex characteristics and growth spurt). Although the first signs of sexual maturity (male ejaculation and female menarche) may not indicate fertility, they mark the onset of reproductive capacity.

When the primary and secondary sex characteristics actually occur may be influenced by diet, activity level, and genetics as well as by the quality of health care in the culture. Early onset is more likely to occur in overweight, less active individuals who have a family history of early onset and who live in an industrialized society.

The timing of the onset of the primary and secondary sex characteristics will also psychologically affect adolescents. Early maturers are generally *pressured more to take on responsibilities like those of adults. They can also be under pressure to begin sexual intercourse early. Late maturers, on the other hand, often have social difficulties because of their extended period of childhood and childish behavior. This latter group, especially boys, will usually carry some adjustment problems into adulthood.*

In addition, a teenager's image of his or her body plays a large role in that teen's level of self-esteem. That image is influenced not only by media and cultural youth/adolescent images but also by what the individual teen believes the opposite sex is looking for or is attracted to.

From a health perspective, nutrition is important to the timing and progression of puberty. Improved nutrition is one reason why puberty onset is usually earlier in industrialized societies than in much of the third world. However, it is important to note that lifestyle behaviors (smoking, low activity levels, poor eating patterns) have the greatest influence on the overall health of teenagers.

Selected Readings

Adelson, J. (1980). *Handbook of adolescent psychology*. NY: Wiley.

Bancroft, J., and J. M. Reinisch. (1990). *Adolescence in puberty*. NY: Oxford University Press.

Hall, G. S. (1904). *Adolescence: Its psychology and its relations to physiology, anthropology, sociology, sex, crime, religion, and education*. NY: Appleton.

Katchadourian, H. A. (1977). *The Biology of adolescence*. San Francisco: Freeman.

Koff, E., J. Reardon, and M. Stubbs. (1990). Gender, body image, and self-concept during adolescence. In *Journal of early adolescence*.

Livson, N., and H. Peskin. (1980). *Handbook of adolescent psychology*. NY: Wiley.

Taitz, L. S., and B. L. Wardley. (1989). *Handbook of child nutrition*. NY: Oxford.

20

Adolescence:
Cognitive Development

This chapter covers cognitive development during adolescence. It begins with an examination of the expanded thinking capabilities of the adolescent as well as of some of the limitations in acquiring this stage. That is, not every adolescent will acquire or use the ability to reason abstractly. One reason for this is adolescent egocentrism, which occurs early in this period. This egocentrism shows itself in three areas of faulty thinking early in adolescence: the imaginary audience, the invincibility fable, and the personal fable.

Advanced moral development is part and parcel of advanced cognitive development. Jean Piaget provided an initial framework (moral realism vs. moral relativism), but it is through the work of Lawrence Kohlberg that development of moral thinking over the lifespan is currently understood. Differences between moral thinking and moral behavior are also discussed.

Finally, the importance of high school as a unifying physical, cognitive, and psychosocial experience is covered, as is career decision making in the adolescent.

ADOLESCENT COGNITIVE DEVELOPMENT

Piaget and Formal Operational Thought

During this period of transition to adulthood, which begins around the age of eleven, the thought processes of adolescents develop some important capabilities. This intellectual maturation, referred to by Piaget as formal operational thought, has a number of characteristics. The major development is in the ability to think in terms of possibilities, to ask and imagine "what if." Basically, adolescents are no longer limited to concrete reality and can now deal with abstractions. In doing so, they form hypotheses (e.g., guesses about possible solutions to problems), test them out, and deduce the best path of action in solving the problem. This is in contrast to a concrete operational child, who tends to solve problems in a logically run trial-and-error fashion. Formal operational thinkers consider possible solutions, mentally examining the possible outcome of each, thereby speculating in advance on which of the hypotheses are likely to be more successful.

Adolescents are also able to separate themselves from actuality and consider other possible alternatives. However, their lack of experience limits their ability to accept these possibilities in practical terms. Adolescents are also able to interpret abstractions such as ideals and values because their thinking is more flexible than that of the younger child in the concrete operational stage. For example, a concrete operational child will say that "a stitch in time saves nine" means that if an article of clothing is falling apart at the seams, one stitch will prevent the article from needing many stitches later on. An adolescent in the formal operations period will be able to abstract from this proverb and explain that it means that if you do a small amount of work ahead of time you reduce the number of problems you may experience later on. This abstract reasoning ability allows adolescents to examine art and literature, understand the symbolism contained therein, and question the moral and social values of their culture. Adolescents are able to consider a number of alternatives, weigh them, and then discard the ones that don't fit. These abilities don't all develop overnight or at the same time. An adolescent may show one skill but not the other at any given time during this development. Not all adolescents or adults use formal operational thought in every situation, even when they have attained it. (See Table 20.1 for a summary of the characteristics found in formal operational thought.)

REVIEWING PIAGET'S THEORY

Piaget's basic description of reasoning processes has been tested and confirmed in other domains, as well as the scientific. However, Piaget's views have been criticized as having two major failings. First, formal operational thought is not universal for all peoples. It is far more likely to be used in technologically advanced societies than in preindustrial societies. Education and culture are strong influences on a child's acquisition of formal operational thought. For example, college students are more likely than high school students to use abstract reasoning. In addition, young school-age children can be taught to use formal operational procedures for problem solving, further indicating the important role of education. Second, even in technologically advanced societies, formal operational thought is not used by all people. It is more likely to be used when reasoning about the familiar

Characteristic	Explanation	Example
Combinational logic	The ability to find all the possible alternatives	When asked what the president could have done in a certain situation, a teenager will produce a great many alternatives, some real and some impractical. If given five jars of colorless liquid and told that some combination will yield a yellow liquid, an adolescent will use an efficient and effective strategy that will produce all possible alternatives.
Separating the real from the possible	The ability to accept propositions that are contrary to reality and to separate oneself from the real world	A teenager can discuss propositions such as "What if all human beings were green?"
Using abstractions	The ability to deal with material that is not observable	An adolescent understands higher-level concepts such as democracy and liberty as well as the abstract meaning of proverbs.
Hypothetical-deductive reasoning	The ability to form hypotheses and use scientific logic	A teenager uses deductive logic in science to test a hypothesis.

Table 20.1   The Formal Operational Stage

(objects, people, situations, events, and so on) than the unfamiliar. Individuals with higher IQs tend to use formal operational thought more often. Emotional factors can also play an important part in applying formal thought (e.g., being depressed reduces the likelihood of formal operational thinking).

A number of findings support the above contentions. Several researchers report that almost 50 percent of adults in the United States appear to never reach the stage of formal operational thought. These studies were based on the success of people in different age groups with solving different formal-operations tasks. Cross-cultural differences have also been discovered. By comparison, individuals in non-Western cultures perform worse when given tests requiring formal operational thought.

The amount of education an individual has seems to be a strong influence on the shift to formal operational thought. Even Piaget later recognized that culture, vocational interests, and educational levels strongly influence the results of tests for formal operations. Additionally, individuals may use formal operational thinking in some areas but may not be able to in other areas. In other words, an adolescent may be able to use such thinking in school but not in interpersonal or social relationships. In conclusion, formal thought is affected by many factors: general intelligence, cultural background, education, and experiences with the particular subject matter.

Piaget's conclusions that adolescents in general are capable of more abstract forms of reasoning than younger children is not in dispute. His critics question whether this occurs solely because the child enters a new developmental stage. They assert that the change is a gradual and unpredictable and depends to some extent on brain reorganization but even more on adolescents' real-life experiences and the amount of practice they have in using their new-found skills.

ADOLESCENT EGOCENTRISM

According to Piaget, preschoolers are not the only ones to be egocentric (see chapter 12 for a general discussion of egocentrism). Whereas preschoolers see themselves almost as the center of the universe, adolescents enter the formal operations stage with a different kind of egocentrism, called by Piaget adolescent egocentrism. Adolescents are concerned primarily with themselves and how others view them. In a sense this egocentrism is a necessary step in the formation of an identity. They imagine that when they walk into a room everyone will not only be looking at them but also evaluating them. Adolescents can now understand the thoughts of others, but they fail to distinguish between the focus of others' thoughts and that of their own.

Relationship to Formal Operational Thinking

The relationship between egocentrism and formal operations thinking is important. The relationship is simple: early in adolescence, egocentrism is high while abstract thinking is just beginning to take hold and is therefore low. As adolescence progresses, these positions reverse. (Basically, the relationship is a very good example of a methodological concept from chapter 2: a negative correlation.) Adolescent egocentrism is also characterized by three interesting but faulty thinking phenomena: the imaginary audience, the personal fable, and the invincibility fable.

IMAGINARY AUDIENCE

In the following example, notice the cause of the daughter's feelings and perceptions:

> Elaine found her daughter, Stephanie, in tears before school one morning. When her mother asked why, Stephanie moaned that she looked awful and that everyone at school would laugh and make fun of her. Elaine looked her over and couldn't find anything wrong and said so, trying to boost her daughter's morale. After a few more tears, Stephanie finally zeroed in on the source of her distress: a few hairs that weren't long enough to fit under her headband. Stephanie knew everyone in class would be criticizing her "ugly" hair.

All parents of teens can relate similar stories. Stephanie anticipated her classmates' reactions, but this anticipation was faulty because she was certain her classmates would see her the same way she saw herself. This phenomena is called the imaginary audience. The adolescent believes that everyone (the audience) is looking at, somehow has intimate knowledge of, and evaluates every action he or she does. This is imaginary because most of the time the adolescent is not the sole focus of attention. The adolescent can become very self-conscious during this time and crave privacy. The self-consciousness that shows itself in the imaginary audience phenomenon slowly fades during later adolescence but never disappears entirely, even in adults. For example, if you worry about how you will look prior to an important event, feeling certain everyone will be staring at you, then you have been thinking with the imaginary audience in mind.

PERSONAL FABLE

As young adolescents reflect on their own thoughts and feelings, they may see themselves as unique. Believing that one is unique is not bad; it is the essence of individuality. However, if this uniqueness is thought of as clearly different from that of others, adolescents can project a future for themselves that seems mythic. Imagining oneself as a great novelist or as president are examples. The importance here is not that these fantasies are impossible. Obviously, some teenagers do go on to become great novelists and presidents. Rather, the personal fable is a way to justify their uniqueness and "guarantee" in their own minds their separate individuality.

INVINCIBILITY FABLE

The invincibility fable is, by definition, in direct conflict with formal operations thinking. Basically, adolescents operating under the influence of the invincibility fable believes the laws of nature do not apply to them. Hence, they believe drinking and driving will not affect them because they can "hold their liquor." Some other beliefs are: drugs will affect other people but not them; sex without contraception is okay because they won't get pregnant; and they don't need to prepare for exams in advance because last-minute studying will do the trick.

PROBLEMS WITH FORMAL OPERATIONS THINKING

A number of behavior characteristics mark the beginning of formal operational thought and the reduction of adolescent egocentrism. With the developing ability to consider alternatives, teenagers become indecisive. They are suddenly aware of the many choices available in every aspect of their lives. Feeling trapped, they often find it difficult to decide between the alternatives.

This awareness of alternatives also breeds argumentativeness. They now begin to see that those whom they once thought perfect are not: their heroes have faults, and most often those "heroes" are the parents. This new awareness results because they want to use every opportunity to practice their reasoning ability and because they are attempting to reconcile reality with fantasy. Finding fault with parents and those in authority is common during this developmental period. Parents should encourage this while avoiding discussions of personality factors that inevitably lead to family discord.

It is interesting to note that many protesters (regardless of the nature of the movement) are young people in this cognitive stage of development. This leads to a kind of hypocrisy on the part of the adolescent. The young person has a difficult time recognizing the difference between expressing an ideal and working toward one. They do not yet realize that thinking about something doesn't make it real. For example, young adolescents' talk about how important it is to clean up the environment is indeed laudable; but talking about this topic while at the same time throwing a candy wrapper on the ground is hypocritical.

As the thought processes mature, adolescents better understand their own identities. By forming adult relationships and deciding what place in society they will take, they move along on their way to adulthood.

MORAL REASONING

Piaget's Views

Until recently, little thought was given to a child's moral development. It has become obvious, however, that in order to achieve some kind of moral code, there has to be advanced cognitive development. This cognitive development does not ensure moral development, but the latter can't be accomplished without it. Piaget laid the groundwork for researching the child's moral development.

Piaget spent a great deal of time not only studying but also playing with children in an effort to understand their moral development. He learned that children up to the age of five will invent their own rules of play and change them at will. Beginning at about age five, a child enters the first of two stages in moral development. The first stage, moral realism, is characterized by the child's belief that rules handed down by parents or teachers (authority figures) are absolute and fixed. What is deemed right or wrong remains inflexible. The child also has the certainty that punishment will follow the breaking of these rules. This notion is called imminent justice. Actions are judged on intentions and resulting consequences during this stage. Pre-schoolers are able to take into account the intentions behind misbehavior when judging the action.

The second stage, moral relativism, is attained around the ages of 10 or 11. This second stage is not attained until the child passes through the first stage. During this stage of moral relativism, the child believes that social rules can be changed either by agreement or consensus. The absolute obedience to authority that marked stage 1 is rejected and replaced by the idea that moral rules result from cooperation, reciprocity, and peer interaction. There is more flexibility in the child's moral judgments. Individual circumstances, emotions, and feelings are all taken into account. No longer is wrongdoing inevitably punished. The child believes in equal justice for all.

Piaget felt that the progress from moral realism to moral relativism involves not only the child's cognitive abilities but also greater exposure to social experiences. The more contact a child has with his or her peers, the greater the likelihood that the child will learn cooperation and be able to compromise. According to Piaget, parents could encourage their children's moral development by being less authoritarian and more egalitarian (democratic).

Kohlberg's Views

Lawrence Kohlberg extended this study into adolescence and adulthood, more specifically defining stages of moral development. In order to study how children reason about difficult moral issues, Kohlberg devised a series of dilemmas, one of the more famous being the dilemma of Heinz:

> In Europe, a woman was near death from a special kind of cancer. There was a drug that the doctors thought might save her. It was a form of radium that a druggist in the same town had recently discovered. The drug was expensive to make, but the druggist was charging ten times what the drug cost him to make. He paid $200 for the radium and charged $2000 for a small dose of the drug. The sick woman's husband, Heinz, went to everyone he knew to borrow the money, but he could only get together about $1000 which is half of what it cost. He told the druggist that his wife was dying, and asked him to sell it cheaper or let him pay later. But the druggist said, "No, I discovered the drug and I'm going to make money from it." So Heinz

got desperate and broke into the man's store to steal the drug for his wife. (Kohlberg & Elfenbein, 1975, p. 621)

The child or adolescent is asked a series of questions that are intended to help him or her understand how the person thinks and arrive at a conclusion. Some of the questions asked included: Should Heinz have stolen the drug? What if Heinz doesn't love his wife? Would that have made a difference? Would Heinz steal the drug if the person dying was a stranger?

Based on his research and the kinds of responses he obtained, Kohlberg concluded that there are three main levels of moral reasoning, with two stages in each level. These levels are identified as preconventional, conventional, and postconventional.

PRECONVENTIONAL

This level involves concern with rewards for good behavior and punishment for misbehavior.

Stage 1. Punishment and obedience orientation ("might makes right"). This stage is characterized by the desire to avoid punishment, and value is placed on obedience to authority.

Stage 2. Instrumental and individual orientation ("scratch my back, I'll scratch yours"). Individuals try to meet their own needs first, wanting what feels good for themselves. There is the desire to be nice to other people so they will be nice back.

CONVENTIONAL

This level pays homage to the social rules and laws of the community, church, society, and culture.

Stage 3. "Good girl"/"nice boy" stage. The reference group decides what is "good" or "bad" behavior, and the child tries to follow these norms.

Stage 4. "Law and order." There is a respect for authority and the desire to follow the "rules."

POSTCONVENTIONAL

At this level the child bases evaluations of what is moral or immoral behavior on individual moral principles rather than on some outside source of authority.

Stage 5. Social contract. Society is governed by rules that benefit all people. If the rules fail, they can be changed or ignored.

Stage 6. Universal ethical principles. The person's moral position is based on universal or fundamental beliefs that transcend established rules.

EVIDENCE FOR KOHLBERG'S VIEWS

According to Kohlberg, most ten-year-olds reason morally at stage 1 or 2. He felt that the individual must be at the cognitive level of early formal operations before stage 3 could be achieved. This occurs around early adolescence. A certain amount of life experience and responsibility is needed before stage 5 can be attained.

According to Kohlberg's research stage 6, which states that people assume personal responsibility for their actions and base their moral judgments on fundamental and universal principles, is extremely rare. Few people are able to achieve this level of moral reasoning, if it exists at all. Mother Teresa, Martin Luther King Jr., and Mahatma Gandhi are some of the very few who are believed to have developed this level of moral reasoning. Since this stage is so rare, it is usually dropped from the rating stages of moral development.

There is strong evidence that Kohlberg's stages develop in this order. In longitudinal studies of teenagers and young adults, it has been found that each stage evolves from and replaces the preceding one. Additional evidence indicates that adolescents can understand moral arguments not only at their own level but also at lower stages or one step higher. They are unable to understand arguments that are two or more steps higher, however.

Based on these observations, Kohlberg saw little progress in moral development during middle adulthood and believed few adolescents developed past stage 4. In fact, many adults do not seem to progress past this stage.

QUESTIONS OF GENDER DIFFERENCES

Kohlberg's theories attracted much attention because until that time little thought had been given to a child's moral development. However, criticism was inevitable. It has been asserted that a bias against females exists in Kohlberg's studies. Girls and women seem to view moral dilemmas differently from their male counterparts. Where males seem to want to avoid interfering with other's rights, females give greater consideration to the human relationships involved. Females are socialized to be caring and nonjudgmental; therefore, they find it harder to judge in absolute terms of right and wrong. Indications are that even though males and females approach moral decisions differently, gender makes no difference in the ultimate decision. Regarding moral development, it would seem that neither sex has an advantage.

MORAL THINKING VERSUS MORAL BEHAVIOR

How does the development of moral thinking affect moral behavior? Young children can tell you that it is wrong to lie and steal while still engaging in such behavior. The same holds true for adolescents and even adults. They tend to look after their own interests and bend the rules to obtain them. This may occur especially when one is under a great deal of peer pressure or when getting caught is very unlikely. Moral thinking and moral behavior are not, then, intimately linked.

Yet the ability to internalize moral thought can affect an individual's actions. The person tries to reconcile beliefs with actions. As children enter adolescence they frequently attempt to match their moral standards to their behavior, discriminating "right" from "wrong" behavior. As adolescents try to understand their own morality, they find it easy to condemn immorality or hypocrisy in those around them rather than in themselves. By exposing adolescents to discussion, interpretation, and role-playing of moral dilemmas, one can help them move to the next level of moral reasoning.

HIGH SCHOOL

The life of the adolescent is centered around high school. High school provides the person with numerous experiences that exercise the intellect. In addition to academic learning, sports, and peer socialization, high school offers a preview of career choices. The importance of the high school experience should not go unnoticed. First, because it provides a proving ground for all the experiences listed above, it may serve a crucial role in the development of formal operational thinking. Since adolescents can observe different situations and outcomes, they can obtain practice in the art of abstract thinking. Second, beyond the obvious opportunities for cognitive development, high school fosters the kinds of physical and psychosocial experiences that are essential for functioning in the adult world. For example, high schools can offer information on drugs, sex education, child development, and relationship building as well as counseling on any difficulty an adolescent may be experiencing. Finally, on a practical level, a high school education has become necessary for most kinds of employment.

The student who leaves school before receiving a diploma greatly reduces his or her career opportunities. Students who drop out face an uphill struggle in starting their careers, since many employers require a high school diploma. The drop-out tends to be a minority-group male from a lower-income family living in the city. Though he has done poorly in school, studies reveal that he is of at least normal intelligence and may even have an above-average IQ.

Reasons for dropping out include poor grades, a dislike of school, being expelled, or needing to support a family. Marriage and/or pregnancy are added reasons why girls drop out. Research has indicated that lack of motivation, low self-esteem, little or no parental involvement, low teacher expectations, and problems with discipline are contributing factors. More than half of the drop-outs questioned shortly after their decision regretted dropping out.

Career Choices STAGES OF CAREER DETERMINATION

Choosing a career is an important issue for the adolescent. Studies show three stages of career decision making. The first, called the fantasy stage, lasts until age 11 or 12. Children at this stage think anything is possible and base their choices on emotion rather than practicality. The second stage occurs around puberty and results in an awareness that jobs may require specific talents or training. This "tentative" stage is an attempt to match the interests of the person with specific abilities or values. In the third stage, the older adolescent or young adult chooses a career after careful planning. During this "realistic" stage, job requirements, talents, abilities, values, and opportunities for training become important considerations.

GENERAL FACTORS AFFECTING CAREER CHOICE

Many factors can affect a career choice. One such factor is socioeconomic status. People are influenced by the lifestyle they grow up in; growing up in a deprived environment will tend to deprive the adolescent of many career opportunities. Also affecting career choice is the fact that familiar surroundings offer a kind of comfort. This means that the low-paying, low-opportunity employment options often found in lower socioeconomic environments may perpetuate themselves.

Parental encouragement for specific careers at or above their own socioeconomic status may serve to reduce the status effect. Parents' encouragement and involvement in their children's education is another factor to be considered. Parents who reward their children for academic achievement and offer not only encouragement but financial support (paying for part or all of college costs) help their children attain higher-status careers than their own.

Level of intelligence also plays a big part in career selection. Some occupations (e.g., doctor) require many years of hard, intense training. This does not mean that high intelligence guarantees "doctorship" for an adolescent. On the contrary, a higher intelligence level actually provides an opportunity for greater career experimentation than does a lower intelligence level. Finally, personality can't be overlooked as an important factor in both career selection and career satisfaction. A successful radio disc jockey has a very different personality from a school librarian. Individuals who know themselves well enough to pick a career that suits their personality are more likely to be satisfied and successful. All these factors are intertwined and cannot be easily separated.

GENDER AND CAREER CHOICE

Daughters today have more opportunities available to them than their mothers did. Sons, however, are still more likely to be upwardly mobile in terms of their careers. Women try to reconcile their personal goals with their career goals. It is a difficult task to combine them. Men tend to separate their goals and see no conflict between job and family or spouse. To succeed in a male-dominated profession, this single-mindedness is essential. Most women consider this sacrifice too high a price to pay for success in a male-dominated profession.

Some women have a fear of success. If they are too successful, they fear they won't be accepted by their peers, especially their male peers. Not all women have this fear of success in all situations.

The good news is that some areas that were once strongly associated with males or females are no longer. Men are more likely to help with the housework and children while supporting their wives' roles in the work force. Women have the freedom to be more assertive in their roles both in and out of the home.

Even with these changes, gender differences are unlikely to disappear. Consider how boring it would be to have two parents very much alike. The important factor, it seems, is to allow each person the freedom to explore his or her individuality.

According to Piaget, adolescents, unlike the concrete operational child, can develop the ability to think abstractly. This means that teenagers can explore different solutions to problems as they arise. Theoretically, any adolescent should have this ability. In reality, however, formal operational thought is most often found in educated people in industrialized societies when they are reasoning about familiar situations. Also, such thinking appears more likely in a school setting rather than when dealing with social or emotional issues.

Related to the onset of formal operational thinking is the appearance of adolescent egocentrism. This occurs when adolescents are preoccupied with how others view them. It occurs most often with regard to the imaginary audience. Basically, each adolescent assumes that he or she is the focus of the attention of all other adolescents. Related thinking problems include the invincibility fable (assuming that the rules of nature do not apply to the adolescent) and the personal fable (assuming that one's life has mythic proportions).

The ability to reason morally should improve during adolescence. Piaget saw moral reasoning as developing in two steps: rules laid out by authorities are absolute and inflexible; and social rules can be changed by agreement or consensus. Kohlberg, however, broke down the development of moral thinking into six stages that roughly correlated with thinking ability, age, and life experience. Of interest is the fact that moral thinking and moral behavior do not always correspond.

High school may serve as a proving ground for the thinking and moral development occurring during adolescence. Not all adolescents go through high school, however, and those that do not have more difficulty later with finding jobs or constructing a career. The development of a career choice goes in three steps: fantasy (anything is possible); tentative (realizing that specific jobs may require specific training); and realistic (where the job requirements or need for training are taken into account). Thus, many factors are involved in deciding on a career, including socioeconomic status, intelligence, gender, and parental encouragement.

Selected Readings

Damon, W. (1984). *Morality, moral behavior and moral development.* NY: Wiley.

Elkind, D. (1974). *Children in adolescence: Interpretative essays on Jean Piaget.* NY: Oxford University Press.

Holland, J. (1973). *Making vocational choices.* Englewood Cliffs, NJ: Prentice-Hall.

Kohlberg, L., and D. Elfenbein. (1975). The development of moral judgments concerning capital punishment. In *American journal of orthopsychiatry,* 45.

National Center for Education Statistics. (1985). *The relationship of parental involvement to high school grades.* Washington, DC: NCES (#NCES-85-250b).

21

Adolescence: Psychosocial Development

*T*his chapter looks at the psychosocial development of the adolescent. By this point, what significantly remains of development is the search for an identity separate from the parents' and peers'. The search will cover the theoretical formulations of Freud and Erikson. The latter provides the best framework for understanding the development of an identity through four identity statuses related to the amount of re-evaluation and choice commitment the adolescent has.

A discussion about the areas of identity development influenced by parents and peers follows. This chapter ends by outlining some factors related to the parent versus peer controversy. An examination of the problem of a generation gap is also included.

THEORETICAL VIEWS OF ADOLESCENCE

The Stormy Decade

The adolescent is faced with many changes. The individual's body is maturing and taking on adult appearances. The thinking processes of the adolescent are maturing and enabling the individual to think in the abstract. However, it is the psychosocial development that molds the adolescent into an adult. The adolescent must decide which lessons of the past will be integrated with present realities and be willing to contemplate the possibilities for the future. This self-examination can best be summed up with the question "Who am I?" Deciding "Who I am" (a search for identity) becomes the most important aspect of the adolescent years.

G. Stanley Hall and most psychologists of the early 1900s thought that this period of adolescent change consisted entirely of storm and stress. The storminess was thought to be the result not only of the changes in body, sex, identity, and independence that were present but also of the adolescent's learning to cope with these changes. The erratic nature of these maturational changes would undoubtedly result in an erratic emotional adjustment period. Hall felt that adolescents could emerge stronger from this stressful time, a view that was widely supported; yet it is a debatable issue today.

Margaret Mead felt society played an important part in contributing to or downplaying this storminess. Societies that provide a calm and gradual transition from childhood to adulthood free their adolescents from this stress and storm. Even though Mead's work has critics, it has shown that the storm and stress of this period are not inevitable.

Psychoanalytic Approach to Adolescence

SIGMUND FREUD

Freud, in his psychosexual theory of development, describes puberty as a reawakening of the sexual urges of the earlier phallic stage (see chapter 13). This approach, which is consistent with the stormy viewpoint of adolescence, describes a period known as the genital stage, which lasts into adulthood. Essentially, the urges and impulses that drove the Oedipal and Electra complexes during the phallic stage re-emerge after a time of dormancy in the latency stage. Because of the sexual changes which are at the core of adolescence, these urges can now be channeled in more appropriate ways, such as through heterosexual relationships outside the family.

Adolescents must free themselves from their parents in order to establish these close relationships. Freud emphasized that not everyone works through this period to attain mature heterosexual love; that is, some people may fixate here as well. However, Freud viewed this stage as having less of an impact than any of the others on normal development. In other words, fixation was possible; it just was not as detrimental as when it happened during the oral, anal or phallic stages. The reason for this was simple: fixation during the genital stage had four prior stages of good development to counterbalance it.

ERIK ERIKSON

Erikson described the adolescent's development during this period as one of defining his or her own identity versus existing in a state of role confusion. To master this stage, adolescents must separate their identities from their parents' identities yet maintain a meaningful relationship with them. They deal with this changing role by calling into question all aspects of their lives. In addition, many expectations and responsibilities are thrust upon them, causing them to further define their own futures.

In trying to achieve this identity, each adolescent uses the two variables of crisis and commitment. A crisis is a period of emotional upheaval and decision making when old values or choices are re-examined. This may occur abruptly or gradually. The outcome of the crisis is a commitment to a plan of action through ideology or a specific role. Realizing that a person could be in either a high or low state of either one or both of these variables, Erikson defined four identity statuses according to the degree of crisis and commitment in each. (See Fig. 21.1 for a graphic presentation of the differences in crisis and commitment among these four statuses.)

Identity Achievement. While searching for an identity the individual passes through one or more of these stages. The ultimate goal, of course, is identity achievement. The individual in this state has devoted much time and effort to a search for choices in response to the crisis. Usually the crisis stage is recently past. The final decision is a strong expression of commitment to some particular behavior role or set of values, a decision the adolescent has reached on his or her own.

Identity Moratorium. An individual can remain in identity moratorium, where the evaluation crisis is ongoing and high as the adolescent searches for answers and choices without making any commitments. A student in college who is trying out various areas of study before deciding on a major is a good example of identity moratorium. This person is on the way to commitment and will probably make identity achievement.

Identity Foreclosure. This status shows itself in two forms. The first is

	Degree of "crisis"	
	High	**Low**
High	**Identity achievement status** (crisis is past)	**Foreclosure status**
Degree of commitment to a particular role or values		
Low	**Moratorium status** (in midst of crisis)	**Identity diffusion status**

Fig. 21.1 The Four Identity Statuses of Erikson

exemplified by the student who passively accepts the career choice or expectations of his parents. Possibly out of avoidance or fear of the evaluation process there is no crisis, just a high level of commitment, making this a very secure status. A second form of identity foreclosure is called the "negative identity": because the parental/societal role is unappealing and because the crisis is still being avoided, the chosen identity (commitment) is the opposite of the expected one. Examples of both forms include becoming a doctor because that is what the parents have been planning for or becoming a juvenile delinquent because it is the opposite of the parental "doctor" plans, respectively. In both cases, the individual puts off making choices for now, often finding out later that unhappiness is a major part of the identity. At that time, the crisis is renewed with the hope of progressing to identity achievement.

Identity Diffusion. This stage is characterized by little or no crisis and little or no commitment. If there was a crisis, no decision was made regarding it and the person is unconcerned over this lack of commitment. This individual may be a loner or drifter with no goals or possibly a fun-seeker who avoids commitments. Usually this person has a low sense of self-esteem.

A number of personality characteristics can be related to these identity stages. Self-esteem, degree of moral reasoning, anxiety and social behavior patterns are just a few. All of these variables affect individuals as they progress through one or more of these identity stages.

It has been found that individuals who have attained identity achievement also attain a deeper sense of intimacy in regard to relationships. People who marry or become parents as a way to define their identity often have not resolved the real issue of their own identity. They may have delayed the issue, but it will surface again later on in life.

PARENTAL VERSUS PEER INFLUENCES ON ADOLESCENT PSYCHOSOCIAL DEVELOPMENT

Is There a Generation Gap?

This search for identity takes a lot of effort and produces much anxiety, but is it necessary? How does the adolescent form this identity? In searching for identity, the adolescent must begin a separation from parental influences. This is seen as the proverbial "generation gap." Partly because of their cognitive maturity, adolescents begin to question all aspects of their relationship with their parents. Research has shown the majority of these conflicts to be over such mundane matters as schoolwork, chores, curfews, and cleanliness. On the one hand, adolescents may see their parents as being too restrictive; on the other hand, they need a base of security and stability during this stressful period of development. A positive development during this period of growth is the adolescent's ability to view parents as individual persons with unique traits and feelings. They can begin to separate their parents from the roles they play as mother and father.

Parents also view this time as a period of upheaval and uncertainty. Their views of their child must develop and change. They need to recognize the adolescent's need for greater freedom in the decision making that affects his or her identity development. There is an uneasy balance between allowing a degree of freedom while maintaining the need for dependence. In order to maintain stability within the family, parents and adolescents both must realize that achieving autonomy does not mean abandoning family ties.

PARENTING STYLES

Parenting styles used with adolescents are broader than the ones used with preschoolers (see chapter13), primarily because the adolescent's search for identity results in the desire to become more involved in the events that will determine his or her future. Whereas the preschooler styles were limited to "authoritarian," "permissive," and "authoritative," styles with the teenager run the gamut from "autocratic" to "ignoring."

Parenting styles affect the amount of tension experienced in the adolescent's progression from dependence to autonomy. Democratic and egalitarian parenting styles are most likely to foster confidence, self-esteem, and autonomy as well as maintain a close child-parent relationship. This reflects the parenting pattern of allowing children the freedom to be heard, and to be listened to, yet at the same time maintaining a disciplined, loving environment. Limits are clearly set, understood, and established with knowledge and input from the adolescent. When discipline is administered, it is explained.

Authoritarian and autocratic parents value strict obedience and feel no need to explain reasons for their decisions. Adolescents of these parents are less likely to think and act for themselves; hence they tend to be more dependent. Permissive, laissez-faire, and ignoring parents (those who are excessively permissive and provide little leadership) don't give the support the adolescent needs during this time. These parents allow their children to drift and make decisions on their own, thus encouraging them to engage in socially deviant behavior.

The degree of parental involvement can affect the adolescent's success in achieving identity. Adolescents who do well in school tend to have parents who value education and take an interest in their children's achievements. Drop-outs view their parents as not having any interest or understanding for the child or education.

The generation gap is not very wide at all. Even though the younger generation is looking for its own identity, adolescents still maintain values and aspirations similar to those of their parents. This is more apparent when adolescents are compared with their parents rather than with the culture as a whole.

The Importance of Peers

As adolescents move away from their parents, peer groups gain in importance. Peers are groups of friends or acquaintances who share similar interests, values, and backgrounds. There are generally two types of peer groups: cliques (which range from three to nine members and are characterized by a closed membership, intimacy, and shared activities) and crowds (larger groups ranging from fifteen to thirty members). One must be a member of a clique before membership in the crowd is acknowledged. Crowd activities are largely social and involve little intimacy. Crowds help peers make the transition from unisex groupings to mixed-sex activities and eventually to paired couples. Adolescents can help each other in a variety of ways to search for and define their own identities. The peer group may act as a sounding board for the adolescent. Within this framework of contemporaries, the adolescent can try out new identities, values, and challenges to their self-esteem. As adolescents question the adult standards and authority around them, it's only natural for them to turn to someone other than these same adults. The peer group provides a source of support during this period of uncertainty. The peer group may also act as "judge and jury" when the adolescent is experimenting with new behaviors. This process of self-discovery can be both painful and embarrassing if the peer group pronounces a negative judgment on particular characteristics.

PEER PRESSURE

Given the importance of peer groups to an adolescent and the fact that over half of the teenager's waking time is spent with these peers, how much influence do peers actually exert? It appears that this power ("peer pressure") is often exaggerated. For example, teenagers were presented with a number of different situations and asked which group, parents or peers, they would turn to for information or support. In situations that involved social or surface issues such as hair styles or feelings about school, adolescents chose their peers as more knowledgeable. However, adolescents reported a closer relationship with their parents in situations where fundamental values and beliefs were indicated. Adolescents are not continuously being bounced from parents to peers. They are able to make choices independent of either group's influence. Peer influence seems to peak in the ninth grade, gradually declining by the junior or senior year of high school.

It is important to realize that while peer pressure may be a strong influence in an adolescent's life, it is not always negative. There can be pressure not to smoke or take drugs but to study hard and dress appropriately. Yet the reality is that some students are drawn into socially unacceptable behavior by their peers. It should be remembered that adolescents choose peer groups that share many of their values and interests. Therefore, a student who chooses to hang around with a peer group who breaks the law must feel some commonality with the members of that group.

SEXUAL IDENTITY

Friendships during adolescence become more intense and intimate. They seem to fill the void teens feel when separating from their parents. Adolescents become more adept at sharing their thoughts and feelings, which may explain why these friendships tend to be so close. The transition from family to peers to close friendships evolves further into opposite-sex friendships and romance. This is a natural progression necessary for the achievement of sexual identity. Sexual activity at this age satisfies a number of important needs. The least important is physical pleasure, and the most important is enhanced communication. The search for maturity, new experience, peer conformity, and the mystery surrounding love are all important needs being attended to.

Parents become uncomfortable with their adolescent's emerging sexuality. Communication between a parent and child is extremely important but oftentimes difficult to achieve. Peers can help with this sexual identity transformation. As boys and girls become aware of each other, there is safety in numbers. By being part of a group, adolescents can think about, talk about, and associate with members of the opposite sex without the intensity of a one-on-one relationship. As intimacy develops, peers can give each other support when faced with rejection. Even when the relationship is progressing, peers can give valuable feedback and validation of feelings being expressed.

By late adolescence the transition to true intimacy occurs. Individuals no longer need the safety of a group or their peers' validation of their own feelings. Sexual behavior typically begins with kissing, followed by breast fondling, then manual-genital contact. The next step is usually sexual intercourse. The age when first intercourse occurs varies widely and is affected by a number of factors. Boys tend to reach sexual maturity later than girls, yet have sex earlier. By age 18, 60 percent of white males have had sex, whereas the same percentage of white females have not had sex until age 19. Likewise, 60 percent of black males have had sex by age 16; whereas the same percentage of black females has not had sex until age 18. Children of parents who run permissive, laissez-faire or ignoring households are apt to be sexually active earliest, followed by those of autocratic or authoritarian parents. Parents who are egalitarian or democratic tend to have children who put off having sexual intercourse, as do adolescents who have high educational aspirations. Girls in single-parent homes tend to engage in sex at an earlier age than their peers. Regular church attendance also is found among teenagers who postpone sexual activity.

The indications are that gender, culture, home, education, religion, and peers all influence an individual's sexual identity. Sexual attitudes have become more liberal in recent decades, with sexual activity beginning at an earlier and earlier age. There are current signs that this trend may be slowing and possibly reversing. (See chapter 22 for a further discussion of teenage sexuality.)

OTHER PSYCHOSOCIAL ASPECTS OF IDENTITY DEVELOPMENT

Career Choice

(For a review of the more cognitively oriented aspects of career choice, see chapter 20.) Another area that adolescents must make decisions about in their already complicated search for identity is that of career choice. It has been found that males and females take different approaches. Besides the differing role models for men and women, males tend to focus on their vocational and personal identities. They seem to be able to compartmentalize their different identities. If a man is asked how his career might affect his future family, the response usually has to do with economics. A woman's response will usually reflect her concern not only with economics but more importantly with her job as a mother and with the family in general. Many women see their identities tied to interpersonal relationships. Certainly, personal characteristics must enter into the decision-making process.

Additional factors the adolescent must consider are intellectual ability and achievement in school. Even though it is true that higher levels of intelligence should open the doors to more aptitude-oriented careers, the relationship between intelligence and vocational choice should not be overemphasized. Being a manual laborer does not mean an adolescent has less intelligence. Job satisfaction is an important factor to consider. The personal experiences an adolescent is exposed to will influence career choice. If adolescents see their parents enjoying their careers, then the adolescents' experiences will be more favorable than if the parents are dissatisfied or never home because of work. The individual's personality and ability to solve problems may help direct the career path. There are practical factors as well, such as a need to enter the work force earlier rather than later, meeting entrance requirements for school, and economics.

Major factors such as gender, socioeconomic status, and the career choices available will affect an adolescent's decisions. A conscious career choice that takes into account an individual's abilities, interests, and goals must also be guided by the opportunity the choice affords, the resources available, and the environment.

GENDER DIFFERENCES

Although career choices may not be finalized by the end of adolescence, these decisions are a vital part of the child's sense of identity, both at the specific vocational level and the more general personal level. Nine out of ten women will be entering the work force this decade. Many of the stereotypes involving career choices for women have been abandoned. Women have the opportunity to enter many nontraditional career fields. There still remain problems, though, for women who face career planning.

Stereotypes about "male" and "female" jobs have declined somewhat over recent years, the greatest decline being in stereotypes of occupations once considered strictly for males. Men are still expected to be the primary breadwinners in the family, and their career choices are expected to reflect that. For a man, his occupational success is reflected in high self-esteem. Adolescents can also see that success in life is often based on career success.

Other Miscellaneous Factors

Many poor and minority groups do not have the career choices available to them that other groups do. A lack of successful role models, discrimination, and a paucity of economic resources all contribute to the problem. Individuals in these groups feel they are at the mercy of the system or that situations are beyond their control. Programs that promote reasonable vocational choices must also battle these basic attitudes of helplessness. There has been some progress in recent years but it has been painfully slow.

Given all the stress and conflict facing the adolescent in gaining this new identity of self, it is amazing that the overwhelming number of teens make such a successful transition. However, serious problems do occur (for a broader discussion of some of these issues, see chapter 22). Drug abuse is one such problem. Given the need to separate or rebel against one's parents or authority figures, a certain amount of experimentation is inevitable. Nine out of ten high school seniors have tried alcohol, two out of three have tried tobacco, and half have tried illegal drugs. Many adolescents will continue using drugs throughout college and into young adulthood.

Illegal drug use is showing a decline among high school seniors. Most adolescents acknowledge that their parents would not approve of their drug use, yet this does not seem to be a reason for the decline. A more probable explanation may be better drug education and the first-hand witnessing of drug addiction among their peers. Alcohol use remains high, however.

Alcohol is a contributing factor in nearly all serious problems associated with adolescence.

The rate of sexual abuse increases at puberty and continues until whatever age the victim is no longer considered a child by society. Typical sexual abuse involves a female adolescent and a father, stepfather, close relative or family friend. Overt force is rarely needed because of the victim's feeling of powerlessness. The adolescent, because of long-term abuse, may fail to learn what a normal adult-child or man-woman relationship should be. Sexual abuse interferes with healthy identity achievement. It may also perpetuate a cycle of abuse that continues from adult to child in subsequent generations. Prevention includes early intervention and counseling. Research has found that fathers who participate in the care of their young children rarely engage in sexual abuse. Perhaps the nurturing feelings that develop through child care inhibits sexual feeling toward the child.

Adolescence was first described as a stormy period by G. Stanley Hall, a viewpoint that was supported by early psychologists including Sigmund Freud. Freud assumed that the genital period was an extension of the phallic period. In essence, the sexual desires for the opposite-sex parent that remained unresolved at the end of the phallic stage re-emerged during the genital stage as yearnings for opposite-sex peer relationships. Although Freud assumed that fixation was also possible at this stage, it was less traumatic because of the successful passage through the other stages.

Erik Erikson saw the purpose of adolescence as the defining of an identity for the teenager. He hypothesized the existence of four different identity statuses based on the level of self-evaluation the adolescent was experiencing and the degree of commitment to a particular life path. These statuses are not considered absolute, but once identity achievement is acquired (usually by the end of college) the adolescent will have attained a greater sense of self-determination and independence.

The social interactions of adolescence represent a switch in emphasis. As time progresses, parents become less important than peers as sources of information and reference. This may serve as the basis for the generation gap.

Another major change that occurs during adolescence is the parenting perspective. That is, the simpler parenting styles appropriate for pre-schoolers now become more complex as teenagers want to become more a part of the decision-making process. Essentially, parenting now becomes an interaction between the parent and the adolescent. The styles that are most conducive to feelings of happiness for both parents and adolescents are those that respect the adolescent's input as important in the family decision process.

Peers become more important over time with respect to behavior choices. That is, peers provide pressure on the adolescent for group-respected behavior. Most often, those behaviors are nondestructive, "posi-

tive" behaviors. This is important with respect to sexual identity and what adolescents perceive as the appropriate developmental identity process.

Other factors influence the identity development of adolescence, including career choice, future career opportunities, different gender expectations with respect to vocation, educational level, drug use, and even sexual abuse.

Selected Readings

Adelson, J. (1980). *Handbook of adolescent psychology*. NY: Wiley.

Elder, G. H. (1962). Structural variations in the childrearing relationship. *Sociometry 25.*

Erikson, E. H. (1968). *Identity, youth and crisis*. NY: Norton.

Field, T., A. Houston, H. C. Quay, L. Troll, and G. Finley. (1982). *Review of human development*. NY: Wiley.

Perlmutter, M. (1986). *Cognitive perspectives on children's social and behavioral development. Minnesota symposium on child psychology*. Vol. 18. Hillsdale, NJ: Erlbaum.

22

Adolescence: Special Issues

*O*ne of the unique aspects of adolescent development is sexuality. Though lacking the fully matured thinking capabilities of adults, adolescents have to cope with such issues as pregnancy, contraception, sexually transmitted diseases, and homosexuality. Changing body physiology and peer involvement impact on the sexual development of the teenager.

Other unique issues that the adolescent has to deal with include drug use and abuse and juvenile delinquency. Psychopathologies that may occur include eating disorders, adolescent schizophrenia, depression, and suicide. This chapter will discuss these and other special issues of adolescence.

SEXUALITY

Adolescent Attitudes on Sexuality

Adolescent attitudes toward sexuality have undergone a revolution since the turn of the century. At that time, 75 percent of all men under the age of 20 were virgins. At the present time, approximately 90 percent of all men under age 20 have had sexual intercourse. In the early 1960s a national survey found that 55 percent of teenage girls reported having intercourse by age 20. By 1988 more than three-quarters of 19-year-old females reported having had sex.

Overall, today's adolescents are more open and honest about sexuality than teenagers earlier in the century. Decisions regarding appropriate sexual behavior are based more on personal values and judgment than on conformity to sexual codes. Most young people continue to oppose "casual sex" (sex only for the sake of physical enjoyment) without a close relationship. Living together is viewed as a personal choice rather than as a violation of a basic principle of personal morality.

The double standard regarding male and female sexuality has been reduced to some degree. Sexual behavior is considered to be a matter of personal choice rather than a social dictate. Female attitudes still tend to be more conservative than male. Women are more likely than men to see sex as part of a loving relationship. Both sexes see sexual intimacy as being proper when one is in love or engaged compared with when an individual is dating without affection. Men expect sexual intimacy earlier in the relationship, while females have more of a tendency to link sexual intimacy to a committed relationship. In the later stages of a relationship, the sex differences in attitudes tend to disappear.

Adolescent Reasoning About Sex

Although teenage experience with sexuality is increasing, cognitive immaturity limits the ability of an adolescent to make a rational decision about sexuality. Especially in young adolescents, formal reasoning ability may be fragile. Teenagers have difficulty thinking through the possible consequences of actions, tend to focus on immediate situations rather than on the future, and may have great difficulty considering the future implications of an unwanted pregnancy. Adolescent egocentric thinking also enters as a dynamic factor; that is, thinking in terms of their own immediate needs rather than seeing any short- or long-term consequences of their behavior. The immaturity of such reasoning is clearly illustrated by an adolescent boy's refusal to use a condom because he finds it inconvenient or emasculating. In addition, as mentioned in chapter 20, it is not uncommon for adolescents to see themselves as invincible and thus to seriously underestimate the chances of pregnancy. When a pregnancy does occur, many teenagers tend to be shocked. Girls are concerned about how to avoid embarrassment and criticism from friends and family. Boys may feel pride at the demonstration of their own virility and give little thought to the responsibility of having a child.

Pregnancy

An increasingly important problem for adolescents today is pregnancy. At the present time, four out of ten 14-year-old girls will become pregnant at least once during their teenage years. Two out of ten teenage girls will give birth at least once during this time, and more than one in seven will undergo at least one abortion during adolescence. Although girls in the teenage years account for only 8 percent of sexually active fertile women, teenagers account for over 46 percent of all out-of-wedlock births. Although this high rate of teenage pregnancy is declining in the United States, it is still significantly higher than in other developed countries. There are more than one million pregnancies a year among teenage girls in the United States.

Teenagers in other countries often have sex at an earlier age, but in the United States they have a much higher tendency to get pregnant.

Such early pregnancies cause significant problems for both mothers and infants. Mothers who keep their children discover how demanding a baby is and tend to keep the infant unattended for increasingly longer periods. Such children frequently end up in the foster care system. Teenage mothers and their babies also face a higher risk of medical complications. These include anemia, prolonged labor, toxemia, low birth weight, prematurity, increased neurological deficits, and increased infant death in the first year. Lack of appropriate medical care rather than inherent teenage medical problems appears to be the cause. (See chapter 5 for a more detailed discussion on the risks of teenage pregnancy.)

Pregnancy is the most frequent reason girls drop out of high school. Mothers who have babies in adolescence tend to have lower incomes, less job satisfaction, less education, and increased depression. If teenage mothers marry, they have a much greater chance of divorcing. Children of teenage mothers often have lower academic achievement and increased incidence of drug abuse, arrest, and teenage parenthood themselves. Teenage mothers tend to have poor parenting skills and to be more impatient, insensitive, and punitive with their children. These children lag behind in social, emotional, and academic development.

The area of adolescent fatherhood has been poorly investigated. Teenage fathers have difficulty dealing with the idea of being a parent. They also tend to be frightened and confused, as well as to feel guilty about the pregnant girlfriend. A substantial number of teenage fathers do not admit parenthood for various reasons, such as disbelief and refusal to accept responsibility. Teenage fathers who do participate in parenting tend to lag behind their peers vocationally, educationally, and emotionally. As with the adolescent mother, the adolescent father is poorly prepared for fatherhood.

Adolescent Cognitions About Sexuality

The risk of pregnancy during the teenage years is high because of immature thinking. Most young women rarely think about the possibility of getting pregnant. Many teens believe they can't become pregnant the first time they have intercourse; they are ignorant about the biology of sexuality. To them contraception reduces the romantic quality and spontaneity of impulsive sexuality.

Much ineffectiveness of sex education during adolescence stems from the limitations of adolescent thinking. Young adolescents have difficulty with formal reasoning, so they have problems seeing and evaluating alternatives and choosing the most appropriate option. Envisioning the future is difficult for teenagers. They tend to think in terms of their own immediate needs rather than considering the consequences for others of their sexual behavior. An adolescent's sense of personal invincibility clouds his or her thinking about the consequences and risks of unprotected sexual intercourse. They underestimate the chance of pregnancy and continue taking risks.

Sex Education: Is It Effective?

A recent study finds that most teenagers feel that sexuality is not openly discussed in their families, and only 10 percent of adolescents surveyed are happy with their parents' approach to sex education. Most teenagers learn about sex from their peers and have no formal sex education from either teachers or parents. Parents of American teenagers are generally in favor of sex education in the schools, and few refuse to let their children participate. However, there is great parental controversy over what should be included in the sex education curriculum. Fears range from teacher encouragement of sexuality to easier availability of birth control devices, which could encourage increased sexuality. Planned Parenthood reports that although parents and children agree that the family should be the first source of sex education, only 30 percent of teenagers discuss contraception with their parents. Only 30 percent of teens take sex education courses in school; these teens are more likely to use contraception than those who have not received the same education. And, strikingly, adolescents whose parents talk to them about sexuality have *decreased* sexual activity. This is likely to result from increased communication and from these teens being more likely to share their parents' values about sex. Such communication effectively transmits values and mores regarding sexuality to the adolescents.

There is little or no evidence that sex education alters personal values about sex or that it increases sexual behavior. It does appear, however, to increase the likelihood that adolescents will use birth control if they engage in sexual behavior.

Sexually Transmitted Diseases (STDs)

Along with sexual activity in the teenage years is a resultant increase in STDs. Such diseases are transmitted primarily through sexual contact and include gonorrhea, syphilis, venereal warts, genital herpes, AIDS, chlamydia, and pelvic inflammatory disease. Teenage girls using oral contraceptives may not realize that they are not protected against STDs. Adolescents tend to believe they are somehow immune to the diseases that affect other people and are more willing to take risks regarding sexual activity. They are also more likely to put off getting medical care and less likely to follow through with treatment. Teenagers are often reluctant to seek help because they feel guilt and embarrassment and are afraid to let their parents know.

Perhaps the most critical factor in sexuality today is AIDS. In 1991 it was estimated that the total number of cases in the United States was over 250,000. Relatively few teens currently show signs of the AIDS virus; however, because of their rate of sexual activity, adolescents are at high risk for coming into contact with the AIDS virus. Transmission of the AIDS virus occurs through sexual contact and use of infected drug syringes. At this time, teens appear to have a modicum of knowledge of AIDS. However, fewer than half of the adolescents asked admit to being selective about sex partners because of the possibility of contracting AIDS. AIDS myths continue to exist. Adolescent selectivity may consist of looking for signs of blisters or other physical manifestations; they are apt to believe they are "safe" if they observe nothing unusual about their sexual partner. Other teenagers feel that if a person comes from a nice background, he or she won't have AIDS. AIDS education is now part of the mandated curriculum for sex education in most states. However, controversy exists over whether or not to teach students abstinence or to emphasize the use of condoms, which provide some protection during sex.

Masturbation

Over the last few decades, the Western world has come to be more accepting of masturbation. In psychological studies done in the late 1970s, 70 percent of boys and 45 percent of girls under the age of 15 admitted masturbating, compared with studies done in the early 1970s in which 50 percent of boys and 30 percent of girls under the age of 15 admitted to masturbation. This is a significant change. Even in this "sexually liberated era" adolescents still view masturbation as shameful and feel guilty when admitting to masturbation. Lower-class adolescents are more likely to view masturbation as abnormal, compared with middle-class adolescents, who are more likely to say that they strongly disapprove of the practice.

Homosexuality

Although openness about homosexuality has dramatically increased over the past few decades, the incidence of homosexuality in Western society has not. Estimates are that from 5 to 10 percent of teenagers maintain exclusively homosexual relationships. Fewer than 10 percent of adolescent girls and fewer than 15 percent of adolescent boys report ever having even a single homosexual contact during their teenage years. However, research has shown that teenage attitudes toward homosexuality have moderated considerably; teenagers have become more tolerant of alternative sexuality over the past few decades.

MENTAL HEALTH PROBLEMS OF ADOLESCENCE

Depression and Adolescent Suicide

Although once thought rare in children and younger adolescents, varying degrees of depression have been found during childhood, puberty, and adolescence. Depression is manifested in different forms at different ages and is thus more difficult to diagnose in youngsters than in adults. Because adolescent defense mechanisms tend to be "acting-out behaviors" (sexual, aggressive or delinquent activity) and because adolescents tend to express their feelings less openly, they generally do not obviously show the hopelessness, help-lessness, and gloomy feelings adult depressives do. What they are likely to show is boredom, restlessness, hypochondriasis, or acting-out behavior.

Although suicide is rare in childhood and infrequent in early adolescence, at about age 15, the suicide rate increases rapidly. Also, since 1950 the overall suicide rate among the 15-to-24-year-old age group has tripled. This is a worldwide phenomenon, with suicide rates increasing in most European countries and the United States. In the United States, approximately 2,000 adolescents aged 15 to 19 commit suicide each year. Among adolescents who commit suicide the ratio is four males to one to female. Boys tend to use more lethal means such as shooting or hanging in contrast to girls, who are more likely to use pills or gas. The warning signs of suicide are numerous. Most individuals who kill themselves have communicated their feelings prior to the attempt. Individuals who have a history of attempting suicide are more likely to make a future attempt. Other signs and warning signals include eating and sleeping disturbances, a decline in school performance, constant depression, reckless or uncharacteristic behavior, and unusually stressful events in the teenager's life.

One factor that can precipitate a suicide attempt is a breakup in a love relationship. Family stressors are also an important factor. These include alcoholism in the family, divorce, a history of mental illness in the family, and parents who are unavailable for one reason or another.

A recently recognized phenomenon is known as cluster suicides. Televised news stories about teenage suicide tend to cause a rise in suicide attempts using similar means. Because of their egocentric thinking, adolescents are particularly vulnerable to being influenced by such information. In Bergenfield, New Jersey, in March 1987, four adolescents killed themselves with carbon monoxide by allowing their car to run in an unvented garage. The next day two teenage girls in Illinois were found dead from similar means. Cluster suicides such as these have been well documented in other areas of the United States. Although the research is scant in this area, TV networks have attempted to ameliorate this problem by presenting educational programs about suicide and interviewing people affected by the suicide. No suicide increase occurred after a number of such programs; however, further research is needed in this area.

Adolescent Schizophrenia

Although rare, schizophrenia is the most frequently occurring psychosis during adolescence. Schizophrenia increases dramatically from age 15 onward and peaks during late adolescence and early adulthood, the time when psychosis is likely to present itself. Symptoms include peculiar speech, incoherent thinking, odd facial movements, lack of obvious emotional tone, hallucinations and delusions, distortions in thinking, poor emotional control, and an overall social withdrawal. Biological and heredity factors appear to play a major role in the development of schizophrenia, although many theorists argue that traumatic experiences in childhood are the most important factor. The prognosis for teenagers who are diagnosed with schizophrenia is poor; 50 percent will show little or no progress and require residential treatment.

In contrast to adolescent schizophrenia, a teenager may experience some psychotic symptoms such as hallucinations or delusions, but these symptoms appear immediately after a significant psychosocial stressor such as divorce of parents or loss of a loved one. Such a reaction is called a brief reactive psychosis and has a much better prognosis than adolescent schizophrenia. With psychotherapy, a teenager can be expected to make a complete recovery, with perhaps residual symptoms of mild depression or anxiety.

Substance Use and Abuse

Although most adolescents do not become serious drug users, drug use among American adolescents is high. Indeed, the highest rates of drug abuse occur during the teenage years. Students are using drugs at an earlier age, even in elementary and junior high school. In a nationwide survey of high school seniors, at least nine out of ten have tried alcohol, half have tried illegal drugs, and two out of three have smoked cigarettes.

LSD use has declined since 1975. The use of marijuana peaked in 1970 and since then has gradually declined. Cocaine use (in powder and crack form) also seems to be decreasing. The perceived risk associated with marijuana use and also peer disapproval have increased over the past fifteen years. The use of barbiturates, cigarettes, and tranquilizers has also decreased over the same period. Alcohol and other drug use has leveled off. Although this trend is encouraging, substance abuse is still a severe problem for adolescents in the United States and other industrialized countries.

There are many for adolescent drug use. Adolescents are naturally curious about new experiences and take risks more readily than adults. A teenager is more likely to use drugs if his or her friends use drugs. Risk of drug abuse is high for teenagers who have had rejecting, overly permissive, authoritarian, and/or hostile parents. Drug-abuse risk is low with adolescents who come from democratic-authoritative family structures.

Drugs are used also to cope with the developmental tasks of the teenage years and the tensions and anxieties associated with these challenges. Substance abuse is associated with teenagers who have other associated psychopathology, such as depression. Such teenagers may have never learned how to cope with peer disapproval and school failures and how to enter into intimate relationships with peers. Some young people use drugs to get away from the hopelessness of their environment, such as a deteriorating, stressful, gang-run neighborhood or an emotionally impoverished family. Parental drug use increases the risk of adolescent drug abuse. And finally, the more parental supervision the adolescent receives, the less likely he or she is to use licit or illicit substances. "Latch-key" children (see chapter 18) are at highest risk for substance abuse.

ALCOHOL

Ninety-four percent of high school seniors have used alcohol. Drinking in this age group is considered "normal." Males are twice as likely as females to drink daily. Socioeconomic status is not related to drinking. Five percent of all high school seniors are drink daily.

In the United States the most powerful predictor of adolescent alcohol use is peer use of alcohol. This differs in other countries. In Israel the most powerful predictor was found to be parental use. Alcohol is related to 30 to 50 percent of all deaths with cars among adolescents.

The *use* of alcohol in adolescents is mainly influenced by environmental factors such as peers. However, the *abuse* of alcohol is strongly influenced by genetic factors. Adoption study data have shown that the biological children of alcoholics are four times as likely to become alcoholics even when adopted into families that are abstinent. Alcoholism is more common in males than females, and an adolescent is at a higher risk of becoming an alcoholic if he or she has an alcoholic father as compared with having an alcoholic mother. Some studies have shown subtle differences in EEGs in the biological children of alcoholics compared with children of nonalcoholics. The more prevalent alcoholism is in the family history of adolescents, the higher the risk of alcoholism in the teenager. An adolescent drinker is more likely to drop out of high school.

TOBACCO

Adolescents who smoke cigarettes daily comprise 20 percent of all high school seniors in the United States. Smoking is influenced by parents and peers; if the teenager has friends or family members or older siblings who smoke, he or she is much more likely to smoke. The use of chewing tobacco has increased in teenagers because of the fear of the health effects of smoking. Surprisingly, slightly more (14.7 percent) high school girls smoke than high school boys (13.1 percent).

Various theories have been advanced to explain smoking in teenagers. Some theories suggest that teenagers smoke to seem older and that late maturing adolescents smoke more than early maturing adolescents. Teenagers who smoke are more likely to be rebellious, to do worse in school, to strive to look older, to participate less in sports, and to have risk-taking personality traits compared with those teenagers who don't smoke.

MARIJUANA

Marijuana use among teenagers has been declining steadily since the 1970s. Approval of marijuana use has also been steadily decreasing among high school and college groups. Still, marijuana remains the most widely used illicit drug in the United States. Adolescents who start to smoke marijuana have many of the same traits as other drug users. Rebelliousness, poor school performance, and turbulent home environments are common in habitual users of marijuana. A motivational syndrome is associated with persistent marijuana use. This syndrome entails a loss of energy, diminished school performance, and a decrease in desire to compete and achieve.

STIMULANTS

The use of amphetamines has also declined somewhat, and only 6 percent of 12-to-17-year-olds have ever experimented with amphetamines. Only 15 percent of current high school seniors have ever tried cocaine, and 5 percent have used crack. It is rare for adolescents to use stimulants regularly. The media campaign against crack and cocaine use appears to have been effective with adolescents. Eighty percent of all high school seniors disapprove of trying cocaine or crack even once. A small subgroup of adolescents becomes physiologically and psychologically addicted to crack.

STEROIDS

Anabolic steroids are synthetic male hormones that stimulate the production of muscle tissue when used in conjunction with exercise. Steroid use/abuse in teenage boys may be the male analog of female bulimia/anorexia. There is much peer and environmental pressure to appear attractive and to conform to societal standards of beauty. Seven percent of high school seniors regularly use steroids, and most of these adolescents are involved in school sports. The side effects of steroids include curtailment of growth because leg bones harden prematurely, shrunken testicles leading to impotence or sterility, depression, irritability, increased aggressiveness, and aggressive outbursts. Although some research indicates steroids cannot be classified as an addictive drug, the psychological component is a powerful pull to continue their use. Adolescent boys who use steroids feel manly, powerful, and attractive; it is difficult for them to stop using a drug that promotes the sense of power they desire.

SUBSTANCE ABUSE EDUCATION

Although some decrease has been noted, drug use among American adolescents is still high. The majority of drug abuse prevention strategies up to this point have been mostly unsuccessful. These drug programs do not remove the environmental problems that lead to drug abuse, such as peer pressure, family problems, and environmental stressors (e.g., poverty). More effective drug education programs will have to teach adolescents other ways of dealing with their stormy emotions and their problems. Information about the dangers of drug abuse appears ineffective. A more recent emphasis has been to teach decision-making strategies and social skills training in order to improve the way troubled adolescents cope with life.

Eating Disorders

Body image is of particular concern in adolescence. Teenagers tend to be preoccupied with their looks, and most are at least partially dissatisfied with their appearance. Puberty is a time of dramatic changes in an individual's body. Boys and girls take on new shapes and appearances. These physiques may not be what the individual expects or the culture promotes. Teenagers are daily bombarded with images of long, lean women and muscular, handsome men. Parents, siblings, and friends also pass judgments on the adolescent's changing body. Teenage girls start getting whistled at, and adolescent boys start commenting on each other's manliness and physical prowess. Another very important factor is that physical attractiveness acts as a catalyst for male-female relationships. This is a time of intense preoccupation with self, one that includes appearance. Adolescent boys are at risk for steroid use in order to develop their muscles. This can be a serious health risk. For their part, adolescent girls are at risk of a psychopathology known as an eating disorder. The two most common forms are anorexia nervosa and bulimia.

ANOREXIA NERVOSA

Anorexia nervosa affects fewer than 5 percent of adolescent females, but of those 5 percent, between 15 and 21 percent die of this self-imposed starvation. Over 95 percent of anorexia sufferers are female. Girls generally develop this disorder at the beginning or end of adolescence. Anorexics have a distorted body image that displays itself as an abnormal fear of becoming obese. They refuse to maintain even a minimal normal body weight and exhibit significant weight loss. Anorexics are preoccupied with food: they talk about it, they cook it, and they urge others to eat. In extreme cases, menstruation may halt, thick, soft hair can spread over the body, and activity increases. Anorexic females can be grossly underweight and still express concern about body fat and losing weight.

Associated features and personality characteristics of anorexia include descriptions of being "normal." As children, these anorexics were described as being "too good," seeming eager to please, dependable, and obedient. Most have been good students and show little overt rebellion toward their parents. The families of anorexics tend to be at least middle class, success-oriented, well educated, and weight-conscious. These teenagers tend to be high achievers, perfectionistic, and above average in intelligence.

Suicide and depression have been linked to anorexia. Psychoanalytic theory explains that an anorexic is afraid of becoming a woman, and therefore maintains a childlike form by extreme dieting. Anorexics have difficulty accepting their sexuality. Family theorists explain anorexia as the result of rigid, overprotective families where conflicts are avoided and family members are enmeshed with one another. Personal identity and independence are discouraged in such families. Losing weight may be a way to gain control within the family rules. Other theorists espouse a biological/genetic basis or a neurological dysfunction. In any event, the cause of anorexia is still unknown.

BULIMIA

Bulimia, sometimes the first stage of development of anorexia nervosa, is characterized by episodic binging, which is generally followed by induced vomiting and the use of diuretics or laxatives. Bulimic binging entails a cyclic pattern of eating extremely large amounts of foods (e.g., a gallon of ice cream and a dozen brownies), feelings of self-criticism, depression and anxiety, stomach pain, self-loathing, induced vomiting, and taking massive amounts of diuretics or laxatives. Combined use of these methods can result in the loss of as much as fifteen pounds within 24 hours. Binges are secret and humiliating. Body weight, however, tends to remain within the average range. The detrimental effects of bulimia include severe damage to the gastrointestinal system; electrolyte imbalance, which may be sufficient to cause a heart attack; erosion of tooth enamel from being frequently bathed in stomach acids; and hair loss.

Bulimia is reported to affect approximately 5 percent of the general population, mostly females. Personality characteristics are similar to those of anorexics and include perfectionism, high achievement, fear of losing control, preoccupation with body image, and unrealistic goals.

Treatment for anorexia and bulimia includes antidepressant medication, group therapy, Overeaters Anonymous, family therapy, and sometimes inpatient treatment, especially in the case of anorexia when this dysfunction may be life threatening.

OBESITY

Ten to fifteen percent of all adolescents are obese, which is defined as being 20 percent over one's ideal weight. Obese adolescents tend to become obese adults. Obesity generally occurs from consistent overeating. An obese teenager may have a particularly difficult time, since physical attractiveness and body image are developed, changed, and emphasized in adolescence. An obese adolescent faces discrimination from peers and decreased social contacts. Healthwise, obesity increases the risk for high blood pressure and coronary disease. There is no easy treatment for obesity. Some success has been reported with multifaceted programs that include increased physical activity, nutritional information, and behavioral programs that work toward decreasing the behaviors that contribute to obesity.

Juvenile Delinquency

Juvenile delinquency refers to adolescents under the age of 16 to 19 years (depending on the state) who break the law. There are two kinds of juvenile delinquents: "status offenders" and "juvenile criminals." The status offender has done something that is not considered criminal except when done by a minor. These acts include drinking alcohol, running away from home, being sexually active, not abiding by parental rules, and truancy. Juvenile criminals have engaged in acts that are considered crimes at no matter what age: rape, murder, robbery, and so on.

Adolescents are responsible for a disproportionate number of crimes. Teenagers commit more than 50 percent of serious crimes in the United States, although they comprise only 38 percent of the population. However, this phenomenon is not unique to the United States; it is world-wide. Boys are four times more likely to be arrested than girls. Teenage delinquents are more likely to be black and Latino than white, and white teenagers are more than twice as likely to be arrested as Asian Americans. Teenagers of low socioeconomic status have a higher arrest rate than those from the middle class. Adolescents at age 15 or 16 exhibit a criminal activity rate about three times that of adolescents at age 12. By age 20, criminal activity has dropped to about half the rate at age 17.

Personality Traits of Delinquents

Some personality traits have been associated with increased risk for juvenile delinquency. Delinquents are likely to be an average of eight points lower in IQ than nondelinquents. Poor verbal skills, poor memory, impulsivity, unconventionality, aggressiveness, drinking, drug use, gambling, and early sexual activity have also been associated with juvenile delinquency. A study in Denmark showed that biological children of chronic criminals had three times the average risk of becoming chronic criminals, despite the stability and noncriminality of adoptive parents. Delinquent males show a history of antisocial behavior dating from early childhood, tend to be muscular in build, and do poorly in school. Delinquency increases when there is a stepfather in the family or the family is headed by a single mother. Adolescents who are poorly monitored by their parents have a far greater risk of becoming delinquent. Delinquents tend to have signs of Attention Deficit Disorder and antisocial behavior as early as age six.

A wide variety of approaches have been used to help prevent or treat juvenile delinquency, and the results have been varied. Most social interventions and treatment programs for juvenile delinquents have not worked. Short-term improvements have been seen, but there is no evidence as yet of any long-term positive effects for society. Adolescent delinquents who are jailed are no less likely to repeat a criminal activity than those who are never caught or are simply given a warning. Time is frequently mentioned as the deciding factor in the decrease of delinquent activity. Most criminals are young.

Adolescence has unique features that challenge the individual. There has been a revolution in teenage attitudes toward drugs and sex. Adolescents are more permissive with regard to sexuality and less interested in illicit drug use than they were even a few years ago. Teenage pregnancy remains an increasingly significant problem. Adolescents are developmentally limited by their ability to make a rational decision and to consider the consequences of sexual activity.

There is no evidence that sex education increases sexual behavior; however, it does increase the likelihood of teenage use of birth control. It is important to note that parental communication about sex has worked to decrease sexual activity in teenagers.

The suicide rate in adolescence is high, with boys who commit suicide outnumbering girls four to one. The adolescent display of depression as a symptom is different from the hopelessness and helplessness characteristic of adult depression. Teenagers' symptoms of depression are complaints of boredom, restlessness, and acting-out behaviors such as aggression or drug abuse.

Although adolescent schizophrenia is rare, it can result in a devastating lifelong mental illness. Illicit drug use in the United States during adolescence has declined or leveled off; however, it is still a severe problem.

During the teenage years, distortions of body image can present themselves as eating disorders in females and steroid abuse in males. Finally, juvenile delinquency remains an important issue in this age group. Adolescents worldwide are responsible for a disproportionate number of crimes. The juvenile delinquent's criminal activity rate is at its highest when he is 15 or 16. There is a significant link also between juvenile delinquency, some early childhood traits (lower IQ, poor school performance, muscular build), and the criminal behavior of biological parents.

Selected Readings

Achenbach, T. M. (1982). *Developmental psychopathology.* NY: Wiley.

Bruch, H. (1978). *The golden cage: The enigma of anorexia nervosa.* Cambridge, MA: Harvard University Press.

Dryfoos, J. G. (1990). *Adolescents at risk: Prevalence and prevention.* NY: Oxford University Press.

Johnston, L. D., P. M. O'Malley, and J. Bachman. (1989). *Drug use, drinking, and smoking: National survey results from high school, college, and young adult populations, 1975–1988.* Rockville, MD: National Institute for Drug Abuse, 59.

Kagan, J. (1983). *Birth to maturity.* New Haven: Yale University Press.

Powers, S. I., S. T. Hauser, and L. A. Kilner. (1989). Adolescent Mental Health. In *American Psychologist 44.*

Shannon, L. W. (1988). *Criminal career continuity: Its social context.* NY: Human Sciences Press.

Trussell, J. (1988). Teenage pregnancy in the United States. In *Family planning perspectives, 20.*

U.S. Department of Justice. (1990). *Crime in the United States.* Washington, DC: Federal Bureau of Investigation.

Index

A

AB error, 109
Abortion, 66–67
　induced, 67
Acceleration, 222
Accidents, 150–151
Accommodation, 28
Acquired Immune Deficiency Syndrome (AIDS),
　　60, 151, 268–269
Adolescence, 265
　attitudes on sexuality in, 265–268
　body image in, 238, 274
　career choice in, 261–262
　cognitive development in, 241–253
　differences in onset, 233–235
　eating disorders in, 274–276
　egocentrism in, 244–246, 266
　and high school, 250–252
　homosexuality in, 269
　juvenile delinquency in, 276
　masturbation in, 269
　maturation differences, 236–238
　mental health problems of, 269–277
　moral reasoning in, 246–250
　parental versus peer influences on, 257–261
　peer relations in, 259–261
　physical development in, 230–240
　pregnancy in, 266–267
　primary versus secondary sex characteristics,
　　232–234
　psychoanalytic approach to, 255–257

Adolescence (cont'd)
　psychosocial development in, 254–264
　schizophrenia in, 270–271
　sexual abuse in, 263
　special issues in, 265–277
　suicide and depression in, 239, 269–270
　theoretical views of, 254–257
Adopted child, 49
Adrenaline, 77
Afterbirth, 71
Age, as cause of birth defects, 62–63
Agent Orange, 64
AIDS (Acquired Immune Deficiency Syndrome),
　　60, 151, 268–269
Alcohol
　adolescent use of, 262, 272
　and birth defects, 61
Amniocentesis, 66
Androgyny, 186–187
Anemia
　iron deficiency, 149
　sickle cell, 48
Animism, 161
Anorexia nervosa, 148, 274–275
Anoxia, 77
Apgar, Virginia, 72
Apgar scale, 72
Aptitude tests, 201–202
Artistic abilities, development of children's,
　　153–154
Assimilation, 28
Associative play, 173